THE N

THE NEW SCHELLING

Edited by
**JUDITH NORMAN AND
ALISTAIR WELCHMAN**

continuum
LONDON • NEW YORK

Continuum
The Tower Building   15 East 26th Street
11 York Road   New York
London SE1 7NX   NY 10010

www.continuumbooks.com

British Library Cataloguing-in-Publication Data
A catalogue record for this book is available from the British Library.

ISBN: 0–8264–6941–8 (HB)
0–8264–6942–6 (PB)

Printed and bound in Great Britain by Antony Rowe, Chippenham, Wiltshire
Typeset by YHT Ltd, London

CONTENTS

CONTRIBUTORS

Manfred Frank is Professor of Philosophy at the University of Tübingen in Germany. He has written more than 130 books and articles that have been translated into over 20 languages. His writings range over themes in German and French philosophy and literature, and philosophical works on aesthetics and subjectivity. His books include *Der unendliche Mangel an Sein. Schellings Hegelkritik und die Anfänge der Marxschen Dialektik* (Suhrkamp, 1975/Fink, 1992); *What is Neostructuralism?* (University of Minnesota Press, 1989); *Stil in der Philosophie* (Reclam, 1992); and *The Subject and the Text. Essays on Literary Theory and Philosophy* (Cambridge, 1997).

Iain Hamilton Grant is currently completing a book-length study of Schelling's speculative physics, specifically with a view challenging current philosophical assumptions concerning antiphysics, on the one hand, and the end of metaphysics on the other. He has written widely on post-Kantian European philosophy (Kant, Schelling, Deleuze, Lyotard) as well as on the physical sciences and technology. He is the translator of works by Lyotard and Baudrillard. He is a senior lecturer in philosophy, science and technology at the University of the West of England, UK.

Jürgen Habermas is a philosopher and sociologist and the foremost living representative of the Frankfurt School of Marxist inflected social theorists. He is Professor Emeritus of Philosophy at the University of Frankfurt and Professor of Philosophy at Northwestern University and has written widely on ethics, politics, history and sociology. Some of his best-known works include *Knowledge and Human Interests* (Beacon, 1971); *Legitimation Crisis* (Beacon, 1975); *Theory of Communicative Action* (2 vols, Beacon, 1981–4); *The Structural Transformation of the Public Sphere* (MIT Press, 1989); *Theory and Practice* (Beacon, 1989); and *Between Facts and Norms* (MIT Press, 1996).

Joseph Lawrence studied philosophy at Tübingen University under Walter Schulz, Dieter Jaehnig, and Rüdiger Bubner, and is now Professor of Philosophy at the College of the Holy Cross in Worcester, Massachusetts. His long-term interests revolve around Schelling's concept of 'philosophical religion', and he has written widely on both Greek and German philosophy, as well as on philosophy and literature. He is the author of *Schellings Philosophie des ewigen Anfangs* (Königshausen & Neumann, 1989), and is currently finishing a book on Socrates.

Odo Marquard is Professor Emeritus of Philosophy at the University of Giessen. He has written widely in defence of scepticism as well as on aesthetics, philosophical anthropology, philosophy of history, the philosophy of myth, and hermeneutics. Some of his writings include: *Farewell to Matters of Principle* (Oxford, 1989); *In Defense of the Accidental: Philosophical Studies* (Oxford, 1991); *Aesthetica und Anaesthetica* (Schöningh, 1989, 1994); *Skepsis und Zustimmung* (Reclam, 1994, 1995); and *Glück im Unglück* (Fink, 1995, 1996).

Judith Norman is an Associate Professor of Philosophy at Trinity University in Texas. Some of her recent articles include: 'Nietzsche and Early Romanticism', in *Journal of the History of Ideas* (2002); 'The Logic of Longing: Schelling's Philosophy of Will' in *British Journal for the History of Philosophy* (2002); and 'Hegel and the German Romantics' in *Hegel and the Arts*, ed. Stephen Houlgate (Cambridge University Press, forthcoming). She has published translations of Schelling and Nietzsche, and is currently translating Nietzsche's late works for Cambridge University Press.

Alberto Toscano received his doctorate from the University of Warwick, for a work entitled *The Theatre of Production: Philosophy and Individuation between Kant and Deleuze*. A former editor of *Pli: The Warwick Journal of Philosophy*, he is the translator and interlocutor of Alain Badiou's *Le Siècle/The Century* (Seuil, 2003), and the editor and translator, with Ray Brassier, of Alain Badiou's *Theoretical Writings* (Continuum, 2004), and, with Nina Power, of Badiou's *On Beckett* (Clinamen, 2003). He is the author of articles on the work of Deleuze, Simondon and Badiou. He is currently a Lecturer in Sociology at Goldsmiths College. Email: a.toscano@blueyonder.co.uk.

Michael Vater received his doctorate from Yale University, and is now Associate Professor of Philosophy at Marquette University. He has translated texts on Schelling's identity philosophy, including: *Bruno, or On the Natural and the Divine Principle of Things* (SUNY, 1984) and 'Presentation of My System of Philosophy (1801)' and 'Further Presentations from the System of Philosophy' (1802) in *Philosophical Forum*, XXXI (2001). He has edited volumes on Schelling and Hegel, and studied Tibetan Buddhism with North American and Indian teachers.

Alistair Welchman has degrees in philosophy and cognitive science from the Universities of Oxford, Warwick and Sussex. He has published a number of articles on Deleuze, Kant and the intersection of European thought with science and technology and has worked for the last several years in the commercial world applying biomorphic computational techniques.

Slavoj Žižek teaches at the Institute for Social Sciences at the University of Ljubljana (Slovenia). He has held posts at Paris-VIII (in psychoanalysis); Cardozo Law School, Columbia, Princeton and the New School for Social Research, and ran for President of the Republic of Slovenia in 1990. He has written widely on philosophy, psychoanalysis, politics and political theory, and film criticism. His books include: *The Sublime Object of Ideology* (Verso, 1989); *Looking Awry* (MIT Press, 1991); *Tarrying With the Negative* (Duke University Press, 1993); *The Indivisible Remainder* (Verso, 1996); *The Ticklish Subject* (Verso, 1999); *Enjoy Your Symptom!* (Routledge, 1992).

ACKNOWLEDGEMENTS

'Several Connections between Aesthetics and Therapeutics in Nineteenth-century Philosophy' by Odo Marquard, translated by Judith Norman from *Schwierigkeiten mit der Geschichtsphilosophie* (Frankfurt: Suhrkamp, 1973) by permission of the publisher.

'Dialectical Idealism in Transition to Materialism: Schelling's Idea of a Contraction of God and its Consequences for the Philosophy of History' by Jürgen Habermas, translated by Nick Midgley and Judith Norman from *Theorie und Praxis* (Frankfurt: Suhrkamp, 1978), by permission of the publisher.

'Schelling and Sartre on Being and Nothingness' by Manfred Frank, translated by Judith Norman from *Der unendliche Mangel an Sein. Schellings Hegelkritik und die Anfänge der Marxschen Dialektik*, 2nd edition, extensively expanded and reworked (Munich: W. Fink 1992), pp. 50–84, by permission of the publisher.

Translations by Nancy McCagney of passages from Nāgārjuna's *Mūlamadhyamakakārikā* that appear in *Nāgārjuna and the Philosophy of Openness* (Lanham MD, 1997) are used by permission of Rowman & Littlefield. Passages translated by Jay L. Garfield that appear in *The Fundamental Wisdom of the Middle Way: Nāgārjuna's Mūlamadhyamakakārikā*, copyright 1995 by Jay L. Garfield, are used by permission of Oxford University Press, Inc.

INTRODUCTION: THE NEW SCHELLING

Judith Norman and Alistair Welchman

A PHILOSOPHER'S PHILOSOPHER

Friedrich Wilhelm Joseph von Schelling (1775–1854) is often thought of as a 'philosopher's philosopher', with a specialist rather than generalist appeal. One reason for Schelling's lack of popularity is that he is something of a problem case for traditional narratives about the history of philosophy. Although he is often slotted in as a stepping stone on the intellectual journey from Kant to Hegel, any attention to his ideas will show that he does not fit this role very well. His later philosophy suggests a materialism and empiricism that puts him outside of idealism proper; his connection with the romantic movement suggests an aestheticism that challenges traditional philosophy as such; and his mysticism allies him with medieval, pre-critical philosophies considered antiquated by the nineteenth century. And if Schelling was not entirely at home with his contemporaries, he seems, on the face of it, to have fared little better with his future: there has been no Schelling school, he has had no followers. No historical trajectory announces Schelling as its point of departure.

And yet Schelling's influence has been an extraordinary one. He has inspired physicists, physicians, theologians, historians and poets. A wildly diverse set of philosophers have claimed that their ideas have resonance with his. Perhaps the question of Schelling's influence can be approached by looking at what Kant says about works of genius – that they should give rise to inspiration, not imitation. Paradoxically, to imitate genius is not to produce an imitation but a new creative work. Whether or not Schelling should be strictly viewed as a genius, Kant's notion suggests a sense in which Schelling should be understood as a 'philosopher's philosopher': he inspired creativity, not repetition. In this perspective, the lack of a 'Schelling school' is a sign of strength; Schelling is continually being rediscovered, and his works have retained a fresh and untimely character. If Schelling does not have any obvious historical successors, it is because his influence cannot be charted by the usual methods. New philosophical tools are needed in order to understand his philosophical significance, his impact on contemporary thought and relevance for contemporary concerns.

Perhaps Schelling's thought presents these challenges because it is 'unsystematic' (although, of course, this does not preclude a certain unity of problematic). This 'unsystem' arises, on the one hand, from Schelling's attempts to produce a philosophical encounter with the irrational and, on the other hand, from the fact that the sheer number of 'systems' he created undermines the notion of unitary system in the sense intended by Kant or Hegel. It is not much of an exaggeration to say that twentieth-century European thought is motivated by a struggle to escape from this notion of a unitary philosophical system imposed largely by German thought in the previous century; consequently, it comes as no surprise that Schelling's thought allies itself with so many different – and mutually incompatible – strands in the contemporary. We see traces of Schelling in both twentieth-century idealism and materialism, in existentialism, Marxism, psycho-analysis and even deconstruction. But it also follows from this notion of 'unsystem' that these alliances or affinities often cannot be expressed in terms of the standard conception of influence, with its institutional presuppositions of schools and expositors that form the concrete correlates of the philoso-phical conception of system. Rather, we need some other conceptualization of Schelling's reach into the present. Karl Jaspers wrote:

> To study Schelling, to look with new eyes at who Schelling is and where he leads, to follow him from his great beginnings, to see through his magic and to let him speak to us from his prevailing modes and ways of thinking – this largely means: to grasp the possibilities and dangers of contemporary philosophy. Schelling's reality, his rich mental life, the way he presents himself is not an example [*Vorbild*] to be copied, but rather a prototype [*Urbild*] of modern possibilities.[1]

The pieces in this collection will view Schelling as *Urbild* rather than *Vorbild*, and explore the possibilities he opened up for modern thought.

DIE SCHELLINGALTER

The periodization of Schelling's works is a subject of heated debate, because a frequent complaint against Schelling is his extreme philosophical volatility. Schelling is described unkindly as a protean thinker, never sticking with a view long enough to develop it. There are two aspects to this charge: fick-leness and lack of rigour. Accordingly, Schelling's defenders often argue for his continuity of vision. Heidegger famously claimed: 'there was seldom a thinker who fought so passionately ever since his earliest periods for his one and unique standpoint.'[2] And Emil Fackenheim turns the complaint against Schelling right around, saying: 'The modern student who fails to perceive a connection does well to suspect that the fault lies, not with Schelling, but with himself.'[3]

Even proponents of the continuity thesis tend to divide Schelling's works into roughly four periods: transcendental philosophy and philosophy of nature; the system of identity; the system of freedom; and the positive philosophy. This classification is certainly an oversimplification, concealing the gradual development and tensions in each of these periods, but it is basically accurate, generally accepted, and taxonomically useful.

Schelling studied at the Protestant seminary in Tübingen from 1790 to 1795; Hegel and Hölderlin were among his close friends and fellow students. Schelling began reading Fichte, and was drawn to the manner in which Fichte was attempting to provide a more fundamental ground for the transcendental structures Kant believed to condition the possibility of experience. Fichte transformed the Kantian system into an idealism by referring all objects of experience entirely to the freely self-positing acts of the absolute subject of consciousness. In early essays such as *Of the I as Principle of Philosophy or on the Unconditional in Human Knowledge* (1795) and *Philosophical Letters on Dogmatism and Criticism* (1795), Schelling pursues this Fichtean line of inquiry. But Schelling quickly became critical of Fichte, and came to believe that a reduction of experience to consciousness illegitimately privileges the subjective pole of consciousness over the objective pole of nature. Schelling began to develop a broader conception of the absolute as a ground of nature and consciousness, being and thought. Schelling hoped that this approach would preserve the autonomy of nature with respect to consciousness while safeguarding human (and divine) freedom.

This line of inquiry led Schelling to split philosophy into two, corresponding parts. A transcendental idealism focuses on the subject of consciousness, tracing the development of the thinking subject from nature. Schelling articulates this project in the *System of Transcendental Idealism* (1800). The complementary project of a philosophy of nature, which Schelling developed in his *Ideas for a Philosophy of Nature* (1797, 1803), focuses on the objective world constructing a speculative system of the laws and forces of nature.

Schelling elaborated this philosophical project at the University of Jena, where Goethe's influence enabled him to secure a position in 1798. In 1801, Schelling turned to arguing (in a Spinozistic – and decidedly un-Fichtean – vein) that the real and ideal aspects of his system stood in a relation of identity or indifference, although they seem separate from a finite, human perspective. This is his second period, his system of identity, articulated in texts such as *Presentation of My System of Philosophy* (1801), *Bruno, or On the Natural and the Divine Principle of Things* (1802), and *System of the Whole of Philosophy and of Philosophy of Nature in Particular* (1804). The question that dogs his philosophy at this point is how conditioned, finite objects (and minds) arise out of this unconditioned, primal identity.

In 1803, Schelling moved first to Würzburg and then, in 1806, to Munich. This is the period of his third philosophical phase, when he began turning his attention to problems involving God and human freedom. If there was a real break in Schelling's philosophy it was here, when he started theorizing a dark, material basis of existence. Schelling no longer thought that the relationship between real and ideal was symmetrical but instead started to theorize that it had the structure of ground and consequent. The material ground has a blunt actuality that does not lend itself to rational exposition, according to Schelling; it is 'unprethinkable' in that we cannot ask about the conditions of its possibility. Our grounding in this material force gives us our individuality and personality, while providing the condition for the permanent possibility of evil, disease, and madness and finally explaining how finite objects are able to arise out of the unconditioned. Schelling developed this notion in the context of philosophies of God, time, and human freedom in a series of texts including *Of Human Freedom* (1809), the *Stuttgart Seminars* (1810), and *Ages of the World {Die Weltalter}* (1811, 1813, and 1815).

Schelling spent the last four decades of his life lecturing in Munich, Erlangen, and Berlin. Kierkegaard, Engels, Bakunin, and Burckhardt were among those who attended his famous lectures. Schelling's later (fourth phase) thought was characterized by a distinction between 'positive' and 'negative' philosophy. Negative philosophy is supposed to be a purely *a prioristic* rational determination of the metaphysical grounds of reality. It treats the essence of things or their abstract possibility (the 'what') as opposed to their existence or concrete actuality (the 'that'), which is the subject of positive philosophy. Existence cannot, in the end, be rationally grounded and philosophy needs an experiential component to describe actuality and complement the speculative inquiries of the negative philosophy. Schelling describes the positive philosophy that integrates this component as a metaphysical empiricism, and worked out positive philosophies of mythology and revelation in a series of lectures delivered in Berlin between 1842 and 1846. His *Philosophy of Mythology* and *Philosophy of Revelation* were not published until after his death in 1854.

Schelling did undoubtedly change his philosophical perspective throughout his long period of intellectual activity, whether or not we agree with Heidegger about how fundamental these changes actually were. The essays in this book will not address the question of the ultimate continuity of Schelling's thought, but rather argue for the rich philosophical potential of the various stages. In other words, this collection does not offer much of a response to the charge that Schelling was a fickle thinker; but it does offer ample evidence that Schelling's thought is both fruitful and rigorous in the extreme.

THE FIRST HUNDRED YEARS

Schelling's reputation has had mixed fortunes. Not only has he been dismissed with the complaint of volatility but for a long time he has been slotted into a facile historical narrative of the triumphal progression of philosophy from Fichte to Hegel in which he was consigned to the role of intermediary, correcting Fichte's shortcomings while cultivating a new set to pass on to Hegel for correction. Accordingly, the task of reviving Schelling has had a lot to do with insisting on his importance outside of this historical position. This entails arguing that Hegel's interpretation is not definitive, and that Schelling's career did not end when Hegel began publishing.

After his death in 1854, Schelling's reputation quickly waned, along with the fortunes of philosophical idealism. He had been subject to a virulent denunciation at the hands of the Young Hegelians who thought that Hegel's brand of idealism lent itself more readily to a permutation into the sort of materialism then in vogue (see Alberto Toscano's paper in this volume). Continental Europe has subsequently seen two revivals of Schelling's thought. Towards the end of the nineteenth century, Schelling enjoyed a first, short-lived renaissance at the hands of such writers as Kuno Fischer, Eduard von Hartmann and Benedetto Croce. After this, his work descended again into relative obscurity – despite Heidegger's important and well-received study of Schelling's *On Human Freedom* – until a second revival on the centennial of his death in 1954. This was the year of an important conference on Schelling in Bad Ragaz, Switzerland (where Schelling had died) which drew renewed attention in Europe to Schelling's works; philosophers such as Jürgen Habermas, Karl Jaspers, Horst Fuhrmans and Walter Schulz contributed important studies arguing for Schelling's historical and philosophical significance. The Jubilee edition of Schelling's works was completed in the same year.

In the English-speaking world, however, neither of these revivals had much effect. This is a fact for which Hegel may be doubly responsible, because the first revival coincided with the rising arc of the Oxford Hegelians, who would naturally have regarded Schelling's significance as very limited. By the mid-1950s, in contrast, both British and American philosophy were dominated by an abrasive variant of the Vienna School philosophy that was so deeply anti-Hegelian that anything even vaguely connected with him – Schelling included – would have been regarded as, at best, nonsense.

The inattention of the English-speaking world is, at last, starting to change. In 1997, Terry Eagleton wrote that 'over the past few years [Schelling] has been shot from Teutonic obscurity to something like philosophical stardom.'[4] There are several reasons for this. Recent resurgence of interest in Heidegger has led scholars to finally attend to a philosopher who was certainly a key influence on the development of Heidegger's thought. David Farell-Krell is perhaps the most notable writer in this tradition. Moreover, recent books by Andrew Bowie, Dale Snow and Edward Allen Beach have helped introduce Schelling to a wider public. Finally Slovenian psychoanalytical theorist, philosophy and film critic Slavoj Žižek has brought Schelling to an audience wider than anyone would have thought possible, not least by insisting on the importance of reading Schelling for viewing Hitchcock (see Žižek's chapter in this volume).

This collection aims to contribute to this on-going discovery of Schelling by showing some of the directions Schelling's thought is leading, and providing translations of classic German studies of Schelling's influence and significance.

THE NEW SCHELLING

Schelling's impact on and relevance for twentieth-century thought can be seen most strongly in four different areas: materialism, existentialism, psychoanalysis and religion.

1. Psychoanalysis

Schelling's connections to psychoanalysis are conceptually clear. He developed a theory of the unconscious as a set of pre-personal drives that matches the contours of Freud's account. Canonical works like Hartmann's groundbreaking *Philosophy of the Unconscious* acknowledge the centrality of Schelling's contribution here.

In his article, 'Several Connections between Aesthetics and Therapeutics in Nineteenth-century Philosophy' (which has been translated into English for the first time for this collection),[5] Odo Marquard argues for a different and more novel 'functional' continuity between Schelling's earlier philosophies of art and nature and Freudian psychoanalysis: 'Freudian psychoanalysis is to a significant degree the disenchanted form of Schelling's philosophy of nature.'[6] Although also interested in the question of the historical influence of Schelling on Freud, Marquard is more deeply concerned with the structural – in fact *functional* – convergence between Schelling's aesthetic and Freud's therapeutic project. He argues that they are formally distinct responses to the same problem, namely the threat posed by the irrational and destructive powers of nature. For Schellingian aesthetics it is the artistic genius that represents an acceptable – sublimated or domesticated – form under which nature can appear. For Freud the therapeutic process performs the same function of providing a forum in which nature can appear but without being a direct threat, albeit in a very different way. This affinity between Freud and Schelling is therefore quite distinct from any questions of historical influence or terminological continuity: they constructed different tools to solve the same problem.

The Slovenian philosopher and film critic Slavoj Žižek has been key in reawakening contemporary interest in Schelling. In his 1996 book, *The Indivisible Remainder: An Essay on Schelling and Related Matters*, Žižek applies a distinctive blend of Lacanian psychoanalysis and pop culture to the task of interpreting Schelling's middle period works. Žižek stresses the Lacanian theme that rational structures of ordinary thought are predicated on some Real, a dejected, obscene surplus of materiality or indivisible remainder that cannot be thought through or thought away. Žižek finds considerable resonance between this and Schelling's theory of a chaotic ground of existence, and spells out the relevance of Schelling for Lacan (and vice versa) in terms of theories of language, time, even physics. Žižek adds to this a dizzying assortment of references to various cultural phenomena, in particular film.

In Žižek's piece for the collection, 'Everything You Always Wanted to Know About Schelling (But Were Afraid to Ask Hitchcock)', he explores the relationship between Lacan, Schelling and Hitchcock. Žižek focuses on Schelling's idea of the unfathomable Real, which he describes as ontologically incomplete, a 'spectral plurality of virtual realities'. Žižek describes three ways of construing this spectral Real in Schelling's *Ages of the World*; and then he generalizes Schelling's point, finding these three versions of the Real played out in a wide variety of Hitchcock's filmic motifs. Schelling becomes a matrix through which to read Hitchcock – a more significant matrix even than Lacanian psychoanalysis. Of course Hitchcock was no reader of Schelling. But Žižek argues that artistic conventions often anticipate the technological means of realizing them, and both Hitchcock and Schelling were aiming at a vision only first realized in the hypertext, which offers a way of presenting reality as virtual, inconclusive, haunted by an abject abyss of traces of possibilities it does not actualize. Hitchcock – and by extension Schelling – prefigure the thought of a fictionalized, virtual reality, in which the virtual is not a qualification on reality, but rather its essence and kernel.

2. Materialism

Schelling has had a stormy relationship with dialectical materialism. Although inspired by his critique of Hegelian idealism, the Young Hegelians repudiated Schelling's theology, and Lukas branded him an irrationalist, largely because of his early theory of a quasi-mystical intellectual intuition.[7] On the other hand, Schelling casts considerable and elaborate doubts on the efficacy of the pure concept as vector of development or ground of material reality. Schelling develops the thought of an 'unprethinkable' material ground prior to reason, and philosophers such as Jürgen Habermas and Ernst Bloch have been very receptive to this idea, agreeing that a purely rational philosophy does not have the resources to account for actually existing material nature. In fact, Marxists have seen Schelling's distinction between negative and positive philosophy as a prototype for a distinction between theory and practice. Habermas goes so far as to describe Ernst Bloch as a 'Marxist Schelling', citing Schellingean inspirations for Bloch's views on nature and history.[8]

In his own treatment of Schelling, Habermas focuses on the works from the time of the *Freedom* essay and the positive philosophy, and the notions of a material ground and pre-personal will. He is interested in the extent to which Schelling succeeded in integrating a sense of historical or empirical contingency into an otherwise transcendental rationalism. In his 1954 dissertation Habermas lays particular stress on the first draft of Schelling's fragmentary, *Ages of the World*; Habermas sees this as the locus for a theory of historical freedom, in which freedom loses its absolute, transcendental character; even God becomes genuinely historical, and individuals are empowered to intervene meaningfully in determining their historical fate. Habermas thinks that Schelling's experiment in historical freedom was ultimately at odds with the rationalist tendency of his metaphysics, leading him eventually to abandon it; Schelling was not able to realize the revolutionary potential of his insight.

Habermas continues these themes in his 1971 article, 'Dialectical Idealism in Transition to Materialism: Schelling's Idea of a Contraction of God and its Consequences for the Philosophy of History,'[9] which appears in English for the first time in this collection. Habermas emphasizes Schelling's theory of a contraction in God, a force that draws things inward and resists expansiveness, acting as a material ground for the actual development of God through history. Habermas focuses on how this force serves to ground not only God but a finite being who has broken from God (but is bound to him by love) and fallen into corruption. This finite creature is social, historical humanity as an '*alter deus*' or other (of the) Absolute. God puts his own fate in jeopardy by relinquishing power to this other, which destroys its connection to nature and inaugurates a period of corruption. Habermas is interested in the extent to which Schelling succeeds in theorizing an actual historical beginning to this *alter deus*, as an actual (as opposed to transcendental) beginning of corruption makes possible the practical demand for an actual end to corruption. This would permit the restoration of an authentic relationship with nature, and the abolition of the political state as a coercive institution that uses domination to establish order.

Judith Norman's article on Schelling and Nietzsche discusses the various affinities and points of contact between these two philosophers of the will. Unlike Schopenhauer, Schelling and Nietzsche were concerned to bring the idea of a material will into relationship with temporality. Specifically, Norman argues that both Nietzsche and Schelling constructed the notion of a will capable of creating the past as a way of affirming the present. For both of them, the will not only intervenes creatively in time – it is involved in a sort of backwards causality that constitutes temporality in the first place. And in both cases, this backwards willing functions within a project of affirmation, as a way of embracing and valorizing the present. Norman argues against seeing this reverse causality as a sort of return of the repressed for either Schelling or Nietzsche; Schelling's notion of reverse causality does not entail the thought of return, while Nietzsche's thought of eternal return is predicated on a decisive overcoming of repression.

Gilles Deleuze refers to Schelling sparingly but approvingly, and the articles by Toscano and Hamilton Grant both explore the Deleuzean side of Schelling. Toscano suggests that materialism can be seen as a type of philosophical *practice* common to both Schelling and Deleuze (-Guattari), specifically the practice of construction. Schelling transformed the Kantian theme of construction in a manner vital to the development of materialism, Toscano argues, giving speculative philosophy a privileged position as a recapitulation of the transcendental production of the Absolute. Schelling's great merit was to bring production into the concept and see philosophy as creative practice; but Toscano thinks that Schelling ultimately fails to make good the promise of this advance. By linking the task of philosophy to construction within the Absolute, and construing the Absolute as a starting point that is given in advance and develops in a necessary manner, Schelling fails to grasp the *specificity* and artifice of philosophical construction. Philosophy remains safely locked within the Absolute and never comes into contact with anything like a non-philosophical exterior. It is the thought of such an exterior, of philosophical construction as heterogenesis, that characterizes Deleuze's more radical materialism, a line of thinking that Schelling inaugurated, according to Toscano, but never fulfilled.

Iain Hamilton Grant's paper, ' "Philosophy become Genetic": The Physics of the World Soul' shares not just a common Deleuzian contemporary intellectual coordination for Schelling with Toscano, but also a Kantian matrix. That is, Schelling exacerbates the productive, constructive or genetic impetus of the critical philosophy, pushing it beyond its representational and therefore idealist frame. At the limit, this requires, as Toscano agrees, an immersion of philosophy itself, the process of thought, in the productive nexus of matter, as well as a strictly correlate intensification of the empirical process of production. The former radicalizes the alleged vitalism of the nineteenth-century *Naturphilosophen*; the latter is, Grant argues, a continual and active un-conditioning of things, almost an *Entdingen*. Along the way Grant recasts the standard debates around Plato and Aristotle in a highly original way ('the *Timaeus* is not a two-worlds metaphysics ... because it has a one-world physics') and performs a *tour de force* by rehabilitating the 'recapitulation' hypothesis of the *Naturphilosophen* – that phylogeny recapitulates ontogeny – in a way analogous to Deleuze's treatment of return in Nietzsche. In both cases, a thought that apparently presupposes a whole idealist identity theory is reconfigured through an account of repetition as a generator of difference. Grant mobilizes recapitulation in the service of a catastrophism that ruins the possibility of the same, arguing that even identity must be constructed, and thereby building an unusual bridge between Schelling's philosophy of nature and philosophy of identity phases.

3. Existentialism

Paul Tillich saw Schelling as the father of existentialism, because his later philosophy explicitly took its point of departure from the notion that concrete existence precedes essence. (Interestingly, this is one of the principle reasons why philosophical materialism has taken such an interest in Schelling.) Indeed, Tillich went so far as to say: 'There are hardly any concepts in the whole of twentieth-century existentialist literature that did not come

from the [Berlin] lectures.'[10] In the case of Kierkegaard this lineage is particularly direct, since he actually attended the lecture series in 1841–2. But
the works of Jaspers and Heidegger, especially Heidegger's famous lectures
on Schelling from 1936 and 1941, also attest not only to Schelling's impact
on their own thought, but also to his wider and continued effects on existentialist thought in general.

Manfred Frank is one of the most significant Schelling commentators in
recent years, and has done groundbreaking work in demonstrating the roots
of Marxism as well as existentialism in the thought of Schelling. His contribution to this collection, 'Schelling and Sartre on Being and Nothingness',
is the first English translation of his important study of Schelling's relevance
for an understanding of Sartrean existentialism.[11] Frank carefully lays out
Sartre's discussion of the nature of consciousness and its relation to the
facticity of being-in-itself in the opening sections of *Being and Nothingness*.
He explains that Sartre has to bend grammar in order to express the manner
in which consciousness *is*, given the fact that its mode of being is to be
nothing; so, for instance Sartre coins passive and transitive forms of the verb
'to be'. Frank argues that Schelling had been driven by the same desire to
distinguish between forms and states of nothingness, and had developed a
sophisticated set of conceptual distinctions that would be useful for an
understanding of Sartre. Both, moreover, were motivated by the same desire
to develop an ontology of freedom. The ontology of the late Schelling, Frank
argues, has 'stupendous similarities' to that of the early Sartre, and Frank
gives us a taste of the productive cross-fertilizations that can occur by
reading the two together.

4. Religion

Philosophers of religion have found considerable inspiration in Schelling,
with Paul Tillich being perhaps the most noteworthy example. Tillich's
central distinction between mysticism and guilt consciousness or philosophy
and religion, and his attempt to overcome this dichotomy through a
metaphysical conception of the will, were inspired by Schelling's late, religious philosophy.

The chapters by Joseph Lawrence and Michael Vater contribute to
ongoing religious appropriations of Schelling's thought in new ways.
Lawrence explores Schelling's conception of radical evil. Given the scope of
the atrocities apparent in the twentieth century and now unfolding in the
twenty-first, Lawrence turns to Schelling not only to understand how and
why evil takes the forms it now does, but also to grasp the possibility of
forgiveness. In his middle period works, Schelling distinguishes between, on
the one hand, the overt evil of incipient irrationality, the chaotic material
ground run amok, and, on the other hand, the subtler (but, Lawrence argues,
ultimately more destructive) evil of a dominating rationalism that conducts
silent genocides in the name of self-interest. These are the twin evils of

suicide bombers and capitalism, or 'Jihad' and 'McWorld', in Lawrence's analysis. Schelling cleared the way for understanding such terrors by seeing hell not as a punishment for evil, but as its condition. Our vibrant, living world necessarily entails the existence of suffering, and the two types of evil are ultimately responses to the crisis caused by ineradicable human suffering. By recognizing this, Lawrence believes, we can not only begin to understand evil – we can finally begin to forgive it.

Finally, Michael Vater's contribution looks at Schelling's system of identity as well as the later system of freedom in light of the tradition of Mahayana Buddhist, anti-metaphysical thought. Vater focuses in particular on the Madhyamika theory of knowledge and reality, and the manner in which it describes the relationship between 'absolute' and 'relative' truths as two ways of speaking about the very same thing(s). Vater uses Buddhist thought as a model of clarity, and therefore a standard by means of which to measure how effectively Schelling's metaphysics is able to avoid a reification of the Absolute. Vater's conclusion is that Schelling cannot avoid this; but it is only by renouncing a philosophical enterprise that the Buddhist tradition succeeds.

* * *

The heterogeneity of the articles collected in this volume is testimony to the diversity and fruitfulness of Schelling's thought, evidence that Schelling articulated a wide range of ideas that other and later traditions would follow through to their limit. Most of all, these articles show that, after 200 years, Schelling is still *new*.

Notes

1   *Schelling: Größe und Verhängnis* (Munich: Piper, 1955), 332.
2   *Schelling's Treatise on the Essence of Human Freedom*, trans. Joan Stambaugh (Athens OH: Ohio University Press, 1985), 6.
3   'Schelling's Conception of Positive Philosophy', in *Review of Metaphysics*, vol. VII, 4 (1954), 565.
4   'Enjoy!' *London Review of Books*, 27 November 1997.
5   The piece originally appeared as 'Über einige Beziehungen zwischen Ästhetik un therapeutik in der Philosophie des neunzehnten Jahrhunderts', in *Schwierigkeiten mit der Geschichtsphilosophie* (Frankfurt: Suhrkamp, 1973) and was republished in *Materialien zu Schellings philosophischen Anfängen*, ed. Manfred Frank and Gerhard Kurz (Frankfurt: Surkamp, 1975), 341–77.
6   'Schelling – Zeitgenosse inkognito' in Baumgartner, H. M. (ed.), *Schelling: Einführung in seine Philosophie* (Munich: Karl Alber, 1975), 22.
7   See Karl Löwith, *From Hegel to Nietzsche*, trans. David E. Green (New York: Anchor, 1967), 114–19.
8   Jürgen Habermas, 'Ernst Bloch: A Marxist Schelling (1960)' in *Philosophical-Political Profiles*, trans. Frederick G. Lawrence (Cambridge MA: MIT Press, 1983), 61–77.
9   The piece originally appeared as 'Dialektischer Idealismus im Übergang zum

Materialismus. Geschichtsphilosophische folgerungen aus Schellings Idee einer Kontraction Gottes' in *Theorie und Praxis* (Berlin: Luchterhand, 1969), 108–61.

10 *Vorlesungen über die Geschichte des christlichen Denkens. Teil II: Aspekte des Protestantismus im 19. und 20. Jahrhundert*, ed. Ingeborg C. Henel (Stuttgart: Evangelisches Verlagswerk, 1972), 123. Quoted in 'Schellings Wirkung im Überblick' by Annemarie Pieper in Baumgartner, *Einführung*, 149.

11 Frank's piece in this collection is a translation of an edited excerpt from part III of the introduction to his seminal book, *Der unendliche Mangel an Sein. Schellings Hegelkritik und die Anfänge der Marxschen Dialektik*, 2nd edition, expanded edn (Munich: W. Fink, 1992), 50–84.

1

SEVERAL CONNECTIONS BETWEEN AESTHETICS AND THERAPEUTICS IN NINETEENTH-CENTURY PHILOSOPHY

Odo Marquard
Translated by Judith Norman

I

This investigation takes its point of departure from two books. One appeared in the first year of the nineteenth century; the other appeared in the last. The one is Schelling's *System of Transcendental Idealism*; the other is Freud's *Interpretation of Dreams*.

Schelling's *System of Transcendental Idealism* appears in 1800, three years after his *Ideas for a Philosophy of Nature*, two years after his work on the World Soul, one year after his *First Attempt at a System of the Philosophy of Nature*. Its concluding and decisive 'Part Six' contains the 'Deduction of a Universal Organ of Philosophy, Or: Essentials of the Philosophy of Art according to the Principles of Transcendental Idealism.'[1] 'Art' – Schelling wrote – 'is ... paramount to the philosopher' (III, 628; STI, 231): 'It is not, however, the first principle of philosophy, merely, and the first intuition that philosophy proceeds from, which initially become objective through aesthetic production; the same is true of the entire mechanism which philosophy deduces, and on which in turn it rests' (III, 625–6; STI, 230) 'The proper sense' – Schelling therefore says – 'by which this type of philosophy must be apprehended is thus the aesthetic sense, and that is why the philosophy of art is the true organon of philosophy' (III, 351; STI, 14). Thus, Schelling clearly understands human reality to be exemplified by art and the artist, and this is reflected in the central position he gives to the philosophy of art.[2] Schelling's *System of Transcendental Idealism* takes an aesthetic perspective on existence; it determines philosophy primarily as aesthetics.

Freud's *Interpretation of Dreams* appears in the final year of the nineteenth century; in point of fact, Jones tells us[3] it appears on 4 November 1899; the title page reads 1900 (according to the wish of the publisher, as with Husserl's *Prolegomena to a Pure Logic*). *The Interpretation of Dreams* is the work in which Freud first formulated psychoanalysis as a theory in a grand style; and it is at the same time the work in which it stops being merely a specialist discipline of medicine. 'Previously' – Freud writes – 'psychoanalysis had only been concerned with solving pathological phenomena';[4] but now that 'the analysis of dreams gave us an insight into the unconscious processes of the mind and showed us that the mechanisms which produce pathological symptoms are also operative in the normal mind ... psychoanalysis became a *depth-psychology* and capable as such of being applied to the mental sciences':[5] 'a path lay open to it' – writes Freud – 'that led far afield, into spheres of universal interest.'[6] Thus the *Interpretation of Dreams* is the first work to justify the claim formulated by old Freud (1938): 'We have known that the delimitation of psychic norms from abnormality cannot be carried through scientifically ... We have therefore established the right to understand normal psychic life through its disturbances.'[7] Thus Freud clearly understands human reality as exemplified by the patient and the one who cures him: the doctor. Freud's *Interpretation of Dreams* takes a therapeutic perspective on existence: it determines (if anything other than philosophy can be spoken of here) philosophy primarily as therapeutics.

II

Thus, two books: Schelling's *System of Transcendental Idealism*, Freud's *Interpretation of Dreams*. They have completely different historical contexts, intentions, and ways of thinking. It seems ridiculous, or at least foolhardy, to discuss them together or to see a connection between them. And yet that is precisely what this study will attempt. Of course, this interest in a connection between Schelling's thesis and that of Freud should only serve to introduce a much more general question, that is of the connection between the philosophical economy of aesthetics and the philosophical economy of therapeutics, discourses that have been developing since the nineteenth century (at the latest) and in striking simultaneity (viz. continuity). As such, this investigation calls the philosophical institution of art 'aesthetics'; and, analogously, it calls the philosophical institution of the art of medicine 'therapeutics'. Is there an objective basis for the chronological connection between the two economies, and if so, what is it? – that will be the question.

III

To go straight to this question with respect to Schelling and Freud: this project would not be worth even discussing, if there were not – in spite of all the differences of their approaches – points of contact.

The distance between them is itself a remarkable fact. This is even the case for their chronological distance – which is deceptive: Freud was born a mere two years after Schelling's death.[8] Moreover, Schelling is certainly not the last philosopher to do aesthetics and Freud is not the first philosopher to do therapeutics: there are intermediaries who are still being discussed. Besides this, they are connected through personal contacts. Maria Dorer pointed to the influence of Freud's teacher, Theodor Meynert, on Freud: Meynert was a student of Griesinger, whose teacher was Herbart.[9] Dorer had not considered that Herbart's teacher had been Fichte (in Jena 1794–97). Schelling was Fichte's student. One of Schelling's followers was the great physiologist Johannes Müller.[10] His student, Ernst Brücke, was Freud's other teacher.[11]

Of course, all these – and other – ties are in no way sufficient to explain what really requires explanation here: there are in fact objective things that Schelling and Freud have in common. We have been alerted to this (more or less in passing) by authors as different as Josef Meinertz[12] (in search of depth psychologists before depth psychology) or Arnold Gehlen[13] (by examining experiments avoided by his archive) or Thomas Mann[14] (living nearby on the most distant magic mountain, in relation to Freud). And in fact, both Schelling and Freud appeal to a very similar set of basic concepts. Both operate, for instance, with a two-tendency theory.[15] Freud understands both of these tendencies as the 'system' of the 'unconscious [*Unbewussten*]' and 'conscious [*Bewussten*]'[16] while Schelling understands them as the 'unconscious [*bewusstlose*]' and 'conscious [*bewusste*] activities'.[17] Both understand the 'unconscious' tendency as 'undetermined', which is to say as a 'formless' and 'freely mobile'[18] 'drive'.[19] Both characterize the 'conscious' through the performance of 'inhibition'[20] and 'repression' (Schelling uses this very term!).[21] Human beings realize themselves on the basis of these 'inhibitions'; they improve and become spiritual (*geistig*) – not only according to Freud,[22] but according to Schelling as well.[23] Both, accordingly, think of the history of the mind as something that happens 'instead' of an immediate gratification: as production of 'illusory products' (Schelling III, 16ff.; *First Attempt*, 1799) and 'compensatory formations'. (Freud X, 256; *Repression*, 1915). Both think of the phenomena of this history as unstable 'syntheses' (Schelling III, 290–1; *First Attempt*, 1799) and 'compromise formations'.[24] Both love to compare these tendencies with the forces of repulsion and attraction.[25] Both think 'genetically'[26] and understand what they are doing as 'construction'.[27] Neither wants to leave room for the accidental.[28] Both are, for this reason, continually being denounced as determinists, fatalists, mechanists. Both essentially attack self-deception by raising the unconscious pre-history of the ego into consciousness:

'the ego ... no longer remembers ... the path that it ... has put aside ... it [has] ... unconsciously and unknowingly laid aside the path to consciousness itself ... [it] finds in its consciousness only, as it were, the monuments, the memorials of the path, not the path itself. But for precisely this reason it is a matter of science ... to allow that ego of the

consciousness to consciously come to itself, which is to say, into consciousness. Or: the task of science is … an *anamnesia*'

This passage could come from Freud, but it is in Schelling.[29] All this –
and much else – does not fail to suggest a certain relationship, at least,
between the two approaches.

The commonality between Freud's and Schelling's theories is no doubt
striking and stands in need of explanation. But it is of interest to the present
investigation in only one, limited aspect: as an important indication of a
connection between aesthetics and therapeutics.

IV

This connection is obviously still opaque. It will become transparent (it
seems) only when we attend to what is both the most central and most trivial
common ground between Schelling and Freud: the fact that they both take
nature seriously. Schelling's early philosophy is distinguished not only by
the central position of aesthetics, but just as much by the central position of
the philosophy of nature. And Freud's theory is indeed characterized not only
by the fundamental validity of the therapeutic optic but at least as much by
its attention to the way the power of nature determines human life. In spite
of all differences, both men are interested in nature precisely as something
not under human control and domination. Perhaps because this conception
of nature holds a central position for Schelling, the aesthetic comes to have a
central position too; and because this idea of nature retains its central
position for Freud, the therapeutic comes to have a central position. The
economy of the aesthetic and the economy of therapeutic – clearly they each
have a strong relation to the empowerment of nature. But if aesthetics and
therapeutics are each connected with the philosophical turn towards nature,
then they are also connected with each other. And so it is the case: aesthetics
and therapeutics and their economies belong together as organs, or more
specifically symptoms, of one and the same basic tendency: of the philosophical empowerment of nature. The path of the philosophy of nature and
the acknowledgement of its power – the path of the nineteenth century –
establishes the philosophical validity of both art and medicine, as the
validity of a presence of nature: an unthreatening presence of nature. That
will be our thesis.

V

If this thesis is right, then it makes sense to carry out the investigation of the
connection between aesthetics and therapeutics and their economies essentially as an analysis of this philosophical turn to nature. That is why this
investigation devotes particular attention to this turn; it will first question
the motives, the impetuses, the conditions of the necessity of this turn; and

then it will devote itself to the following answer: philosophy was forced to turn to nature because of a weakness in historical reason 'from a cosmopolitan point of view'.[30] Reason's impotence establishes the power of reason's other, the power of nature.

The star witness for this argument (not the only witness, and a reluctant, although impressive one) is precisely that book with which this whole investigation began: Schelling's *System of Transcendental Idealism*. It is about 'history',[31] and it testifies to reason's weakened state, its impotence. As 'reason of the present', its principal concern is only with the theoretical reason of the epistemological subject as researcher in the natural sciences (STI, Part III), and the moral reason of the convictions of the private individual (STI, Part IV). And so, according to Schelling's philosophy, the reason of the present is not the reason of society. But the 'reason of society' (III, 592; STI, 202) is what controls both society's antagonistic relation to the state of things and also society's natural attitude to a 'cosmopolitan constitution' – and Schelling's transcendental system situates this reason in an imperceptibly distant future (III, 602; STI, 210). And so, according to Schelling's philosophy, the reason of society is not a reason of the present. This withdrawal of reason, in part into the infinitely distant future and in part into the private chamber of mere theory and interiority, is definitive of its impotence. But by virtue of its impotence (where, as the reason of the present, it denies itself to society and, as reason of society, it denies itself to the present) reason is forced to entrust the social present and the reality of history to something that is not realized reason – to *nature*. Schelling's transcendental system explicitly acknowledges precisely this result not only by working together with the philosophy of nature, but even in the transcendental system itself. Part V of the transcendental system – which is a philosophy of nature *in nuce* – is no mere pastoral interlude, but is in fact the early Schelling's basic statement on 'history'. Precisely 'the transcendental philosopher', Schelling writes, 'assuredly recognizes that the principle [of nature] is that ultimate in ourselves ... on which the whole of consciousness, with all its determinations, is founded' (III, 610; STI, 217). Nature expresses itself through the weakness of reason as the 'final thing' in history, as its decisive power; reason and its history bring us back to nature.

VI

Disclosing this pent-up power of nature is a necessary act of enlightenment. But coming to terms with this power is an act of resignation: the force that falters through the weakness of reason is compensated by a 'sublation'[32] of nature in history; 'nature' becomes an embodiment of those pent-up problems whose resolution forces historical reason into a state of resignation. Precisely through this fundamental resignation a question now arises and becomes impossible to dismiss: how do we live with nature if it has this sort of inviolable power over history?

With respect to this power of nature, Schelling – and with him the greater part of the 'romantic' philosophy of nature (Oken most decisively) – had tried to help by accepting, praising and referring what he could not sublate to the truth, which would play the role of rescuer. 'All power of healing' – Schelling said – 'is only in nature';[33] 'Come to physics' – he called – 'and see the truth!'[34] However, this 'romantic' transfiguration of nature is fundamentally unstable; thus, in the history of the philosophical turn to nature, it is only one response, and indeed a transitory one. Schopenhauer[35] replaces it with a desperate position on the power of nature, Feuerbach[36] through an abstract-sensualistic one, Nietzsche[37] with a Dionysian one, Freud with a sober sceptical one. But none of these strategies dispels the power of nature; they only serve to remove its pleasant predicates and reveal its threatening ones. This indicates what could be called nature's *définition noire*: nature, which had always somehow stood under the sign of 'possibility' in point of fact maintains absolutely no relations to anything. Its seemingly beneficial originality and immediacy reveals it to be the seat of wreck and ruin, as compulsion to strife and destruction, as 'death drive'. Previously seen as healthy and sound, nature is oppressed from now on by its irrevocability: the 'eternal return of the same', the 'repetition compulsion'. But this *définition noire* is the true definition: it is true in precisely the sense that everything that nature doubtlessly and genuinely 'is as well' (namely: a contemporary authority and a paradisiacal refuge as compensation for objectification) is no match for its *'définition noire'*, and is forced into its service. There is obviously, on the basis of the mere turn to nature and immediacy, no chance for an effective and liveable distinction between negation and liberation. In its dominant tendency, the presence of this powerful nature 'only as nature' is not the presence of something healing but rather of destruction.

VII

Precisely because of this the whole philosophical turn to nature simultaneously exhibits an unwillingness to let the sought-after nature appear *as* nature, 'no questions asked'. The philosophy of this turning instead feels compelled to find methods of presenting this nature that can tame it and render it unthreatening. Among these methods were the attempts by romantic philosophy of nature to combine this uncanny nature with a good deal of rationality: the determinations of the 'I' and the 'organic' cures correspond to this.[38] These methods also include the desire of even the middle period Schelling to subordinate this nature by construing it as the 'ground in God'.[39] These methods also include the very real efforts of these very philosophers of nature who – on the way to an enchantment of romantic philosophies of nature – clearly see the destructive power of this nature: the call for a redemptive 'saintliness' belongs to Schopenhauer's philosophy of the aimless cycle of willing; the call for an 'overman' who finds this 'most difficult thought' 'easy and blessed' belongs to Nietzsche's philosophy of '*amor fati*' of the 'eternal return of the same'. In general, nature's seizure of power ushers in a search for ways to endure it; there is clearly no way to acknowledge the power of nature without at the same time appealing to those forms of its presence as non-nature that block its appearance as complete inhumanity.

Among these forms, those devoted specifically to coping with nature now become particularly important. The most significant of these are medicine and the art of genius. Where reason is forced to gather courage and acknowledge the power of nature (and thereby risk its own negation) – this is precisely where it needs artists and doctors as the organs of a (respectable) fear of this courage. Ultimately, they are functionally related: the art of genius and the art of medicine are granted – with respect to the perilous turn to nature as rescuer – a common philosophical role as humanity's simultaneously necessary and impotent attempt to rescue itself from this rescuer. That is true for the nineteenth century. And precisely because this problem of rescuing yourself from the rescuer arises unavoidably from this century's philosophical turn to nature, philosophy has to supersede this turn by transcendentally ennobling precisely these *modi vivendi* with a nature that has attained power.

VIII

This seems to be the reason why Schelling's transcendental system could not finish with its Part V – although this is where the turn to nature is made into a definitive solution of the problem of history. Schelling writes: 'the transcendental philosopher assuredly recognizes that the principle [of nature] is that ultimate in ourselves . . . but the *self itself* is not aware of this' (III, 610; STI, 217): the 'self itself' does not dare see it. It only dares to see and accept this power of nature in the moderating reflection of an 'aesthetic intuition', (III, 611; STI, 218) so 'that,' Schelling writes, 'this reflection of absolute unconsciousness . . . is only possible through an aesthetic act of imagination' (III, 351). This is why Part VI of the transcendental system belongs to Part V. It belongs to Schelling's philosophy of nature insofar as the philosophy of nature is superseded by the aesthetic. But this connection is general: precisely because the world proves all-too-natural it needs to be 'justified as an aesthetic phenomenon'.[40] It is precisely the turn to nature that compels philosophy to become primarily aesthetic; the art of genius gains fundamental philosophical validity precisely with respect to the power of nature, and specifically given its power to avoid, its ability to save; it offers a form in which nature can be present in an 'unthreatening' manner.

The art of genius is suitable for this role because its agent, the aesthetic genius, maintains a particularly close relation to the problems particular to an overpowering nature.

On the one hand, the aesthetic genius is particularly exposed to this problem of overpowering nature. This is because genius, by virtue of definitions that have been in effect since Kant and up through Freud, *is* precisely this nature; and he is for this reason radically compelled to solve the problem of how a person can be nature and nonetheless live as a person.

On the other hand, the aesthetic genius is a particularly good match for this problem of an overpowering nature. He has the astonishing ability to transform this history-threatening and history-negating nature from a real fate into a game of the imagination, thus rendering it unthreatening. He does this not only by evoking the multiple shapes of nature with lamentation and longing so that it is a 'lost' and 'distant' nature and not a dangerous-present one; but also by capturing the threatening 'presence' of this nature in an artwork. All the aspects of this nature that the genius needs to avoid in order to live, namely its destructiveness, are thus defused into a poetic subject. The wreckage, destruction, 'shattering' as well as all of his demands – indeed, precisely those that re-enforce the interiority of the individual: the regression to the primary and primitive, the search in general for imperfection, the passion for wounds and conflict, for the asocial, for nothingness and for death, the ecstasy of self-dissolution and the lust for evil, the compulsion to perfections of deficiency, a virtuosity in delaying, the urge to absurdity, and the enthusiasm of failure – the aesthetic genius 'poeticizes' all this, precisely in order not to have to 'be' it; he paints the devil on the wall so that it won't come; he acts as the mouthpiece of nature to avoid the sin of being it rather than poeticizing it.[41]

However, this investigation does not concern aesthetics so much as the question that arises when aesthetics abandons its solution before its problem. And this is just what it does. The aesthetic gives up because it does not succeed in providing and maintaining enough unreality and aesthetic immunity to prevent this nature and the threat it poses to history from returning into reality. An indication of this capitulation is the immediate, excessive expenditure of additional energy to rescue this unreality, as seen in the economy of irony. It can almost be said that the aesthetic disqualifies itself through this lack of unreality more than through any lack of reality: its power of avoidance becomes unbelievable, its ability to save becomes dubious. Its continually urgent programme of serving as an unthreatening presence for the all-too-threatening nature – the aesthetic no longer fulfils this. But what fulfils this programme if not the aesthetic? That is now the question. How is it possible to live with a nature that has power over history when it no longer suffices to live with it 'aesthetically'?

IX

The most obvious answer to this question is medicine: it is the place people turn to in the difficult business of living and getting along with their natural aspect. With respect to the ongoing philosophical turn to nature and the need to confront the threat nature poses to history, when it is no longer enough to 'poeticize' this threat as a crisis of interiority, then it must ultimately come down to an attempt to 'heal' it as a 'disease' and in this way render it unthreatening and liveable for humans. Where the turn to nature persists and with it the programme of its unthreatening presence, then within philosophy the crisis of the aesthetic leads to an economy of the therapeutic: because 'the poet' proves to be a failure as 'transcendental doctor', the real doctor succeeds him in the post of guardian of 'transcendental health'.[42]

This changing of the guard was already imperative in the early nineteenth century – at a time, that is, when medicine had not yet become an exact science and was not yet particularly successful at curing diseases. At least two phenomena at precisely this historical juncture signal this imminent change: philosophy begins turning to medicine, and medicine begins turning to philosophy.

Philosophy, then, takes a striking turn to medicine. Schelling is again representative of this change. During precisely the time (somewhere between 1800 and 1806) when he distanced himself from the actual project of carrying out his aesthetics, he gave medicine a significant philosophical revaluation. Medicine clearly plays an important role in his life during the years in which his philosophy is developing in a new direction: Schelling's own therapeutic experiments – whatever they may have been – drove him out of Jena; he stopped off in Bamberg where he worked together with the physicians Marcus and Röschlaub who were instrumental in getting Schelling a professorship in Würzburg between 1803 and 1806; finally, Baader, who had started out as a doctor himself, was expecting him in Munich. In addition, medicine was becoming increasingly philosophically significant for Schelling: he had already given a central position to the 'theory of disease' in his *First Attempt at a System of the Philosophy of Nature* (II, 220–39). Physicians were well-represented in his *Journal for Speculative Physics* – think of Eschenmayer who still was a physicist then, and Hoffmann, who published a *Construction of Disease* there. In 1802 – the year of his honorary doctorate in medicine from Landshut – Schelling gave a lecture on medicine as part of his *Lectures on the Method of Academic Studies*.[43] This was decisive for his philosophy of nature; beginning in 1806 – immediately following his lectures on the philosophy of art[44] – Schelling, together with Marcus, published the *Journal of Medicine as a Science* (1806–8), its motto: *iairos philosophos isotheos*. In the Preface Schelling writes: 'if researchers of nature are all ... priests ... of certain natural forces: then the doctor preserves the holy fire in the centre ... Medical science is the crest and blossom of all natural sciences';[45] and the (speculative) natural sciences are, for Schelling, the foundational sciences. So medicine acquires a fundamental philosophical role in Schelling's philosophy precisely when art loses it. And this is generally the case: where aesthetics retreats, therapeutics takes over.

At the same time, medicine takes a striking turn to philosophy: the doctors respond to their philosophical payoffs not only by producing new medical theories but by becoming philosophers themselves. What matters –

demands Kieser, for instance, in his 1817 *System of Medicine* – 'is to bring higher, philosophical insights to bear on a ... doctrine of disease and treatment'[46] as in, for instance, a 'philosophical history of medicine'.[47] Many philosophies of disease are conceived – understanding disease as disharmony, repression or even original sin. Moreover, 'romantic philosophies of nature' are, to a surprising extent, being written by doctors themselves: Kielmeyer, Eschenmayer, Windischmann, Ritter, Treviranus, Oken, Troxler, Schubert, Baader, and Carus (to name only a few): these men were indeed doctors, pharmacists, professors of medicine. And finally, it was in precisely this first half of the nineteenth century that a genre developed in philosophy that had until then been the almost exclusive domain of doctors: 'anthropology'. A host of pertinent titles appeared as well as a (clearly very psychiatric-oriented) *Journal for Anthropology* under the direction of Friedrich Nasse. It was indeed – as Heinroth said in his 1822 *Textbook for Anthropology* – an 'age when anthropology was a favorite topic for researchers'.[48] In 1810, Franz von Paula Gruithuisen had already written in his *Anthropology or On the Nature of Human Life and Thought for Prospective Philosophers and Physicians* that 'even those philosophers who are neither anatomists nor doctors say that this research must come from the hands of anatomists and doctors'[49] because 'nobody is in a better position to find what is hidden in humans than the research physician'.[50] So the fact that its practitioners were doctors does not speak against the philosophical importance of these anthropologies, but rather for the philosophical importance of doctors: the minor value this 'merely physiological' anthropology is granted today (just read what Steffens wrote about it[51] and you have read the book itself) is completely inappropriate: not only does it have a clear advantage among all forerunners of today's anthropology in that it actually called itself 'anthropology'; it also anticipates the later discipline's thesis: 'Judged according to his physical powers ... one soon detects in [man] a weakness and lack, by virtue of which he cannot be compared to animals ... But by virtue of his mind' – which 'is a thing ... utterly distinct from nature' and which 'never appears'– 'he is lifted above nature':[52] that is not a quote from Scheler, but rather an assertion by Joseph Ennemoser, a professor of medicine at Bonn, taken from his 1828 *Anthropologischen Ansichten*.[53] Of course Herder had said similar things as well. But now doctors are saying these things; they are authorized to formulate fundamental philosophical theses, and we need to ask: how did doctors come to assume this role? The answer suggested here is just this: the philosophical authority of doctors is part of a philosophical economy of therapeutics that develops when philosophy turns to nature as a decisive power and when, at the same time, aesthetics as the philosophy of life is no longer equal to this nature and stops being effective.

X

This thesis indicates a transcendental reshuffling and as such, it draws attention to a rather significant set of events within nineteenth-century philosophy: a changing of the guard between aesthetics and therapeutics, which, at first, and to a great extent, occurs in the subtler form of a changing of economies. It is part and parcel of such a change that the powers that replace each other also develop an interest in each other. Accordingly, in precisely the nineteenth century we see an increasing aesthetic interest in medicine and medical interest in aesthetics.

Aesthetics, then, displays a growing interest in medicine: poetry and literature begin to pay increasing attention – precisely during this period – to patients and the doctors who treat them. This situation can hardly be summarized more succinctly than Hans Robert Jauss does when he writes: 'The current popularity of the doctor as central figure and modern hero in novel and film makes it easy to forget that his literary role in the past was less laudable; specifically, throughout the centuries he was primarily a comic figure ... The change to a serious perception of the literary role of the doctor probably took place in the 19th century.'[54] A corresponding change is most likely taking place with the patient. It would be nice to have a study of the figures of the doctor and patient in nineteenth-century literature. At any rate (even looking only at Robert Guiskard, the conclusion of *Wilhelm Meister*, E. T. A. Hoffmann's doctor figures, and above all at the sharp rise in doctors' poetry at the end of the century) it is clear that in precisely the period in question, the doctor and the patient (which is to say the protagonists of the therapeutic) receive growing recognition, even in literature, of their increasingly philosophically significant role as heirs to the aesthetic solution: art and literature set off for the magic mountain.

At the same time, there is a growing medical interest in aesthetics: in precisely the nineteenth century, artistry becomes increasingly treated as a set of medical-pathological findings. A prelude to this is the historical convergence of publications in aesthetics and anthropological medical philosophy, even in the eighteenth century: Baumgarten's *Aesthetica* appeared in 1750, and in 1772 Platner published the first instalment of his *Anthropology for Doctors and the Learned*. Since then, beauty and art became a regular theme for medical-philosophical anthropologies: doctors became increasingly involved in aesthetics – whether (like Schiller already) they had left medicine and become exclusively artists, or whether they (like Carus for instance) made a point of remaining doctors, in spite of their artistic endeavours. But increasingly, aesthetics began being treated medically. And so the debate over 'the problem of genius' is part of this historical change, a debate that, from the time of Moreau and Lombroso up through Lange-Eichbaum and Benn (which is to say from at least the second half of the nineteenth century up through the present) has tried to link 'genius and madness'. Of course this has been a time-honoured tradition since Plato's *Ion*.

What is new about it though, is that madness has changed from 'enthusiasm' to a pathological syndrome: and aesthetic productivity becomes a surrogate for therapy. This leads to an attempt to grasp aesthetic symbols as symptoms. But all this is expected: where therapeutics succeeds aesthetics as the incumbent fundamental philosophy, philosophy itself demands a medical diagnosis of the problem of aesthetics. That is why this medical aspect of aesthetics readily takes over even the philosophy of philosophers. This is where Nietzsche's idea of a 'physiology of the aesthetic' belongs;[55] this is where Nietzsche's genius-madness discussion belongs, a discussion he had with Freud's friend Josef Paneth in Nice in 1884. But equally, this is where Schelling's genius-madness theory from the *Stuttgart Seminars* (1810) belongs (VII, 470); and recently, Pöggeler has called attention to the extent to which Schopenhauer's theory of genius was (even in 1819) bound up with a theory of 'madness'. Incidentally, Freud understood this theory of madness (to which he was alerted by Otto Rank in 1910) as the anticipation (of which he was not previously aware) of his own theory of neurosis. And so, in the end, even Freudian psychoanalysis, with its philosophical attraction, is positioned within an economics of therapeutics that developed through a growing crisis in aesthetics.

XI

Together with Schelling, Freud was the point of departure for this investigation. Schelling's philosophy represented aesthetics, Freud's theory represented therapeutics. But at the same time, the similarities between them attracted our attention. The ensuing discussion was, of course, only a few thoughts by way of an attempt to understand the path from Schelling to Freud in nineteenth-century philosophy; this path was seen as a type of changing of the guard from aesthetics to therapeutics, a change that had become unavoidable due to the continuing weakness of reason and resignation on the part of the philosophy of history – which is to say, the continuing power of nature.

But at the same time, this also represents an attempt to understand the similarities between Schelling and Freud. And so this whole discussion is just as much an attempt to uncover the common ground between them. In this changing of the guard, the players may change but the role remains the same. Only because aesthetics and therapeutics, when they achieve prominence in this period, are performing basically the same function – only because both are supposed to tame the threatening rescuer, nature, into an unthreatening state – only then can they indeed serve as functional replacements. So if Schelling's theories and those of Freud are related in this changing of the guard, they are related functionally and what follows from this functional relationship is what generally follows from relationships: not only quarrels, but above all similarities. This implies that Freud's psychoanalysis gets its philosophical position within a changing of the guard from aesthetics to therapeutics consistent with the form of a repetition of figures of thought in transcendental philosophy's turn to nature (which at the beginning of the nineteenth century naturally does not yet lead primarily to therapeutics but still leads to aesthetics). It is, therefore (one can say, without it being sufficiently covered in this short analysis), not an 'antithesis' but rather a 'state' of this transcendental philosophy, and so this is precisely the similarity between Schelling and Freud that has been our theme all along. Three aspects of this are to be stressed.

First, there is a fundamental similarity in the character of their actions: because both concern nature under the conditions of the weakness of historical reason – that is, because both concern this nature as an unresolvable power, both remain unique in at least being able to *remember* this power that they cannot 'sublate'. Schelling does this trustingly, and modifies this memory aesthetically; Freud does it anxiously, and modifies this memory therapeutically. But for both, the priority is *anamnesis*.[56]

Second, there is a fundamental similarity in the character of their hopes: both need to hope (Schelling does so with enthusiasm, Freud with scepticism) that the lack of threat that memory on its own cannot supply to nature, nature can in the end supply to itself. Where the goat is gardener, one can only hope that goats will really be able to garden. But this hope requires the theory of a special 'cunning of reason' – the theory of a 'rationality through nature': Schelling presents it as theory of an 'absolute productivity' of 'nature' that has 'inhibitions' and thereby becomes spiritual (*geistig*); Freud presents it as the theory of natural drives that through 'goal-actions' are compelled to become spiritual; but both are basically theories of sublimation.

Finally, there is a third fundamental similarity in the character of their disappointments: both approaches hold that 'good' sublimation does not last and conclude with the thesis that the threat posed by nature cannot be overcome. Schelling left the formulation of this disappointment to Schopenhauer: 'the will, which is *natura naturans*',[57] writes Schopenhauer, is essentially 'self-torture' and 'only a continuously inhibited striving, a delayed death'.[58] Freud formulated this disappointment in the theory of the overpowering 'death drive' and writes: we 'cannot … conceal from ourselves: that we have unexpectedly sailed into the harbor of Schopenhauer's philosophy' (XIII, 53). Even in the way it manifests disappointment, Freud's psychoanalysis repeats the motives and fates of the former transcendental-philosophical turn to nature.

XII

With this, we end the examination. It followed a transcendental-philosophical programme of a discussion of function. Accordingly, it had – through a number of suggestions – spoken only about a function in whose performance aesthetics and therapeutics in this period developed a relationship and rivalry, and received the same philosophical honours. It did this not as the completion of a thesis, but rather as the attempt to formulate a working hypothesis to be put to the test in the future. Here, where the rational 'history from a cosmopolitan point of view' and the justice actualized in it for the sake of freedom do not seem to fulfil humanity, nature should do it; but this dangerous rescuer needs to be presented in an unthreatening manner, in order to be liveable. An unthreatening presence of nature: this was, at first, the art of genius; but when it proved to be too weak, it became the art of healing. Aesthetics and therapeutics – when they came to prominence in the nineteenth century, these had, minimally, a common function. Both can be defined as attempts to preserve humanity under the impression of the impotence and resignation of historical-cosmopolitan reason – that is, under the pressure of an overpowering nature. Both operate in the place of the philosophy of history, but also instead of its bad negation.

Notes

[Editors' note: we have attempted to preserve Marquard's reference information, but have sometimes removed involved discussions. Where possible, an English version of the cited text is also mentioned, although Marquard's notes are not always accurate enough to allow this.]

1   F. W. J. Schelling (*Sämtliche Werke* [Cotta: Stuttgart und Augsburg, 1856/61]), vol. III, 612–29; *System of Transcendental Idealism* (STI) (1800), trans. Peter Heath (Charlottesville: University Press of Virginia, 1978), 219–36. [References to this work will be to this volume, followed by the page number from the Heath translation. Further references to Schelling's collected works will be by roman volume number and page followed by English short title (and page number, where a translation exists, or date otherwise).]

2   Within the *System of Transcendental Idealism* (see III, 349; STI, 12) and as the third philosophy 'above' the philosophy of nature and transcendental philosophy: see especially IV, 86 and 89 (*On the True Concept of the Philosophy of Nature*, 1801).

3   E. Jones, *Sigmund Freud. Life and Work I* (London: Hogarth, 1954), 395.

4   S. Freud (*Gesammelte Werke*, London: Imago Publishing Co. Ltd., 1940ff.) XIV, 73; *Autobiographical Study* (1925) in *Historical and Expository Works on Psychoanalysis*, trans. James Strachey (London: Penguin, 1986), 231. [References to Freud will be given by roman volume number and arabic page followed by the short title and date of the corresponding English translation where possible.]

5   XIII, 228; '*Psychoanalysis*' (1923) in *Historical and Expository Works*, 151.

6   XIV, 73; *Autobiographical Study*, 231.

7   XVII, 125; *Outline of Psychoanalysis* (1940) in *Historical and Expository Works*.

8   Schelling died on 20 August 1854; Freud was born 6 May 1856.

9   See M. Dorer, *Historische Grundlagen der Psychoanalyse* (Leipzig: Verlag von Felix Meiner, 1932) especially 71–106, 128–43, 148–54, 160–70. Theodor Meynert (1833–92) was professor of psychiatry in Vienna. Wilhelm Griesinger (1817–68) was professor of psychiatry in Berlin (Charité).

10 Johannes Müller (1801–58) was professor of comparative anatomy and psychology, first at Bonn, then, as of 1833, in Berlin.

11 See Freud XIV, 35ff.; Ernst Brücke (1819–92) was a friend of Helmholtz, Du Bois-Reymond, and Ludwig as well as a professor of physiology in Vienna.

12 J. Meinertz, *Philosophie, Tiefenpsychologie, Existenz. Tiefenpsychologische Keime und Probleme in der Philosophie des deutschen Idealismus und in der Existenzphilosophie* (Munich: Ernst Reinhardt, 1958), 64–100.

13 A. Gehlen in particular discovered an 'invisible "red thread"'from Fichte to Freud. See 'Über die Geburt der Freiheit aus der Entfremdung', in *Archive für Rechtes- und Sozialphilosophie* 40 (1952/53), 338–53.

14 Thomas Mann, *Die Stellung Freuds in der modernen Geistesgeschichte* (lecture, 1929, in *Gesammelte Werke in 13 Bänden* [Frankfurt/Main: S. Fischer, 1960/1974], X, 256–80) stresses in particular Freud's 'unconscious heritage' from romanticism (particularly from Novalis) and interprets psychoanalysis – here accepted fully and in every way – as 'that form of appearance of modern irrationality that unambiguously opposes every reactionary abuse', 280.

15 For the expression 'tendency' see for instance Schelling III, 17 (*First Attempt at a System of the Philosophy of Nature*, 1799) and Freud XIII (*Psychoanalysis* and *Theory of the Libido*, 1923). It cannot be argued here the extent to which this two-tendency theory is related to the tradition of 'hylomorphic' two-principle doctrines.

16 Freud II/III, 614ff. (*Interpretation of Dreams*); see the excellent summary XII, 218.

17 *Basic Concepts of the Transcendental System* (III, 348–9ff); also 'the unconscious' (III, 351) and 'unconscious' (III, 450); 'a region lying outside the ordinary consciousness' (III, 527ff.).

18 See Schelling's theory of *amorphon* (III, 31ff.); 'Dynamic philosophy sees the formless as original ... In the pure productivity of nature this is still not a determination, and thus not a shape either' (III, 31n2; *First Attempt*, 1799). Thus the reference to the 'Proteus of nature' (*On the World-Soul*, 1798). See Freud's theory of the free motility of the libido (XI, 358; *Introductory Lectures in Psychoanalysis*, 1917, XVII, 73; *Outline of Psychoanalysis*, 1938) as a theory of 'indifference' (XIII, 273; *The Ego and the Id*, 1923).

19 This term is also used by Schelling (III, 19; *First Attempt*, 1799, III, 290–1; *Introduction to an Attempt at a System of the Philosophy of Nature*, 1799) in connection with the use of the term in Fichte and Schiller.

20 This is a basic concept of Schelling's (1799) *First Attempt* (III, 15ff). See the corresponding theory of limitation of the transcendental system. In Freud 'inhibition' becomes in part the name of a symptom (*Inhibitions, Symptom and Anxiety*, 1926), but in general means 'goal inhibition'. See XII, 154ff.

21 For Freud, 'the doctrine of repression ... is the cornerstone ... of psychoanalysis' (X, 54; *On the History of the Psychoanalytic Movement*, 1914). For Schelling see II, 374 (*On the World-Soul*, 1798) and – in the form of 'pressed back (reflected)' – see II, 304 (*Introduction*, 1799).

22 Theory of sublimation: see XXII, 230–1 (*Psychoanalysis* and *The Libido Theory*, 1923).

23 Theory of potences: see IV, 77 (*General Deduction of the Dynamic Process*, 1800) and the *Transcendental System* (II, 450).

24 See Freud II/IIII, 690 (*On Dreams*, 1901), XIII, 222 (*Psychoanalysis* and *The Libido Theory*, 1923), XIV, 71 (*Autobiographical Study*, 1925).

25 See Schelling (III, 264 ff.; *First Attempt*, 1799, III, 299; *Introduction*, 1799; and in particular II, 177ff. *Ideas for a Philosophy of Nature*, 1797).

26 Schelling II, 39 (*Ideas for a Philosophy of Nature*, 1797); compare III, 378, 397, 427. See Freud VIII, 411 (*Interest in Psychoanalysis*, 1913).

27 See Schelling in *Transcendental System* (III, 371; 376); Freud XIV, 43ff. (*Construction in Analysis*, 1937).

28 See Schelling II, 398 (*Transcendental System*, 1800). See Freud XIII, 413 (*Short Sketch of Psychoanalysis*, 1928).
29 X, 94–5 (*On the History of Modern Philosophy*, 1827). See also *Transcendental System* III, 345, 351.
30 In the Kantian sense from 'Ideas for a Universal History from a Cosmopolitan Point of View' (1784) (in *On History*, ed. Lewis White Beck [Indianapolis: Bobbs-Merrill, 1963]). What the Kantian formula suggests is that the concrete historicity of reason cannot be determined (as is common these days) by renouncing the 'philosophy of right' but only by turning towards it: Hegel's philosophy of history is deliberately a part of the philosophy of right; and Schelling draws 'the conclusion ... that the only true object of history can be the gradual development of a cosmopolitan constitution, since this is the only ground of a ["universal"] history' (III, 592–3; STI, 202–3). 'Impotence of reason', which is to say its loss of this concrete historicity (in contrast to Scheler's notion) is not an eternal constitution but rather a primarily Western state of weakness of reason.
31 It aims 'to set forth ... a progressive history of self-consciousness ... with precision and completeness' (III, 331; STI, 2) and in order to 'enumerate only those actions which constitute epochs, as it were, in the history of self-consciousness, and establish them in their interrelations with one another' (III, 398; STI, 50). The aim of the history is for its agent – the 'I' in Schelling's vocabulary, the only creator *vere accusabilis*, as we can say – to be inspected, totally and unconditionally, justified before itself and satisfied with itself, because a rational and humane world has arisen through its history.
32 In the Hegelian sense of creating a 'mediated' presence.
33 VII, 19; *Presentation of the True Relation of the Philosophy of Nature to Fichte's Improved Doctrine*, 1806.
34 IV, 76; *Universal Deduction of the Dynamic Process*, 1800.
35 Whose philosophy is here treated as a form of 'philosophy of nature' in every respect.
36 Whose 'new philosophy' (not least because it claims to be anthropology: see section IX) can, at any rate, be seen as a (disenchanted) form of 'philosophy of nature'.
37 See, as basic principle for my interpretation, F. Nietzsche *Gesammelte Werke*, 23 vols (Munich: Musarion, 1922–9) XVIII, 88: ' "Return to nature" is increasingly understood in a way contrary to Rousseau. Away from idyll and opera!' (*The Will to Power*, 1884–8 aphorism, 117).
38 See Schelling III, 341; STI, 6: 'The completed theory of nature would be that whereby the whole of nature was resolved into an intelligence'.
39 See Schelling's, 1809, *Philosophical Inquiries into the Nature of Human Freedom* (*Werke* VII), James Gutmann, trans. (La Salle IL: Open Court, 1986.)
40 F. Nietzsche, *Werke* III, 10, 46 (*The Birth of Tragedy*, 1872, 2nd edition, 1886).
41 See S. Kierkegaard, *Sickness unto Death* (1849), ed. and trans. by Howard V. and Edna H. Hong (Princeton NJ: Princeton University Press, 1983).
42 See Novalis, *Werke*, Wasmuth, ed., (Heidelberg: Lambert Schneider, 1957), III Fragment 1833 (1798).
43 Lecture 13, V, 335–343 (1803). Schelling emphasizes at the same time: 'the science of medicine ... presupposes not only the philosophical development of the spirit, but the fundamental principles of philosophy as well' (V, 340–1).
44 The last of which was held in Würzburg 1804–5.
45 VII, 131 (1806). In 1808 Schelling became an honorary member of the Physical-Medical Society in Erlangen.
46 Dietrich Georg Kieser (1779–1862), *System der Medicin: zum Gebrauch bei*

akademischen Vorlesungen und für practische Ärzte (Halle: Hemmerde & Schwetschke, 1817–19), I, iv.

47 'Entwurf einer philosophischen Geschichte der Medicin', in Kieser *System* I, 1–96.

48 Johann Christian August Heinroth (1773–1843; professor of psychiatric medicine, Leipzig*), Lehrbuch der Anthropologie*, 2 vols (Leipzig: Vogel 1822, 2nd expanded edition 1831), vii.

49 *Anthropologie oder von der Natur des menschlichen Lebens und Denkens für angehende Philosophen und Ärtze* Franz v. Paula Gruithuisen (1774–1852) was professor of, amongst other things, zootomy, and later astronomy in Munich.

50 Joseph Ennemoser (1787–1854; professor of medicine at Bonn), *Anthropologische Ansichten oder Beiträge zur besseren Kenntniß des Menschen* (Bonn, 1828), v.

51 Henrich Steffens, *Anthropologie* (Breslau, 1822), I, 3ff.

52 Ennemoser, 33.

53 *Anthropologischen Ansichten*, 38–9. Compare M. Scheler's (1927) *Die Stellung des Menschen im Kosmos* (Bonn: Bouvier, 1998).

54 H.R. Jauss, *Die Ärztesatire in Marcel Proust 'Auf der Suche nach der verlorenen Zeit'*, in: *Die Waage* 4 (Aachen, 1959), 109.

55 F. Nietzsche XV, 389 (*On the Genealogy of Morals*, 1887).

56 Compare Schelling X, 94–5 and IV, 77 (*Universal Deduction of the Dynamic Process*, 1800): 'The Platonic Idea that all philosophy is remembrance is true in this sense; all philosophy consists of remembering the state in which we were one with nature'. And Freud XI, 451–2 (*Introductory Lectures in Psychoanalysis*, 1917): 'We can express the goal of our concerns in different formulas: making the unconscious conscious, raising up the repressed, filling in the amnesiac holes, these all amount to the same thing.'

57 A. Schopenhauer (1848), *Die Welt als Wille und Vorstellung* (Leipzig: Hesse & Becker, 1919), II, 653.

58 A. Schopenhauer (1819), ibid. I, 367.

2

EVERYTHING YOU ALWAYS WANTED TO KNOW ABOUT SCHELLING (BUT WERE AFRAID TO ASK HITCHCOCK)

Slavoj Žižek

Schelling with Hitchcock – just another postmodern eccentricity? The aim of this short essay is to dispel this first impression. My first *theoretical* encounter with Hitchcock occurred when I noted a strange coincidence of dates: two decades ago, while I was reading for the first time Lacan's *Seminar I*, I stumbled upon the passage in which Lacan elaborates his notion of the gaze through critical reference to Sartre's *L'être et le néant*:

> I can feel myself under the gaze of someone whose eyes I do not see, not even discern. All that is necessary is for something to signify to me that there may be others there. This window, if it gets a bit dark, and if I have reasons for thinking that there is someone behind it, is straight-away a gaze.[1]

My first association here was, of course, Hitchcock's *The Rear Window* – and it is easy to imagine my surprise when I took note of the fact that both Lacan's seminar and Hitchcock's film were made in the same year (1954). Is this notion of the gaze not perfectly rendered by the exemplary Hitchcockian scene in which the subject is approaching some uncanny threatening object, usually a house? In this scene, the objective shot of the person approaching the uncanny Thing (rendering the subject *not* in a direct frontal view, from the point-of-view of the Thing itself, but from the side) alternates with the point-of-view shot of the person fascinated by the Thing. Here we encounter the antinomy between the eye and the gaze at its purest: the subject's eye sees the house, but the house – the object – seems somehow to return the gaze ... No wonder, then, that the so-called Post-Theorists speak of the 'missing gaze', complaining that the Freudo-Lacanian 'gaze' is a mythical entity nowhere found in the actuality of the spectator's experience: this gaze effectively is missing, its status being purely fantasmatic.

Lacan's notion of gaze thus involves the reversal of the relationship between subject and object: the gaze is on the side of the object, it stands for the blind spot in the field of the visible from which the picture itself photographs the spectator.[2] 'The splinter in your eye is the best magnifying glass' – this aphorism from Adorno – undoubtedly a mocking reference to the famous Biblical passage about the detractor who sees the splinter in his neighbour's eye, yet does not see the timber in his own eye – does it not render in a precise way the function of the Lacanian *objet petit a*, the blind spot without which nothing would be really visible? In Hitchcock's *Shadow of a Doubt*, there is a brief passage which fully bears witness to his genius: it literally stages the magnifying force of the 'splinter in the eye'. The young FBI detective investigating Uncle Charlie takes his young niece Charlie out for a date; we see them in a couple of shots walking along the streets, laughing and talking vivaciously – then, unexpectedly, we get a fast fade out into the American shot of Charlie in a state of shock, gaping with a trans-fixed gaze at the detective off screen, blurting out nervously 'I know what you are really! You are a detective!' . . .

Of course, we do expect the detective to use the opportunity and to acquaint Charlie with Uncle Charlie's dark side; however, what we expect is a gradual passage: the detective should first break the cheerful mood and address the serious issue, thus provoking Charlie's outburst when she realizes how she was being manipulated (the detective asked her for a date not because he liked her but as part of his professional work). Instead of this expected gradual passage, we are directly confronted with the traumatized Charlie. (One could argue that, with her shocked gaze, Charlie does not react to some previous words of the detective: what happened is that, in the middle of the frivolous conversation she all of a sudden grasps that there is something other than flirting going on. However, even in this case, the standard procedure in filming the scene would have been to show the couple pleasantly talking; then, all of a sudden, Charlie would be struck by the fateful insight. The key Hitchcockian effect would thus be missing: the direct jump to the shocked gaze.) It is only *after* this shocking discontinuity that the detective voices his suspicions about Uncle Charlie's murderous past. To put it in temporal terms: it is as if, in this scene, the effect precedes its cause – we are first shown the effect (the traumatized gaze) and then given the context responsible for this traumatic impact – or are we? Is the rela-tionship between cause and effect really inverted here? What if the gaze here is not merely the recipient of the event? What if it somehow mysteriously generates the perceived incident? What if the conversation that follows is ultimately an attempt to symbolize/domesticate this traumatic incident? Such a cut in the continuous texture of reality, such a momentous inversion of the proper temporal order, signals the intervention of the Real: if the scene were to be shot in the linear order (first the cause, then the effect), the texture of reality would have been left undamaged. That is to say, the Real is discernible in the gap between the true cause of the terrified gaze and what we are given to see later as its cause: the true cause of the terrified gaze is not what we are shown or told afterwards, but the fantasized traumatic excess projected by the gaze into the perceived reality.

The ontological consequence of this paradoxical status of the Gaze is *the virtualization of our life-experience*, the explosion/dehiscence of the single 'true' reality into the multitude of parallel lives, which is strictly correlative to the assertion of the proto-cosmic abyss of chaotic, ontologically not yet fully constituted reality – this primordial, pre-symbolic, inchoate 'stuff' is precisely the neutral medium in which the multitude of parallel universes can coexist. In contrast to the standard notion of one fully determined and ontologically constituted reality, with regard to which all other realities are its secondary shadows, copies, reflections, 'reality' itself is thus multiplied into the spectral plurality of virtual realities, beneath which lurks the pre-ontological proto-reality, the Real of the unformed ghastly matter. And this brings us to Schelling, the first to clearly articulate this pre-ontological dimension with his notion of the unfathomable Ground of God, something in God that is not-yet-God, not yet the fully constituted reality – it is Schelling, more than Lacan, who forms the true focus of my philosophical interest in Hitchcock.

In what does Schelling's philosophical revolution consist? According to the standard academic *doxa*, Schelling broke out of the idealist closure of the Notion's self-mediation by way of asserting a more balanced bi-polarity of the Ideal and the Real: the 'negative philosophy' (the analysis of the notional essence) must be supplemented by the 'positive philosophy' that deals with the positive order of existence. In nature as well as in human history, the ideal rational order can only thrive against the background of the impenetrable Ground of 'irrational' drives and passions. The climax of philosophical development, the standpoint of the Absolute, is thus not the 'sublation [*Aufhebung*]' of all reality in its ideal Notion, but the neutral medium of the two dimensions – the Absolute is ideal-real ... Such a reading, however, obfuscates Schelling's true breakthrough, his distinction, first introduced in his essay on human freedom from 1807,[3] between (logical) Existence and the impenetrable Ground of Existence, the Real of pre-logical drives: this proto-ontological domain of drives is not simply 'nature', but the spectral domain of the not yet fully constituted reality. Schelling's opposition of the proto-ontological Real of drives (the Ground of being) and the ontologically fully constituted Being itself (which, of course, is 'sexed' as the opposition of the Feminine and the Masculine) thus radically displaces the standard philosophical couples of Nature and Spirit, the Real and the Ideal, Existence and Essence, and so forth. The real Ground of Existence is impenetrable, dense, inert, yet at the same time spectral, 'irreal', ontologically not fully constituted, while Existence is ideal, yet at the same time, in contrast to the Ground, fully 'real', fully existing. This opposition, the one between the fully existing reality and its proto-ontological spectral shadow, is thus irreducible to the standard metaphysical oppositions between the Real and the Ideal, Nature and Spirit, Existence and Essence, and so forth.

The notion of a pre-ontological Real is crucial not only with regard to the history of ideas, but even with regard to art and our daily experience of reality. Recall the protracted stains that 'are' the yellow sky in late Van Gogh or the water or grass in Munch: this uncanny 'massiveness' pertains neither to the direct materiality of the colour stains nor to the materiality of the depicted objects – it dwells in a kind of intermediate spectral domain of what Schelling called *geistige Koerperlichkeit*, the spiritual corporeality. And is not the entire contemporary popular (but not only popular) culture populated by entities located in this pre-ontological domain? Recall, from the Stephen King horror tradition, the spectral figure of a young boy, not yet sexualized, who is 'undead', a living dead, utterly corrupted *and* innocent, infinitely fragile *and* all-powerful, the embodiment of Evil in his very purity. Do we not encounter the same figure in modern art a century ago, from the poems of Georg Trakl to the paintings of Edvard Munch, in the guise of the asexual spectral young boy, this 'unborn' who stands simultaneously for vulnerable innocence and utter corruption?

In more general terms, the spectral Real appears in three versions: the shadow of the spectral entities that accompanies fully constituted reality; the inscription of the gaze itself into the perceived reality; the multiplication of realities themselves – the idea that what we perceive as reality is just one in the multitude of alternatives. The link between these three versions is easy to establish: the gap that separates reality from its proto-ontological spectral shadow is not simply 'ontological' (in the naïve sense of the inherent properties of the objects themselves); it concerns the way the subject relates to reality – in short, this gap marks the inscription of the subject's gaze into the perceived reality. To put it in standard Kantian terms, reality is accompanied by its spectral shadows only insofar as it is already in itself transcendentally constituted through the subject. And the moment the gaze is included in the picture, we no longer have *one* fully constituted reality accompanied by its multiple shadows, but a multitude of realities that emerge against the background of the indistinct pre-ontological Real. The inscription of the gaze itself into the perceived reality is thus the 'vanishing mediator' between the two extremes, the *one* reality accompanied by proto-ontological spectral shadows and *multiple* realities emerging out of the abyssal plasticity of the Real. And the ultimate irony is that this same point holds for Schelling's writing itself, for the very text(s) in which he deployed this pre-ontological dimension of proto-reality, his *Weltalter* fragments: there are three consecutive drafts, as if we have the three alternative-reality versions of the same text.

The closest one can get to this spectral dimension in our experience of reality itself is, perhaps, the countryside in extreme places like Iceland or the Land of Fire at the southern tip of Latin America: patches of grass and wild hedges are intersected by the barren raw earth or gravel with cracks out of which sulphuric steam and fire gush out, as if the pre-ontological primordial Chaos is still able to penetrate the cracks of the imperfectly constituted/

formed reality. In cinema, this medium of the 'undead' image, this uncanny in-between dimension is clearly discernible in what is arguably the most effective scene in *Alien 4: Resurrection*: the cloned Ripley (Sigourney Weaver) enters the laboratory room in which the previous seven aborted attempts to clone her are on display – here she encounters the ontologically failed, defective versions of herself, up to the almost successful version with her own face, but with some of her limbs distorted so that they resemble the limbs of the Alien Thing – this creature asks Ripley to kill her, and, in an outburst of violent rage, Ripley effectively destroys the entire horror-exhibition.

One finds the three versions of the spectral Real at their purest in the work of Hitchcock. In his films, the same visual or other motif *insists*, imposing itself through an uncanny compulsion and repeating itself from one film to another, in totally different narrative contexts. Best-known is the motif of what Freud called *Niederkommenlassen*, 'letting [oneself] fall down', with all the undertones of melancholic suicidal fall[4] – a person desperately clinging by his hand onto another person's hand: the Nazi saboteur clinging from the good American hero's hand from the torch of the Statue of Liberty in *Saboteur*; in the final confrontation of *The Rear Window*, the crippled James Stewart hanging from the window, trying to grab the hand of his pursuer who, instead of helping him, tries to make him fall; in *The Man Who Knew Too Much* (remake, 1955), on the sunny Casablanca market, the dying Western agent, dressed as an Arab, stretches his hand towards the innocent American tourist (James Stewart) and pulling him down towards himself; the finally unmasked thief clinging from Cary Grant's hand in *To Catch a Thief*; James Stewart clinging from the roof funnel and desperately trying to grasp the policeman's hand stretching towards him at the very beginning of *Vertigo*; Eva Marie-Saint clinging from Cary Grant's hand at the edge of the precipice (with the immediate jump to her clinging to his hand in the sleeping car's berth at the end of *North by Northwest*). Upon a closer look, we become aware that Hitchcock's films are full of such motifs. There is the motif of a car on the border of a precipice in *Suspicion* and in *North by Northwest* – in each of the two films, there is a scene with the same actor (Cary Grant) driving a car and dangerously approaching a precipice; although the films are separated by almost 20 years, the scene is shot in the same way, including a subjective shot of the actor casting a glance into the precipice. (In Hitchcock's last film, *The Family Plot*, this motif explodes in a long sequence of the car that rushes down the hill, since its brakes were meddled with by the villains.) There is the motif of the 'woman who knows too much', intelligent and perceptive, but sexually unattractive, with spectacles, and – significantly – resembling or even directly played by Hitchcock's own daughter Patricia: Ruth Roman's sister in *Strangers On a Train*, Barbara del Geddes in *Vertigo*, Patricia Hitchcock in *Psycho*, and even Ingrid Bergman herself prior to her sexual awakening in *Spellbound*. There is the motif of the mummified skull that first appears in *Under Capricorn* and finally in *Psycho* – both times, it terrifies the young woman (Ingrid Bergman, Vera

Miles) in the final confrontation. There is the motif of a Gothic house with big stairs, with the hero walking up the stairs where, in the room, there is nothing, although he previously saw a feminine silhouette on the first-floor window: in *Vertigo*, it is the enigmatic episode of Madeleine seen by Scottie as a shade in the window and then inexplicably disappearing from the house; in *Psycho*, it is the appearance of the mother's shadow in the window – again, bodies which appear out of nowhere and disappear back into the void. Furthermore, the fact that in *Vertigo* this episode remains unexplained opens up the temptation to read it in a kind of *futur anterieur*, as already pointing towards *Psycho*: is the old lady who is the hotel-clerk of the house not a kind of strange condensation of Norman Bates and his mother – the clerk (Norman) who is at the same time the old lady (mother), thus giving in advance the clue on their identity, which is the big mystery of *Psycho*? *Vertigo* is of a special interest insofar as, in it, the same figure of the spiral that draws us into its abyssal depth repeats itself and resonates at a multitude of levels: first as a purely formal motif of the abstract form emerging out of the close-up of the eye in the credits sequence; then as the curl of Carlotta Valdes' hair in her portrait, repeated in Madeleine's haircut; then as the abyssal circle of the staircase of the church tower; and, finally, in the famous 360° shot around Scottie and Judy-Madeleine who are passionately embracing in the decrepit hotel room, and during which the background changes to the stable of the Juan Batista Mission and then back to the hotel room; perhaps, this last shot offers the key to the temporal dimension of 'vertigo' – the self-enclosed temporal loop in which past and present are condensed into the two aspects of the same endlessly repeated circular movement.

It is this multiple resonance of surfaces that generates the specific density, the 'depth' of the film's texture: a set of (visual, formal, material) motives 'remain the same' across different contexts of meaning. How are we to read such persisting gestures or motifs? One should resist the temptation to treat them as Jungian archetypes with a deep meaning – the person clinging to another's hand expressing the tension between spiritual fall and salvation. We are dealing here with the level of material signs that resists meaning and establishes connections that are not grounded in narrative symbolic structures: they just relate in a kind of pre-symbolic cross-resonance. They are neither signifiers nor the famous Hitchcockian stains, but elements of what, a decade or two ago, one would have called cinematic *écriture*. In the last years of his teaching, Lacan established the difference between symptom and *sinthom*: in contrast to symptom, which is a cipher of some repressed meaning, *sinthom* has no determinate meaning – it just gives body, in its repetitive pattern, to some elementary matrix of *jouissance*, of excessive enjoyment – although *sinthoms* do not have sense, they do radiate *jouis-sense*. Hitchcock's *sinthoms* are thus not mere formal patterns: they already condense a certain libidinal investment. As such, they determined his creative process: Hitchcock did not proceed from the plot to its translation in cinematic audio-visual terms. He rather started with a set of (usually visual) motifs that haunted his imagination, imposing themselves as his *sinthoms*; then, he constructed a narrative that served as the pretext for their use. These *sinthoms* provide the specific flair, the substantial density of the cinematic texture of Hitchcock's films: without them, we would have a lifeless formal narrative. So all the talk about Hitchcock as the 'master of suspense', about his unique, twisted plots, and so forth, misses the key dimension. Fredric Jameson said of Hemingway that he selected his narratives in order to be able to write a certain kind of (tense, masculine) phrase. The same goes for Hitchcock: he invented stories in order to be able to shoot a certain kind of scenes.

Within the narrative space itself, this explosion of a single reality gives rise to the implicit resonance of multiple endings. The most obvious and well-documented case is, of course, that of *Topaz*: before deciding on the ending of *Topaz* that we all know, Hitchcock shot two alternative endings, and my point is that it is not sufficient to say that he simply chose the most appropriate ending – the ending we have now rather in a way presupposes the two other, with the three endings forming a kind of syllogism – Granville, the Russian spy, (Michel Piccoli) telling himself 'They cannot prove anything to me, I can simply leave for Russia' (the first discarded ending); 'But the Russians themselves now do not want me, I am now even dangerous to them, so they will probably kill me' (the second discarded meaning); 'What can I do then if in France I am outcasted as a Russian spy and Russia itself no longer wants me? I can only kill myself . . .' – the ending that was effectively adopted. There are, however, much more refined versions of this implicit presence of alternative endings. Already the denouement of Hitchcock's early melodrama *The Manxman* (1929) is preceded by two scenes that could be read as possible alternative endings (the woman kills herself; the lover never returns).

Hitchcock's masterpiece *Notorious* owes at least a part of its powerful impact to the fact that its denouement should be perceived against the background of at least two other possible outcomes that resonate in it as a kind of alternative history.[5] In the first outline of the story, Alicia wins redemption by the film's end, but loses Devlin, who is killed rescuing her from the Nazis. The idea was that this sacrificial act should solve the tension between Devlin, who is unable to admit to Alicia his love for her, and Alicia, who is unable to perceive herself as worthy of love: Devlin admits his love for her without words, by dying in order to save her life. In the final scene, we find Alicia back in Miami with her group of drinking friends: although she is more 'notorious' than ever, she has in her heart the memory of a man who loved her and died for her, and, as Hitchcock put it in a memo to Selznick, 'to her this is the same as if she had achieved a life of marriage and hap-piness'. In the second main version, the outcome is the opposite; here, we already have the idea of a slow poisoning of Alicia by Sebastian and his mother. Devlin confronts the Nazis and flees with Alicia, but Alicia dies in the process. In the epilogue, Devlin sits alone in a Rio cafe, where he used to meet Alicia, and overhears people discussing the death of Sebastian's wanton

and treacherous wife. However, the letter in his hands is a commendation
from President Truman citing Alicia's bravery. Devlin pockets the letter and
finishes his drink ... Finally, the version we know was arrived at, with a
finale which implies that Devlin and Alicia are now married. Hitchcock then
left this finale out, to end on a more tragic note, with Sebastian, who truly
loved Alicia, left to face the Nazis' deadly wrath. The point is that both
alternative endings (Devlin's and Alicia's death) are incorporated into the
film, as a kind of fantasmatic background of the action we see on the screen:
if they are to constitute a couple, both Devlin and Alicia have to undergo the
'symbolic death', so that the happy ending emerges from the combination of
two unhappy endings – these two alternative fantasmatic scenarios sustain
the denouement we actually see.

This feature allows us to insert Hitchcock into the series of artists whose
work forecast today's digital universe. That is to say, art historians often
noted the phenomenon of the old artistic forms pushing against their own
boundaries and using procedures that, at least from our retroactive view,
seem to point towards a new technology that will be able to serve as a more
'natural' and appropriate 'objective correlative' to the life-experience the old
forms endeavoured to render by means of their 'excessive' experimentations.
A whole series of narrative procedures in nineteenth-century novels announce
not only the standard narrative cinema (the intricate use of 'flashback' in
Emily Brontë or of 'cross-cutting' and 'close-ups' in Dickens), but sometimes
even the modernist cinema (the use of 'off-space' in *Madame Bovary*) – as if a
new perception of life was already here, but was still struggling to find its
proper means of articulation, until it finally found it in cinema. What we
have here is thus the historicity of a kind of *futur anterieur*: it is only when
cinema arrived and developed its standard procedures that we can really
grasp the narrative logic of Dickens's great novels or of *Madame Bovary*.

And is it not that today we are approaching a homologous threshold: a
new 'life experience' is in the air, a perception of life that explodes the form
of the linear centred narrative and renders life as a multiform flow – even and
up to the domain of 'hard' sciences (quantum physics and its multiple reality
interpretation, or the utter contingency that provided the spin to the actual
evolution of the life on Earth – as Stephen Jay Gould demonstrated in his
Wonderful Life, the fossils of Burgess Shale bear witness to how evolution
may have taken a wholly different turn) we seem to be haunted by the
chanciness of life and the alternate versions of reality. Either life is experienced as a series of multiple parallel destinies that interact and are crucially
affected by meaningless contingent encounters, the points at which one series
intersects with and intervenes into another (see Altman's *Shortcuts*), or different versions/outcomes of the same plot are repeatedly enacted (the 'parallel
universes' or 'alternative possible worlds' scenarios – see Kieslowski's *Chance*,
Veronique and *Red*; even 'serious' historians themselves recently produced a
volume, *Virtual History*, the reading of the crucial Modern Age century
events, from Cromwell's victory over the Stuarts and the American war of

independence to the disintegration of communism as hinging on unpredictable and sometimes even improbable chances). This perception of our reality as one of the possible – often even not the most probable – outcomes of an 'open' situation, this notion that other possible outcomes are not simply cancelled out but continue to haunt our 'true' reality as a spectre of what might have happened, conferring on our reality the status of extreme fragility and contingency, implicitly clashes with the predominant 'linear' narrative forms of our literature and cinema – they seem to call for a new artistic medium in which they would not be an eccentric excess, but its 'proper' mode of functioning. The notion of creation also changes with this new experience of the world: it no longer designates the positive act of imposing a new order, but rather the negative gesture of choice, of limiting the possibilities, of privileging one option at the expense of all the others. One can argue that cyberspace hypertext is this new medium in which this life experience will find its 'natural', more appropriate, objective correlative, so that, again, it is only with the advent of cyberspace hypertext that we can effectively grasp what Altman and Kieslowski – and, implicitly, also Hitchcock – were effectively aiming at.

This, perhaps, also points towards what a proper 'Schellingian' remake of a Hitchcock film would be: to stage, in a well-calculated strategic move, one of the alternative scenarios that underlie the one actualized by Hitchcock, like the remake of *Notorious* with Ingrid Bergman surviving alone. This would be a proper way to honour Hitchcock as the artist that belongs to our era. Perhaps, more than de Palma's and others' direct *hommages* to Hitchcock, the scenes that announce such a proper remake are to be found in unexpected places, like the scene in the hotel room, the place of crime, in Francis Ford Coppola's *Conversation* – Coppola certainly is not a Hitchcockian. The investigator inspects the room with a Hitchcockian gaze, like Lila and Sam do with Marion's motel room in *Psycho*, moving from the main bedroom to the bathroom and focusing there on the toilet and the shower. This shift from the shower (where there are no traces of the crime, where everything is clean) to the toilet sink, elevated it into the Hitchcockian object that attracts our gaze, fascinating us with its premonition of some unspeakable horror, is crucial here (recall Hitchcock's battle with censorship to allow the inside view of the toilet, from where Sam picks up a torn piece of paper with Marion's writing of the amounts of spent money, the proof that she was there). After a series of obvious references to *Psycho a propos* of the shower (quickly pulling open the curtain, inspecting the hole in the sink), the investigator focuses on the (allegedly cleansed) toilet seat, flushes it, and then the stain appears as if out of nowhere, blood and other traces of the crime overflowing the edge of the sink. This scene, a kind of *Psycho* reread through *Marnie* (with its red stain blurring the screen) contains the main elements of the Hitchcockian universe: it has the Hitchcockian object, which materializes some unspecified threat, functioning as the hole into another abyssal dimension (is flushing the toilet in this scene not like pushing the wrong button that dissolves the entire universe in the science-fiction novels?); this object that simultaneously attracts and repels the subject can be said to be the point from which the inspected setting returns the gaze (is it not that the hero is somehow regarded by the toilet sink?); and, finally, Coppola realizes the alternative scenario of the toilet itself as the ultimate locus of mystery. What makes this mini-remake of a scene so effective is that Coppola suspends the prohibition operative in *Psycho*: the threat *does* explode, the camera *does* show the danger hanging in the air in *Psycho*, the chaotic bloody mess erupting from the toilet.[6] (And is not the swamp behind the house in which Norman drowns the cars with the bodies of his victims a kind of gigantic pool of excremental mud, so that one can say that he in a way flushes the cars down the toilet – the famous moment of the worried expression of his face when Marion's car stops immersing into the swamp for a couple of seconds effectively signals the worry that the toilet did not swallow the traces of our crime? The very last shot in *Psycho*, in which we see Marion's car being pulled out of the swamp, is thus a kind of Hitchcockian equivalent to the blood re-emerging out of the toilet sink – in short, this swamp is another in the series of the entrance points to the pre-ontological Netherworld.)

And is not the same reference to the pre-ontological Underworld also operative in the final scene of *Vertigo*? In the pre-digital times, when I was in my teens, I remember seeing a bad copy of *Vertigo* – its last seconds were simply missing, so that the movie appeared to have a happy ending, Scottie reconciled with Judy, forgiving her and accepting her as a partner, the two of them passionately embracing ... My point is that such an ending is not as artificial as it may seem: it is rather in the actual ending that the sudden appearance of the Mother Superior from the staircase below functions as a kind of negative *deux ex machina*, a sudden intrusion in no way properly grounded in the narrative logic, which prevents the happy ending. Where does the nun appear from? From the same pre-ontological realm of shadows from which Scottie himself secretly observes Madeleine in the florist's in *Vertigo*.[7] It is the reference to this pre-ontological realm that allows us to approach the quintessential Hitchcockian scene that was never shot – precisely because it renders the basic matrix of his work directly, its actual filming undoubtedly would have produced a vulgar, tasteless effect. Here is this scene that Hitchcock wanted to insert in *North by Northwest*, as reported in Truffaut's conversations with the Master:

I wanted to have a long dialogue between Cary Grant and one of the factory workers [at a Ford automobile plant] as they walk along the assembly line. Behind them a car is being assembled, piece by piece. Finally, the car they've seen being put together from a simple nut and bolt is complete, with gas and oil, and all ready to drive off the line. The two men look at each other and say, 'Isn't it wonderful!' Then they open the door of the car and out drops a corpse.[8]

Where did this corpse emerge, fall, from? Again, from the very void from which Scottie observes Madeleine in the florist's – or, from the void from which blood emerges in *Conversation*. (One should also bear in mind that what we would have seen in this long shot is the elementary unity of the production process – is then the corpse that mysteriously drops out from nowhere not the perfect stand-in for the surplus-value that is generated 'out of nowhere' through the production process?) This shocking elevation of the ridiculously lowest (the Beyond where shit disappears) into the metaphysical Sublime is perhaps one of the mysteries of Hitchcock's art. Is not the Sublime sometimes part of our most common everyday experience? When, in the midst of accomplishing a simple task (say, climbing the long line of stairs), we are overwhelmed by an unexpected fatigue, it all of a sudden appears as if the simple goal we want to reach (the top of the stairs) is separated from us by an unfathomable barrier and thus changed into a metaphysical Object forever out of our reach, as if there is something that forever prevents us from accomplishing it. And the domain where excrements vanish after we flush the toilet is effectively one of the metaphors for the horrifyingly-sublime Beyond of the primordial, pre-ontological Chaos into which things disappear. Although we rationally know what goes on with the excrements, the imaginary mystery nonetheless persists – shit remains an excess that does not fit our daily reality, and Lacan was right in claiming that we pass from animals to humans the moment an animal has problems with what to do with its excrements, the moment they turn into an excess that annoys it.[9] The Real in the scene from *Conversation* is thus not primarily the horrifyingly disgusting stuff re-emerging from the toilet sink, but rather the hole itself, the gap that serves as the passage to a different ontological order. The similarity between the empty toilet sink before the remainders of the murder re-emerge from it and Malevitch's 'Black Square on White Surface' is significant here: does the look from above into the toilet sink not reproduce almost the same 'minimalist' visual scheme, a black (or, at least, darker) square of water enframed by the white surface of the sink itself? Again, we, of course, know that the excrements that disappear are somewhere in the sewerage network – what is here 'real' is the topological hole or torsion which 'curves' the space of our reality so that we perceive/ imagine excrements as disappearing into an alternative dimension which is not part of our everyday reality.

Along the same lines, two scenes are crucial in *Mulholland Drive*, David Lynch's masterpiece: (1) the scene in the night club in which a Latina girl sings a passionate love song and, after she collapses, her singing *goes on* – a rendering of the Real of the Voice similar to that at the beginning of Sergio Leone's *Once Upon a Time in America*, in which we see a phone ringing loudly, and when a hand picks up the receiver, the ringing goes on; (2) the test shots of the young heroine (Naomi Watts): when, in front of a group of cinema people, she enacts a love scene with an older experienced actor, one is embarrassed by the excessive *intensity* of the acting, which becomes 'more real than reality' – in the strict homology with the first scene in which the voice, when deprived of its bodily support, regains an additional force. One cannot but be shocked at how, when let free to act, this allegedly shy, small-town girl is able to display such an intense erotic engagement.

The shot of the voice continuing to sing even when its bodily support collapses is the inversion of the famous Balanchine ballet staging of a short piece by Webern: in this staging, the dancing goes on even after the music stops. We have thus, in one case, the voice that insists when deprived of its bodily support, and, in the other case, the bodily movements that insist when deprived of their vocal (musical) support. The effect is not simply symmetrical, because, in the first case we have the undead vocal drive, the immortal life, going on, whereas in the second case the figures that continue to dance are 'dead men dancing', shadows deprived of their life-substance. However, in both cases, what we witness is the dissociation between reality and the real – in both cases, the Real persists even when reality disintegrates. This real, of course, is the fantasmatic Real at its purest.

Of course, in all these cases, the shock effect is followed by an explanation which relocates it back into ordinary reality: in the night club scene in *Mulholland Drive*, we were warned at the very outset that we are listening to a pre-recorded music, that the singer just mimics the act of singing; in the case from Leone, the phone we continue to hear ringing after the receiver is picked up is another phone, and so on. However, what is nonetheless crucial is that, for a short moment, part of reality was (mis)perceived as a night-marish apparition – and, in a way, this apparition was 'more real than reality itself', because, in it, the Real shined through. In short, one should discern which part of reality is 'transfunctionalized' through fantasy, so that, although it is part of reality, it is perceived in a fictional mode. Much more difficult than to denounce-unmask (what appears as) reality as fiction is to recognize in 'real' reality the part of fiction. Is this not what happens in transference, in which, while we relate to a 'real person' in front of us, we effectively relate to the fiction of, say, our father? Recall also *Home Alone*, especially Part 2: in both parts, there is a cut two-thirds into the film; although the story seems to take place in a continuous diegetic place, it is clear that, with the final confrontation between the small kid and the two robbers, we enter a different ontological realm: a plastic cartoon-space in which there is no death, in which my head can explode, yet I go on as normal in the next scene ... Again, part of reality is here fictionalized.

Symmetrical to this short-circuit between fiction and reality is another, obverse, case of the dialectic of semblance and Real that makes it clear how 'returns of the Real' cannot be reduced to the rather elementary fact that the virtualization of our daily lives, the experience that we are more and more living in an artificially constructed universe, gives rise to the irresistible urge to 'return to the Real', to regain the firm ground in some 'real reality'. *The real that returns has the status of a(nother) semblance: precisely because it is real – on account of its traumatic/excessive character, we are unable to integrate it into (what we experience as) our reality, and are therefore compelled to experience it as a nightmarish apparition.* This is what the captivating image of the collapse of the World Trade Center was: an image, a semblance, an 'effect', which, at the same time, delivered 'the thing itself'. This 'effect of the Real' is not the same as what, way back in the 1960s, Roland Barthes called *l'effet du réel*: it is rather its exact opposite, *l'effet de l'irréel*. That is to say, in contrast to the Barthesian *effet du réel* in which the text makes us accept as 'real' its fictional product, here, the Real itself, in order to be sustained, has to be perceived as a nightmarish irreal spectre. Usually we say that one should not mistake fiction for reality – recall the postmodern *doxa* according to which 'reality' is a discursive product, a symbolic fiction that we misperceive as a substantial autonomous entity. The lesson of psychoanalysis – and of Schelling – is here the opposite one: *one should not mistake reality for fiction* – one should be able to discern, in what we experience as fiction, the hard kernel of the Real that we are only able to sustain if we fictionalize it.

Notes

1   Jacques Lacan, *The Seminar, Book I: Freud's Papers on Technique* (New York: Norton, 1988), 215.
2   Jacques Lacan, *The Four Fundamental Concepts of Psycho-Analysis* (London: Tavistock, 1979), 264.
3   See F. W. J. Schelling, 'Philosophical Investigations into the Essence of Human Freedom and Related Matters', in *Philosophy of German Idealism*, ed. Ernst Behler (New York: Continuum, 1987).
4   See Sigmund Freud, 'The Psychogenesis of a Case of Homosexuality in a Woman', *The Pelican Freud Library*, vol. 9: Case Histories II (Harmondsworth: Penguin Books, 1979), 389.
5   See the fascinating report in Thomas Schatz, *The Genius of the System* (New York: Hold & Co., 1996), 393–403.
6   Hitchcock's obsession with cleanness is well-known: in an interview, he boasted that he always leaves the restroom so clean that no one would have guessed, upon inspecting it, that he was there before. This obsession also accounts for the obvious pleasure-in-disgust Hitchcock finds in the small filthy details that characterize the Cuban mission in Harlem in *Topaz*, like the official diplomatic document stained by the grease from a sandwich.
7   When Lesley Brill claims that in *Under Capricorn* a kind of underworld creature is trying to drag Ingrid Bergman back into hell, one is tempted to say that the nun that appears at the very end of *Vertigo* belongs to the same evil netherworld – the paradox being, of course, that it is a *nun*, a woman of God, who embodies the force of Evil that drags the subject down and prevents her salvation.
8   Francois Truffaut, *Hitchcock* (New York: Simon & Schuster, 1985), 257.
9   It's similar with the saliva: as we all know, although we can without problem swallow our own saliva, we find it extremely repulsive to swallow again a saliva which was spat out of our body – again a case of violating the Inside/Outside frontier.

3

DIALECTICAL IDEALISM IN TRANSITION TO MATERIALISM: SCHELLING'S IDEA OF A CONTRACTION OF GOD AND ITS CONSEQUENCES FOR THE PHILOSOPHY OF HISTORY

Jürgen Habermas
Translated by Nick Midgley and Judith Norman

Schelling is not a political thinker. At three points in his philosophical career he produced a theory of the political order or (in the language of the system) a deduction of the state. But his political thought never went beyond these occasional sketches. What is surprising is not the author's obvious lack of interest in this subject, and the consequently sporadic nature of these three attempts at a deduction, but rather their mutual incompatibility. Each of the deductions starts from a different point and leads to results incompatible with the other two.

THREE DEDUCTIONS OF THE STATE

In his philosophy of nature, the young Schelling had made broad speculative use of the faculty of judgement employed so restrictedly by Kant. Along with his first attempt systematically to complete this philosophy of nature with a philosophy of mind,[1] Schelling attempted to vindicate the constitutive validity of the Ideas of the Kantian philosophy of history. The theoretical scruples of the critique of pure reason that Fichte, it seems, had been the first to think through, were used for the practical end of a 'perfectly just order'. It was within this framework that Schelling reclaimed Kant's theory of justice for identity philosophy. Men, as rational beings, act freely – it is at the free discretion of every individual to limit his action so as to allow for the possibility of other people's free acts.

But the most holy (the perfectly just order) must not be left to chance; rather, 'it must be made impossible, through the constraint of an unbreakable law, that the freedom of the individual should be abolished [*aufgehoben*] in the interaction of all'.[2] 'A natural law on behalf of freedom' is required: a just order established in accordance with the principles of practical reason, but guaranteed by the automatic sanctions of state power. It must be able to function like natural mechanism.[3] A rational, natural right would (in an entirely Kantian sense) be permanently grounded in the republican order of each state, and in the cosmopolitan federation of all states together. Such a universal legal constitution, however, is 'realisable only by the species as a whole, that is, only by way of history'.[4] Its gradual emergence is 'the single true object of history'. This idea of historical *deliberation* (*Geschichtsbetrachtung*) deftly converts identity philosophy into a driving force (*spiritus rector*) of history itself.

How could something rational ultimately emerge from the inescapable contradiction of all individual actions, from the completely lawless play of freedom, unless history as a whole arose from an absolute synthesis of all actions,

in which, because it is absolute, everything is so far weighted and calculated so that everything that may happen, however contradictory and discordant it may seem, still has and discovers its ground of union therein.[5]

In the face of the superior standard of absolute identity, the agent's experience of moral freedom is reduced to mere appearance, just like the knower's experience of natural causality. The Christian baroque allegory of the world drama provides a harmonious resolution to this difficulty:

If we think of history as a play in which everyone involved performs his part quite freely and as he pleases, a rational development of this muddled drama is conceivable only if there be a single spirit who speaks in everyone, and if the playwright, whose mere fragments are the individual actors, has already so harmonized beforehand the objective outcome of the whole with the free play of every participant, that something rational must indeed emerge at the end of it. But now if the playwright were to exist independently of his drama, we should be merely the actors who speak the lines he has written. If he does not exist independently of us, but reveals and discloses himself successively only, through the very play of our own freedom, so that without this freedom even he himself would not be, then we are collaborators of the whole and have ourselves invented the particular roles we play.[6]

This God who reveals himself in history has, in fact, borrowed the traits of his divinity (traits that are not historically revealed so much as aesthetically transfigured) from a philosophy of art, and one that translates Bruno's Renaissance into the language of Novalis.

Schelling's second attempt at a theory of the political order refers to the first tacitly and negatively (if at all). Ten years after the *System of Transcendental Idealism*, the Schelling of the 'Stuttgart Seminars'[7] states laconically that:

> We all know of efforts that have been made, especially since the advent of the French Revolution and the Kantian concepts, to demonstrate how unity could possibly be reconciled with the existence of free beings; that is, the highest possible freedom of the individuals. Quite simply, such a state is an impossibility. Either the state is deprived of the proper force or, where it is granted such [force], we have despotism.[8]

Alluding to Fichte, Schelling remarks that it is no accident that the most rigorous theorists of the Idea of a completely just order tend to get caught in the worst despotisms. This is the place where the deduction of the state is connected to the philosophy of the *Ages of the World*, and indeed provides it with a proof of that event that is beyond experience but whose consequences are forced upon us; an event that Schelling, after 1804, describes mythologically as the fall of the first man from God. Schelling views the factual existence of the state as the 'greatest proof' that man is sinking back into nature. Humanity has lost its 'unity' through that act, just as nature has lost its 'unity' through man. As rational beings separated from God, men can no longer look for true unity *in* God; they must now look for their own unity without being able to find it: 'The natural unity, this second nature superimposed on the first, to which man must necessarily take recourse, is the [modern] state; and, to put it bluntly, the [modern] state is thus a consequence of the curse that has been placed on humanity.'[9]

Schelling once considered institutionalized legal compulsion to be an advantage of the state because it guaranteed the legality of actions through a natural mechanism; now, however, he considers it a moral defect. But this just shows the problem with a system that discounts distinctions from the philosophy of reflection and, like Hegel, only recognizes the power of second nature as permanently grounded when it has taken the form of ethical life (*Sittlichkeit*):

> The state, even if it is being governed in a rational manner, knows well that its material power alone cannot effect anything and that it must invoke higher and spiritual motives. These, however, lie beyond its domain and cannot be controlled by the state, even though the latter boasts with being able to create a moral setting, thereby arrogating to itself a power equal to nature. A free spirit, however, will never consider [such] a natural unity sufficient, and a higher talisman is

required; consequently, any unity that originates in the state remains inevitably precarious and provisional.[10]

The human race will not have a true unity as long as the political unification of society is based on the state's methods of physical compulsion.
To find its true unity, humanity needs the ability 'if not to abolish the
state outright, then at least to ensure that the state will progressively divest
itself of the blind force that governs it, and to transfigure this force into
intelligence.'[11]

Schelling was spared the traditionally obligatory discussion of the best
form of the state by the barely concealed anarchistic consequences of this
idea. In 1800 he had clearly opted for the democratic republic; in 1810 this
had become a matter of indifference. The state as a state, which is to say the
institution of compulsion in which dominance is the undisputed substance of
the political, remains an unmistakable sign that the (originally sound) order
of humans and nature is still in a state of corruption.

Four decades later, Schelling's third attempt at a theory of the political
order[12] led him to reject both the earlier theories. It would be contrary to
truth itself 'to sublate the state itself, that is the state in its fundamentals,
whether practically through state revolutions (the planning of which is
criminal) . . . or theoretically through doctrines that can make the state as
just and acceptable as possible to the I.'[13]

Schelling is not talking about any of the early socialist theories flooding in
from France, and certainly not the *Communist Manifesto*, which had achieved a
certain publicity a few years earlier; Schelling means the moderate Rous-
seauism of the philosopher of Königsberg, the doctrine that Schelling
himself, in his earlier years, had emphatically embraced and accorded speculative importance:

> Reason in the service of the I can only be sophistical where a practical
> rather than a pure theoretical interest holds sway; and it can con-
> sistently lead only to the full self-rule of the people (the undiffer-
> entiated masses) where (because the appearance of constitutionality is
> unavoidable) the people must be both overseer and underling, as Kant
> explains: overseer as the united people themselves, underling as scat-
> tered masses.[14]

In his late philosophy Schelling still associates the state with the fall of the
first man; but now the appearance of the state is not conclusive evidence of a
perverted world but rather the healing power against this very perversion.
Man is indebted to the state, as the earthly representative of the intelligible
order from which he tore himself away:

> The state is this external order of reason equipped with compulsive
> force, whose material presence is a mere fact and has a mere factual

existence, but which is made holy by the law living within it that is neither from this world, nor from men, but which has been written directly by the intelligible world. The law that has become a factual [*tatsächlichen*] power is the answer to that deed [*Tat*] through which man placed himself outside reason; it is reason in history.[15]

Here, without the Hegelian mediation of morality and ethical life, ontological positivism leads to a direct identification of the authority exercised by existing states with the necessary assertion of a hypostasized ethical order abstractly opposed to humanity. In this stage of the world historical process, the state is *eo ipso* the court of restitution:

> The state is the intelligible order itself become factual in opposition to the factual world. This gives it a root in eternity; it is the enduring foundation for the whole life of mankind and all further development, which can never be sublated nor further investigated; it is the precondition that everyone must be called upon to preserve, both in genuine politics as well as in war for the sake of the state.[16]

In 1810, by contrast, Schelling stated that: 'The most convoluted situation arises with the collision among various states, and the most blatant phenomenon of the unattained and unattainable unity is that of war.'[17]

There would be no reason to recall these three contradictory attempts at a deduction of the state if it served merely to document the intellectual history of Schelling's linear development from revolutionary minded Tübingen seminarian to church-conservative state philosopher of the 'Romantic' reaction under Friedrich Wilhelm IV. For his generation, the path from republican to monarchist, however nearsighted it may have been, was not even original. But what is unique is the detour through the second version of the philosophy of the state, which leads to the denial of the state as such. I want to determine the systematic context that gives rise to this theme in order to interpret it as a valid symptom of a crisis in which Schelling alone, of all the great idealists, is brought to the very edge of idealism itself.

THE CORRUPTION OF THE WORLD AND THE PROBLEM OF AN ABSOLUTE BEGINNING

Hegel's famous assessment of Schelling's concept of absolute identity and its corresponding act of intellectual intuition still applies to the Schelling of the *Bruno*.[18] This identity philosophy was not 'serious about alterity and alienation, or the overcoming of this alienation'; in fact, its Absolute lacked 'the seriousness, the suffering, the patience and labour of the negative'.[19] But in a treatise published two years earlier as a continuation of the *Bruno*, Schelling had quietly anticipated this criticism from the preface to the *Phenomenology of Spirit*. In the text on *Philosophy and Religion*, intellectual intuition is defined in a positive sense for the last time;[20] and for the first time, 'the origin of finite things from out of the Absolute' appears as such an urgent problem that Schelling feels he has to deny that the Absolute makes a continuous transition into reality. Rather, this would be conceivable only as a 'complete break with absoluteness, through a leap'.

Instead of starting from intellectual intuition (like a shot from a pistol),[21] Hegel, in 1807, determined the 'beginning' of philosophy as the beginning of the 'emergence from the immediacy of substantial life',[22] which is to say from the form of consciousness in which it had always already found itself as a knowing enmeshed in exteriority. The appearing spirit frees itself from the immediacy of sense certainty to attain pure knowing, and in so doing, it attains the concept of science as the result of the experience of consciousness. The phenomenology of spirit, which begins by developing the truth of the standpoint of pure knowledge (reinen Wissen) is, for this reason, the pre-supposition of pure science (reinen Wissenschaft), which is to say logic. This was indeed the sequence in which the system was originally conceived. At the beginning of the first volume of the greater Logic, however, Hegel poses the same question for discussion: with what must science begin?[23]

He objects to the hypothetical or problematic experience that begins with an arbitrary appearance as an 'alien assumption and presupposition', which it uses to establish the very thing assumed through the logical movement of the investigation itself; that is, it uses it precisely to retrospectively establish what was initially merely presupposed to be the true beginning, just as the phenomenology of consciousness leads from its external appearance back to pure science. But philosophy as a system does not allow the beginning to be provisional merely because the absolute ground appears only in the result: 'it must determine the nature of things and their content'. As Hegel already expressly concluded in the Heidelberg Encyclopedia (§ 36), the science of the appearing spirit makes as bad a candidate for the absolute beginning of philosophy as any of the philosophies of the real do – they all presuppose the Logic. The old Hegel regarded the Phenomenology of Spirit as a peculiar work, incapable of reorganization; he famously excludes it from his system, and recycles its title for a sub-section in the philosophy of subjective spirit.

In the first chapter of the greater Logic, this liquidation is already partly complete: 'if no presupposition is to be made and the beginning itself is taken immediately' (instead of letting it be mediated by pure knowledge, the standpoint of the Phenomenology of Spirit), 'then its only determination is that it is to be the beginning of logic, of thought as such ... The beginning therefore is pure being.'[24] Of course Hegel does not leave it at that. In order to isolate pure being as such, pure knowledge must 'step back' from this, its content. Hegel tries to use the argument that it is in the nature of beginning itself to be being and nothing else: 'we should be without a particular object, because the beginning, as the beginning of thought, is supposed to be quite abstract, quite general, wholly form without any content; thus we should have nothing at all beyond the general idea of a mere beginning as such.'[25] In addition, the concept of the beginning as such cannot reach abstract being as something immediately objective, because the beginning reveals itself equally as a beginning of thought.

However much logic wants to devote itself to being for the sake of its beginning, being does not throw off the determinations of thought. Consequently, the difficulty remains that from the outset, the logical forms are interpreted precisely in their ontological sense as forms of self-conscious spirit. The third book of the *Logic* addresses this difficulty:

> It is true that the pure determinations of being, essence and the Notion constitute the ground plan and the inner simple framework of the forms of the spirit; spirit as *intuiting* and also as *sensuous consciousness* is in the form of immediate being; and, similarly, spirit as *ideating* and as *perceiving* has risen from being to the stage of essence or reflection. But these concrete forms as little concern the science of logic as do the concrete forms assumed by the logical categories in nature, which would be *space and time*, then space and time self-filled with a content as *inorganic nature*, and lastly, *organic nature*. Similarly here, too, the Notion is to be regarded not as the act of the self-conscious understanding, not as the *subjective understanding*, but as the Notion in its own absolute character which constitutes a *stage of nature* as well as of *spirit*. Life, or organic nature, is the stage of nature at which the Notion emerges, but as blind, as unaware of itself and unthinking; the Notion that is self-conscious and thinks pertains solely to spirit. But the logical form of the Notion is independent of its non-spiritual, and also of its spiritual, shapes. The necessary premonition on this point has already been given in the Introduction. It is a point that must not wait to be established within *logic* itself but must be cleared up *before* that science is begun.[26]

The *Logic* explicitly needs a pre-concept (*Vorbegriff*) of logic that could become a concept only by going through the real philosophies of nature and spirit – but logic, for its part, presupposes this. In the end, philosophical science in general must make do without an absolute beginning: whatever beginning it takes as its point of departure proves to be merely derived, because the progressive process of determination and the regressive process of grounding belong to one another.[27]

> In this manner philosophy exhibits the appearance of a circle which closes with itself, and has no beginning in the same way as the other sciences have. To speak of a beginning of philosophy has a meaning only in relation to a person who proposes to commence the study, and not in relation to the science as science.[28]

Hegel acknowledges the embarrassment: a philosophical introduction to philosophy is absolutely impossible. In fact, he must be content with a didactic introduction, with the proviso that this sort of historical, rationalizing introduction cannot achieve what is truly possible only philosophically.[29] This propaedeutic, which the novice must cast aside on coming of age, remains outside the system. With the problem of its own entryway, philosophical idealism becomes entangled in a hermeneutic circle in which it refuses to believe. A beginning of the system is not conceivable within the system. And yet this is what Schelling is looking for. Before turning to the details of his attempt, I want now to clarify the motive for his attempt, in comparison with Hegel.

The circle in which philosophy moves forwards as much as backwards into itself, without beginning or end, a circle in which philosophy is enclosed just as much as it encloses itself, is not external to the world that has attained self-certainty in absolute knowledge: this certainty consists in knowing that the highest level anything can reach is that on which its decline begins.[30] The conclusion of Hegel's *Logic*, namely the achieved unity of method and system, is in truth the completion of the span of history: it bends its line back in a circle. To this extent, the free release of the absolute Idea into the immediacy of nature needs no special grounding. Schelling, who thinks he detects a 'blockage of movement' between the *Logic* and the *Philosophy of Nature* (henceforth a *topos* of the entire Hegel critique) sees the merciless and magnificent consistency of a system that, just when the *Logic* comes to an end, understands that it is shut in a circle. The absolute idea would not have achieved its level if it did not, at just that moment, begin its decline. If there is redemption, then it is only in the self-sacrificing completion itself. Eternal life is only actual as redemption from eternity through immortal death. Schelling approaches this thought with horror: if our world were divine, there would be no redemption – this is what Hegel had shown.

From this standpoint, Hegel had rightly defended his claim of the thoroughgoing rationality of actuality against the reproach that he de-emphasized both the individual and finitude as it appears in the form of pain, falsity and evil. Even in the *Logic*, the life of the concept produces a concept of life as fractured and, in particular, the feeling of this fracture:

> *Pain* is therefore the prerogative of living natures; because they are the existent Notion, they are an actuality of infinite power, such that they are within themselves the *negativity* of themselves, that this *their negativity* is *for them*, and that they maintain themselves in their otherness. It is said that contradiction is unthinkable; but in fact, in the pain of a living being it is even an actual existence.[31]

It is rather the other way around: because this reproach is of so little concern to Hegel he must suspend the genuine doubt that moves Schelling. Because, in the self-uniting and self-closing system that has no beginning or end, Hegel nonetheless accommodates the tension between the Absolute and the finite (where only a leap should be possible, according to Schelling) in all its unbearable severity – he immortalizes, as the infinite unity of negativity with itself, that mercilessness that cannot last and yet is always there: 'by virtue of the freedom which the Notion attains in the Idea, the Idea possesses within itself also the *most stubborn opposition*; its repose consists in the security and certainty with which it eternally creates and eternally overcomes that opposition, in it meeting with *itself*.'[32] This peace had come to terms stoically with irrevocability: reconciliation succeeds only by passing into another alienation; in succeeding, it fails again.

Schelling, on the other hand, *had* at one point thought he had been blessed with reconciliation through the intellectual intuition of the Absolute. Even in the 1806 *Aphorisms on the Philosophy of Nature*, absolute identity still appeared to him to be the 'All-blessed outside of all conflict' – there is no death in the universe. Because he had assured himself that divine life was love playing with itself (the very thing that Hegel was reproaching him with) without any consideration for 'the labour of the negative', the experience he had in the meantime of the 'harshness and truncation of things' was a deep emotional shock that awoke in him a motive quite foreign to Hegel. Philosophy which, as idealism, continues to try to know the inter-connectedness of being overall, now stands before this task: to confront a fundamentally perverted world, and, for the sake of its possible redemption, to try to comprehend how such a world originates out of the Absolute. This entails going beyond theodicy, beyond the justification of the world (once again achieved with greatest rigour by Hegel) in order to think the world historically as a theogony. This requirement arises, as Schelling confesses in the last notes before his death, 'entirely practically',[33] after a final despair has seized philosophy – an incomparably different shape of that 'self-completing scepticism' that Hegel had already claimed for his phenomenology. It is incomparable because *this* despair can no longer find satisfaction in a dialectic of life without beginning or end. This movement requires an *actual* beginning as the condition for the possibility of having *actual* end. Schelling joins Hegel in opposing those who play down the conflict in life, because life itself essentially involves conflict.

> They want to use peaceful universal concepts to settle a conflict that only a deed decides. They want to generate the result of a life that should be struggled through, of a history in which, as in actuality, scenes of war alternate with peace, pain with pleasure, danger with salvation – and they want to generate these results out of a mere connection of thoughts that are as arbitrary in their beginning as in their succession.[34]

Only the next sentence shows the difference from Hegel:

> But no-one believes that he travels the path of true science unless he
> sets out from something that is *actually* a beginning, something that
> allows for thinking, thus something which is *in itself* un-prethinkable
> [*Unvordenklichen*] and first ... and progresses through intermediate
> stages up to that which is *actually* the end. Everything that does not
> *begin* in this way ... is merely apparent, artificial, made-up science.[35]

Using the conception developed in the *Ages of the World* of longing for an
actual beginning and an actual end, Schelling undermines the insight into
the vanity of a life that is always the same, in which only something
determined to die enjoys its completion.

> If the old saying – that there is nothing new under the sun – were in
> some sense to prove true; and if the question: 'what is it that has
> happened?' were always correctly to be answered: 'just what will one
> day happen'; and if the question: 'what is it that will happen?' were
> always correctly to be answered: 'just that which has happened before' –
> then it would certainly follow that the world has in itself no past and
> no future, that everything which has happened in it from the begin-
> ning and everything which will happen up to the end belongs to a
> single overarching time; that the authentic past, the universal, the past
> as such, is what came before and outside of the world; that the
> authentic future, the universal, the absolute future is what is to be
> looked for after and outside of the world. And so a great system of
> times would unfold for us.[36]

Schelling would like to establish the beginning as historical so that he can
begin the system absolutely. All the same, he certainly owes his beginning to
a *petitio principii*. Philosophy is driven by the 'lively feeling of this indis-
putable other', a feeling that crops up everywhere as a reluctance, and makes
it difficult for goodness to be actualized; but philosophy is driven just as
much by a consciousness that this otherness needs to be sublated, a consciousness that is posited in the same feeling as a practical, pre-theoretical
need. If we idealistically presuppose the systematic interconnectedness of the
world, then the origin of fragmentation and corruption (in an aimless world
that has turned into pain and a reproach against humanity)[37] must already be
included in a beginning that begins above all conflict. This is the only way
that an overcoming of corruption, an actual end of evil, can be presented as a
historical possibility: *nemo contra Deum nisi Deus ipse*.

In his doctrine of radical evil, Kant had already shown how this incon-
trovertible force of active denial could be traced back to a natural ground in
which 'the subjective highest ground of all maxims is intertwined and
likewise rooted in humanity itself'.[38] However, in order to grasp the natural
ground itself as the ground of the perverted world as well as the perverted

heart, it was necessary to go beyond the sort of determinations of finite freedom (and indeed finitude itself) that transcendental idealism provided, and that could be found in the objective idealism of the philosophy of nature as much as in the *Phenomenology of Spirit*. Thus, what seems to be called for is not a relation of faculties of knowledge to one another, a dialectic of understanding and reason that understands itself as movement of spirit, but something that precedes reason itself, a ground on which reason denies its own grounding without being able to seize hold of this grounding as such. Matter is such a ground. It is no accident that matter is the 'Cross of all Philosophy':

> The system that wants to explain the origin of things from on high, comes almost necessarily to the thought that the products [*Ausflüsse*] of the highest original force [*Urkraft*] must finally lose themselves in a certain exteriority, where only a shadow of essence, a smallest scrap of reality remains, a something that can be said to be but really is not ... Proceeding in the opposite direction, we also claim an exteriority under which nothing is; for us it is not the last, the product, but the first, from which everything begins, not mere lack or near total deprivation of reality, but active denial.[39]

This non-being that is not a reality, and yet undeniably has a fearful reality,[40] is put forward as the historical beginning of the system. Hegel, on the other hand, says of this same matter (which concerns 'the exposition of God as he is in his eternal essence before the creation of nature and finite spirit' which is to say logic), that it is pure thought.[41]

THE GROUNDING OF A MATERIALIST *AGES OF THE WORLD* IN THE DIALECTIC OF EGOISM AND LOVE

Of course, a historical-materialist beginning will not help in constructing the interconnectedness of the world as a theogonical process unless the material in question can be seen as both the matter of the Absolute itself *and* the condition of the possibility of a break in the Absolute. Schelling allied himself with the apocryphal tradition in which the required relation was already prophesied, albeit in mythical language – the tradition of Jewish and Protestant mysticism.[42] Three topoi are relevant in this context: first, the representation of a nature in God; second, that of God's retreat back into himself, of a self-limitation of God;[43] and finally the idea of the fall of the first man, who dragged creation down with him and opened history up to the goal of the restoration of an original state. All three are connected in curious ways with the intuition of a force that draws things together, a contraction.

1. The Sohar, the great Kabbalistic text from thirteenth-century Castille, presents the doctrine of the two hands of God; he points with the left and dispenses mercy with the right. The attribute of stern judgement is also

called 'the wrath of God'. This inextinguishable, fiery wrath that blazes in the ground of God is reined in by God's love, mitigated by his mercy. But though the flames are held back, they can always strike out and consume the sinners – as a deep hunger, held back only with difficulty by the gentleness of God. This, of course, had been Jakob Böhme's formula; in his doctrine of the 'source spirits' (*Quellgeistern*) Böhme again brought to light the world of the Sephiroth, the attributes of God. This source of wrath also appears in the complementary picture of pure darkness and the harshness with which things are drawn together, a kind of contraction. Just as in winter, Böhme adds, when it is bitterly cold and water freezes into ice, this force of contraction is what provides true permanence ('since rigidity causes a body to draw together and keep together, and hardness dries it up, so that it continues to exist as a creature').[44]

2. God as an eternal nature produces this first contraction in himself and communicates it to creation as well; this contraction must not be confused with that other process of shrivelling through which God literally makes room in himself for the world (in himself, because in the beginning he can have nothing outside himself); that is the contraction as act of creation. A few decades before Böhme, Isaak Luria, the Kabbalist from Safed, used the picture of the Zimzum to conceptualize a backward movement of God into himself, a self-banishment from his own midst. God shrinks into his depths for the sake of revelation; denying himself, he clears the way for creation. As the formula of the later Kabbalists has it, 'God drags himself back from himself into himself.'

3. What is common to both Luria and Böhme is the doctrine of the fall of Adam Kadmon, the original man, who also frees himself from the bond of original creation through a contraction. Furthermore, like that first will of God/nature, he undertakes this contraction in order to be something for himself, although human free will alone is his point of departure. Given the fact of this created individual will, nature in God retroactively assumes the meaning of divine egoism too: 'Every will that goes into itself and seeks the ground of its living content … comes into an ownness [*ein Eigenes*].' This quotation from Böhme applies to the initial birth in God as much as to the first man's renunciation, which pulls creation down into the abyss and almost knocks God himself off his throne.

Schelling let himself be guided by experience of the corruption of our world; translated into philosophy, the topoi discussed above are well suited for dealing with this experience. Schelling shows just how deep that experience goes in a remarkable discussion of the connection between nature and the spirit world after the death of his beloved Caroline:[45]

Every step that leads upwards is delightful, but those reached by falling are horrible. Does not everything bear witness to a fallen world? Did these mountains grow as they stand there? Did the ground which bears us arise from a raising up or a sinking back? And a strong, fixed order did not rule here, but rather, after a limited lawfulness in development, chance settled in. Or who will believe that the waters that were clearly at work everywhere – tearing apart these valleys and leaving behind so many sea creatures in our mountains, and all according to an inner law – who will accept that a divine hand stored hard rock formations on slippery clay, so that they would consequently slide down and bury peaceful valleys sown with human dwellings in terrible ruin, and bury joyful wanderers in the middle of the path. Oh those ruins of ancient human glory that are sought by inquisitive travellers in the deserts of Persia and the wastelands of India – they are not the true ruins; the whole earth is one great ruin, where beasts live as ghosts and men as spirits, and in which many hidden forces and treasures are held fast as if through invisible powers and under the spell of a magician.[46]

A baroque worldview, exaggerated to the point of absurdity and couched in romantic language. Specifically, Schelling cites the following phenomena as proof 'of the power that the outer has over the inner in this life':[47] first, the power of chance and free will, which is to say the dark remainder of some fundamental irregularity, something that eludes all scientific rationalization; second, the frailty and transitoriness of all life – illness and the universal necessity of death; third, the phenomena of the so-called evils of nature, namely everything in nature that is harmful, poisonous, and just gruesome;[48] and finally the presence of evil in the moral world, including general misfortune, want and suffering that society only intensifies: 'To put the finishing touches on the image of a humanity that has entirely succumbed to a material and, indeed, existential struggle, we merely need to add all those evils that can only originate in the state, such as poverty or mass hysteria.'[49]

All the same, from out of the pain of life we always experience something of the longing 'for unknown, nameless good' as well – a longing that we ourselves share. Schelling uses several examples to illuminate the structure of the negative. Because error can be both highly spiritual and, at the same time, untrue, it does not consist of a lack in spirit, but is instead perverted spirit; error is not privation of truth, but itself something positive. In fact, spirit is understanding emerging from a lack of understanding – it has its basis in madness. Men without madness have minds that are empty and barren. What we call understanding, spontaneous, active understanding, is nothing other than well-ordered madness. Virtue is the same; in the absence of self-will, virtue is powerless and without merit. 'This is why the saying is completely true [the reference is to Hamann], that someone with no strength for evil is also incapable of good ... The soul of all hate is love, and calm appears only in the besieged and excited centre of the most violent wrath.'[50]

Error, madness and evil seem to break forth when a relative non-being rises above being, in the reversal and elevation of matter over that which is refracted in it and which must appear as the essence. In short, evil arises out of the self-willed sovereignty of a 'barbarian principle which, conquered but not annulled, is the true foundation of everything great'.[51]

A single quote will demonstrate that this category originated in the mystical tradition:

> Mere love for itself could not be, could not subsist, for, due to its expansive and infinitely communicative nature, such love would dissolve if it were not imbued with a contractive force. God can consist of pure love alone no more than man. If there is love in God, there is also wrath, and it is this wrath or God's own proper force that lends support, ground, and permanence to love.[52]

Schelling refers to the power of drawing things together (a power that rules in all beings) as the basis lying at the ground of existence.[53] Its essence is amphibious because it simultaneously withdraws and grounds; it is itself not real and yet it is the only thing that bestows reality; it engulfs itself in itself and flees, and nevertheless, in this concealment it provides a ground and basis for the only thing that reveals itself. As long as such matter complies with love, love is its essence (*Wesen*); if, however, it raises itself above love, the horrific (*Unwesen*) becomes essential, and with it that control of the outer over the inner of which the corrupted world bears universal witness.

> It can have no true life such as exists only in the original relation; it does indeed have a life of its own but a false life, a life of lies, the growth of unrest and corruption. The most striking comparison is offered by illness, which, as the disorder coming from a misuse of freedom in nature, is the true counterpart to evil or sin.[54]

The inversion (*Umkehrung*) of the principles (which are what they are only in relation to one another, but can, nevertheless, be so in either a true or a false way) leads Schelling back to the notion of a misuse of 'freedom'. For freedom to be misused implies, on the one hand, that it must be absolute freedom, but on the other hand, that it cannot be the freedom of the Absolute itself, because it is not acceptable to think that God is the author of the unholy. The perversion (*Verkehrung*) of the principles and the corruption of the world must therefore result from the exercise of a freedom which is *like* God without being him – the freedom of an *alter deus*, namely Adam Kadmon, the first man. Schelling introduced this idea of another Absolute in 1804: 'The counterpart is an Absolute that has all the same properties as the first; it would not be truly absolute and in itself unless it could grasp itself in its selfhood, in order to truly be *the other Absolute.*'[55]

My claim is that the construction of this *alter deus* is the true theme of the *Ages of the World*, even though the individual fragments do not reach their intended systematic goal – the point at which creation *praeter deum* turns into creation *extra deum*. In other words, if it succeeds in presenting the myth of Adam Kadmon and in deducing the category of another Absolute out of an actual beginning of the Absolute, then enough has been done in theory to satisfy the practical need for demonstrating the *possibility* of an actual end to the corruption of this world – at least according to idealistic criteria. It would demonstrate that the unholy does not come from eternity, and thus does not need to last for eternity; a pattern of thought, by the way, that Marxists right up to the present day employ when they argue that the historical origin of domination proves that it can be sublated. Thus, Schelling tries to construct a God who at first is nothing but God – and consequently cannot have anything in or outside of himself except what he is; but out of whose original omnipotence another God can be thought to emerge, viz. the first man furnished with God's own Absoluteness. God's omnipotence is complete only when he lets something like himself come into existence, something to which (for the sake of strict identity) God can also lose his own power: with him, the first man, God puts his own fate in jeopardy. God assumes the risk that the other God will misuse his freedom, that is to say will fracture the bond of principles indivisible in God himself and overturn their relationship. In this way, God assumes the Promethean task of producing the corrupted creation again, as it were, this time by means of a nature that is itself corrupted, only historically. In the fall of the other God, the original God is brought down too, delivered up to history; his own fate is abandoned to the subject of this history – to social humanity. Even the Kabbala regarded the Messiah as merely the seal on a document that must be written by men *themselves*.

Schelling constructs this God in the first fragment of the *Ages of the World*, using as construction material the mystical category of contraction. In fact, he begins with a notion of God as the ungrounded, the *Ensof*, the will that wills nothing. The mystics called this divinity, which is above God himself, pure joy, absolute bliss, grace, love and simplicity; philosophically, this freedom is literally All and Nothing, the absolutely inaccessible. We can at best represent it for ourselves by analogy:

> If we were to assume that a personal God is something that compre-
> hends itself, then it would not be able to exist from pure love alone any
> more than any personal essence could, man for example. This is because
> this love, which is by nature infinitely extended, would melt away and
> lose itself without a force holding it together and giving it perma-
> nence. But this force cannot exist without love any more than love can
> exist without this withstanding force.[56]

Of course, a beginning still has not been posited. The first efficacious will is the one in which God draws himself together; the beginning is a contraction of God: 'Attraction is at the beginning. All being is contraction.'[57] In all the writings from around the time of the *Ages of the World*, there are few propositions that Schelling was as concerned to prove as this one. He kept trying to establish the plausibility of this methodical materialism:

> In development, the lower necessarily precedes the higher. The negating, enclosing, fundamental force must exist so there can be something to bear the grace of the divine essence and carry it upwards; for otherwise this grace would not be able to reveal itself. Wrath must come before love, severity before mildness, strength before gentleness. Priority stands in an inverse relation to superiority.[58]

God draws himself together, which means that he includes what he is as love within himself as nature. The contracting force is made into the centre of his existence. In the beginning, the Absolute is the God confined in his own being – a sort of first creation of God through himself. Then comes the second, true, creation, in which the world emerges in its ideal form because the conflict of principles induced by the contraction of God must be resolved. A phase of rotary motion (*Umtrieb*) precedes this decision.

> Through that contraction, active will again senses love as the first will, so that it again resolves to expand: But through the separation, the other will is excited in it anew, as the desire to exist. And since active will cannot leave this second will (given that existence depends on it being both wills) contraction arises again immediately out of expansion, and there is no way out of this.[59]

After he has pulled himself together into a contracted state, God longs to spread out again in the quiet nothingness he was in before; but he cannot do this, because it would mean again giving up his self-created life. This contradiction seems irresolvable, and it would really be so, if God were not able to open up a new dimension where the incompatible becomes compatible. God can break the spell of eternal time and relax the constraint of the simultaneity of the principles. He steps back into the past, takes what was united in himself as his principles, and posits them as a sequence of periods: as ages of the world.

In the phase of rotary motion, something like an inner time was already posited:

> But first and foremost, this time is not a persisting, orderly time; rather, each moment is overcome by a new contraction, by simultaneity, and it must devour the very offspring it has just created ... we require a personality that is different from the first (the enclosed God),

a personality that decisively sublates the simultaneity of the principles in it, and that posits Being as the first period or the past, that which is as the present, and the essential and free unity of the two enclosed in the first as the future. Only through a personality like this can the time hidden in eternity be expressed and revealed, and this occurs when the principles that co-existed in eternity as simultaneous potencies of Being come forth as periods.[60]

In this way, a beginning of time is first posited; it is inconceivable 'that something like the past not be posited as the future; because every moment of time arises only in this polarised distinction.'[61] Also, the first decision of the confined God is to draw himself back entirely into the past, and indeed as another act of contraction, but now in Isaak Luria's sense of the term. Luria interpreted God's withdrawal into himself not as a closing up so much as a making room in himself for another. It is a contraction in the higher dimension of time that supersedes the first 'spatial' contraction and, as such, returns into itself in order that, lowered to a potency, it can set free and actualize what had previously been confined.

But if, through this debasement and self-confinement, God for the first time is subordinated to love, then love overcomes him, and creation is this overcoming of divine egoism through divine love; in creation, the principle of the first contraction (which had retreated into the past) remains in the present as matter. Schelling describes the way in which the first force contracts into itself again using the image of the father being created through the son – as, in fact, his self-replication, 'so that what produces the first thing is itself again produced by it.'[62]

The son is the redeemer . . . because the father is himself a father only in and through the son. For this reason, the son is again the cause of the Being of the father, and here the famous saying of the alchemists holds particular weight: the son's son is, who the son's father was.[63]

Eternity, for its part, was once described as a 'child of time'.[64] Only on the horizon of the disclosed ages of the world, the opening up of time, does eternity exist as something that exceeds its horizon – the comparative of both past and future, more past than the past itself, more future than the future, but existing only through both. In the present, the confined God who has decided upon the world lets his eternity be worked out, as it were, through time. The creation of the ideal world of nature and spirit takes place as a continuous bisecting of past and present. Only at the end is an essence created that is wholly present; only man, as the consciousness that makes historicity possible, keeps past and future completely separate. He stands on the threshold of the future and can pass beyond it. If he were to take that step over into the age of the future, then, in a single stroke, time and eternity would be brought into the highest completion and the world ages, which are separated at present, would be brought together and united.[65]

This is the crucial threshold in the theogonical process. Up to this point, the God who has stepped back into the past can supervise events (as the father who is conceived through his son in continual separation). In delivering himself to the power of the one he has empowered, he stays in charge until he is opposed by man who, as the other God, can take charge. At this moment, the proposition comes true: 'He freely gives up his own life, as his own. He is himself the first example of that great and insufficiently comprehended doctrine: he who finds his life will lose it, and he who loses his life will find it.'[66]

God would have been able to find his life in his *alter ego* if this first man had decided on love: in love, things are connected 'each of which could be for itself and yet is not and cannot be without the other'.[67] In the earlier text that Schelling is referring to here, it is stated even more clearly: 'if each thing were not a whole but only a part of the whole, then there would not be love: however there is love, because each thing is a whole, and yet is not and cannot be without the other.'[68]

From this point on, the meaning of the theogonical process as a whole reveals itself, the answer to the question as to the motive of that unfathomable act of the first contraction of God, which is surpassed and taken back in a second contraction, and thus the answer to the question of why is there *something* rather than nothing. God controls everything; his domination is limited only by the fact that it is *necessary*. This domination as a having-to-dominate is the condition that God cannot rise above (*aufheben*), 'since he would need to rise above himself'.[69] He can only free himself from this single limitation imposed by his own unlimited dominion if something uncontrollable presents itself to him, viz. something like him, something that he indeed *could* rule, but *would* not rule – because he could only have it by not having, in love. In this sense, it is said that only through love and subordination to glorification can God gain power over the conditions of his existence, conditions that he cannot rise above without rising above himself. He only gains dominance by dominating something like himself, but something that specifically evades domination. Absolute control over everything, even over this absoluteness itself, is completed by *renouncing the domination* that is made possible by the production of another Absolute, and thus in the union with something that is utterly uncontrollable. This is the esoteric meaning of the overcoming of divine egoism through divine love. Of course this love must also be *willed* by the other Absolute, because otherwise it would not be an Absolute. For the sake of love, God must take on the risk that his counterpart might refuse him – and dissolve the unity of principles that was indissoluble in God himself. This is what explains that brutal fact of a perversion (*Verkehrung*), which we immediately perceive in the corruption of the world, a world that has slipped out of God's hands, whose history is handed over to the 'inverted [*umgekehrten*] God' of social mankind.

In the condition of 'materialism' where the outer has control over the inner, men forfeiting their true unity with God must seek a natural unity, viz. in the state that now enforces the unity of free subjects with physical force. The original God has been inverted in the human race: the former has control over everything but could rule over no one, whilst men rule without control, and thus only want to control the uncontrollable, other men, without being able to control the controllable, viz. a nature that is alienated from man. Nevertheless this human race is still a God (although in a perverted way) because it makes its own history, and is thus the subject of its history without being able to be it *as* a subject (since this would make history into another creation). In the idea of the fallen *alter deus*, the Absolute's mediation through history is posed as a task that is itself to be solved historically – a task for which there is the prospect of a solution.

THE IDEA OF THE CONTRACTION OF GOD AND ITS CONSEQUENCES FOR THE PHILOSOPHY OF HISTORY

The category of 'ages of the world' that arises from the contraction of God is such an intensely historicist way of constructing history that it treats the deliverance of the Absolute into history as settled fact; but at the same time, this historicity arises so unmistakably out of God that a final contraction of the inverted God ought to bring about the restoration of the corrupted world. The very first sentence of *Ages of the World* declares this to be the goal of a historical-idealist philosophy: 'The past is known, the present is recognized, the future is divined. What is known is recounted, what is recognized is presented, what is divined is prophesied.' Nowhere is the distance separating Schelling from Hegel laid out as precisely as it is here. History is the subject matter of the highest science; in its essence, philosophy is history, in its presentation, it is a fable. If philosophy is not in a position to describe what *it* knows with the same simplicity and directness that characterize how every other piece of knowledge is recounted, this only shows that at present we have not yet attained true science: 'The opinion that philosophy can finally be turned into actual science by means of dialectic ... reveals a restricted outlook, inasmuch as the very existence and necessity of the dialectic proves that the true science has not yet been found.'[70]

The philosopher is the *historian* of the Absolute; which is why Schelling regrets not being able to remove everything dialectical from the core of history, 'although I will try as much as possible to deal with it in introductions, passing remarks, and notes'.[71] Dialectic is for Schelling what historical reason was for Hegel, a form of subjective spirit. To Hegel, history seems like an unsuitable but indispensable introduction to the dialectic; to Schelling, dialectic seems unsuitable for the presentation of history. Nevertheless, dialectic also remains indispensable for Schelling, as we are dealing with the history of the Absolute, we require the standpoint of an achieved mediation of both in order to be able to 'recount' comparatively, as is done by the historian, but also, and most perfectly, by the epic poet.[72]

Hegel can presuppose this standpoint; from his perspective, Schelling's procedure is easy to criticize:

> when it is a question, not of *truth* but merely of *history*, as in pictorial and phenomenal thinking, we need not of course go beyond merely narrating ... But philosophy is not meant to be a narration of happenings but a cognition of what is true in them, and further, on the basis of this cognition, to comprehend that which, in the narrative, appears as a mere happening.[73]

The dialectic, which is handled as a mere form of presentation for the historical (insofar as it concerns the history of the Absolute), counts as an 'intelligent reflection' for Hegel:

> Even though it does not express the Notion of things and their relationships and has for its material and content only the determinations of ordinary thinking, it does bring these into a relation that contains their contradiction and allows *their Notion to show or shine through* the contradiction.[74]

In fact, the *Ages of the World* rarely frees itself from its dialectical images to reach the concept. But this is justified by the fact that Schelling does not recognize the objective concept as a form of the Absolute's self-mediation. Subjectively, the concept must indeed raise itself above history; objectively, however, it is always outdone by it; this reduces it to an indispensable but inadequate means of constructing the historical object. For Hegel, on the other hand, 'time' is just an intuited concept – in grasping its concept, spirit gets rid of time.[75] If Schelling had written a *Logik*, the third book would have been subordinate to the second, the concept to the essence. Philosophy cannot in itself perform the still unfinished task of mediation, because the corrupt world is not a negation that requires the determinate negation of Absolute Knowledge in order to then comply with it.

Contraction is made of sterner stuff than negation, equipped, as it were, with a surplus of moral energy above and beyond the logical categories. It is no accident that Schelling (pre-dialectically in a certain sense) retains the notion of principles or potencies that nevertheless always stand in relations of dialectical correspondence. The mediating movement is not some third thing that is replaced by the potencies; but at the same time, it is not a dialectic that lets the principles as its moments perish from and in each other. Rather, the movement, the contraction, only sticks to the one principle (and in fact to the lower one) that determines its relation to the higher, as well as the higher principle's mode of reaction. Love's action is to let egoism act, according to whether egoism keeps love locked up inside itself, or whether, closing itself off, it makes itself the ground of the freely flowing love. Contraction can either hold back a crisis or initiate one but it cannot itself control the crisis, so, like the drawing-together force that overcomes itself, it must let itself be divided by and through love. Once an event has been authorized, it must be allowed to occur. In this way, the negative gains the substantial character of a contraction that is both less destructible and more forgiving than the diremption of life into the abstract universal and isolated individual; the concrete universal acquires a self-comprehending but transitory unity from the contradiction given in a contraction. Hegel was only able to construct unity, diremption of unity, and the unity of the two, but not something like a positively posited *false unity*. For him, certainly, the life of the Idea itself is the existing contradiction: 'if an existent in its positive determination is at the same time incapable of reaching beyond its negative determination and holding the one firmly in the other, then it is not the living unity itself, not ground, but in the contradiction falls to the ground.'[76]

So unity disintegrates into its abstract moments and only remains as this diremption. Schelling, on the other hand, thinks of the inverted relation between existence and base as still being a unity: 'for it is not the separation of forces that is in itself disharmony, but rather their false unity, which can be called a separation only in relation to the true unity.'[77]

While Hegel (in the example of the state, for instance) must draw the conclusion that a whole stops existing at all as soon as the unity of its concept and reality is broken, Schelling can still conceive the state precisely in its uncanny form as the 'terrible reality' of a *false unity*. According to Hegel, such a reality does not correspond to the concept, but merely appears; it is accidental, arbitrary and external and has no power, not even the power of the negative. 'In common life, any freak of fancy, any error, evil and everything of the nature of evil, as well as every degenerate and transitory existence whatever, casually acquires the name of actuality. But even our ordinary feelings are enough to forbid a casual (fortuitous) existence getting the emphatic name of an actual.'[78]

On the contrary: the false unity, the ground's domination over love confers the demonic equality of blindingly brilliant appearance, even of blindness itself, upon accident, chance and mere appearance (given the control of the outer over the inner). The self-comprehending spirit is not *eo ipso* in control:

> Whoever is somewhat acquainted with the mysteries of evil ... will know that the most intense corruption is precisely the most spiritual one, and that under its sway everything natural, and consequently also our sensibility and even the most base pleasure, will disappear; such corruption will turn into cruelty, and a character of demonic-devilish evil is far more of a stranger to pleasure than a good one. Hence, if error and evil are both spiritual in kind and origin, the spirit itself cannot possibly be the highest form.[79]

But the task expected of social mankind in its role as fallen *alter deus* –
how is it possible? How is the mediation of the Absolute and history possible, if not through the comprehension of the concept?

The opaque interconnectedness of this world over and above the historically active human race becomes peculiarly objective via the almost Kantian
abstraction of an original and originary evil deed, one that cannot be logically deduced: the fall of the first man from God. Because corruption is
anticipated as a sort of general thesis, the history of mankind can no longer
be comprehended as moral self-liberation along the lines of a phenomenology
of spirit. Given the fact that the movement of history occurs on a different
level from the act that first grounds history, man can confront the consequences of that act but cannot confront the act itself as its own act.
According to Hegel, every step of the subject's development into the
objective begins as the subject is repulsed by the objective with the
uncomprehended harshness of exteriority; finally, however, the subject comes
to experience, in its own body, only what it has itself produced, and is forced
to recognize this experience as such. In Schelling's conception, on the other
hand, nature that has been reduced to the inorganic remains absolutely
external to man. The identity of mankind with nature has been disrupted at
such an elemental level that even on the path to a working appropriation, an
ineradicable remainder of unconquerable chance must be left behind. At
every stage in the mediation of the human race and nature, the subject finds,
outside the traces of its own history, this sort of an older and darker force in
the object, a force that could never be wholly dominated; the subject does
not experience *simply* the impediments of its own historical activity in the
blows of fate. But even more, it seems to offer the only possible path for
precisely this historical activity: to rid the corrupted world of its materialism
through material production itself, to break the spell of the outer over the
inner through active externalization itself. In fact, this is already set out in
the dialectic of contraction. Only the contracting force of matter is able to
give strength to the enclosed forces of love, to unlock and contend with the
will of the ground that has once again contracted to a dark core: love is
merely 'an in-between', itself lacking initiative.

Although the historical idealism of the *Ages of the World* contains crypto-
materialist elements of this kind, Schelling certainly never seriously drew
out the materialist conclusions. Nevertheless, we are compelled to draw
systematic consequences, because at precisely this juncture there is a clear
turning point in the biography of the work, one that runs right through the
middle of the suddenly abandoned project of the *Ages of the World*. Whether
or not he was aware of it, Schelling shied away from these consequences and
was therefore forced to revise his premises.

A first approximation of the historico-philosophical consequences of
Schelling's idea of the contraction of God, insofar as they concern us, can be
found in the religio-historical example of Sabbatianism. This heretical
movement, which continued to horrify Orthodox Judaism well into the

eighteenth century, dates back to 1665–6, when Sabbatai Zevi first revealed himself as the Messiah, and then, summoned before the sultan, converted to Islam. The highest dialectical doctrine, which is an extreme variation of Urian mysticism, not only justified antinomian actions but promoted them. Because the consuming positivity of evil can only be overcome through wickedness itself, the magic of interiority that had, until then, determined the mystical direction of Judaism, suddenly turned into a magic of apostasy. The weak will not prevail over the strong in this corrupted world through rigorous adherence to the Torah; rather, the world is sunk so deep in corruption that it can only be restored by an even greater depravity. The Messiah himself must descend into the realm of evil in order to release the imprisoned divine love. The apostasies of the Messiah would be followed by the mass conversion of the heretical congregation to Catholicism and Islam. The canonization of sin let anarchy loose in the sanctum of the law itself. Denied any sort of politico-historical confirmation, radical praxis transposed itself into religious criticism; the rationalism of natural rights inherits the unfulfilled transformation of Sabbatianism into emancipation, even if it is just an emancipation from the ghetto. It is only a step from mystical heresy to the enlightenment: Jonas Wehle, the head of the Prague mystics in 1800, cites the authority of both Sabbathai Zevi *and* Mendelssohn, Kant *and* Isaak Luria.[80]

Similarly, in 1811, the mystically inspired Schelling stands both close to and far from the consequences of an atheistic materialism. In connection with that 'greatest proof of man's sinking back into nature', which is to say the state as the physically enforced natural unity of social man, Schelling notes: 'Once nature's existence was threatened by man, and once nature was forced to constitute itself as its own *proper* world, it appeared that everything was directed at the preservation of this external foundation of life.'[81]

On the one hand, humanity as the *alter deus* makes its own history; on the other hand, as the inverted God it has destroyed the connection with nature and lost its dominion over it; under these conditions, how can mankind break the control of the outer over the inner unless it takes on the outer *externally* and, in that effort (which, in Schelling's words, is directed towards the preservation of the external foundations of life), mediates itself with nature in social labour. This is not such an absurd thought because Schelling himself sees that the power of the outer can only be overcome (which is to say it can only be broken) insofar as men understand that they should turn it against itself – through the mastery of nature. The passage above continues:

Everything, even the most precious being, must perish in collision with nature, and the best forms must join forces with this externality, so to speak, if it is to be tolerated. However, what persists in this struggle, and prevails as something divine against this overpowering force of external nature will have proven itself under fire, and it must veritably contain a divine power.

This passage seems to agree: man can regain control over nature using technology directed to the outside rather than through a magic of interiority that is always qualified by contemplation.

But if the argument ever reached this point, wouldn't the historical process automatically shed its theogonical skin? As the subject of a history that is no longer synchronized with nature in accordance with identity philosophy, humanity is set free; it can put aside as a superfluous hypothesis the idea of 'the complete humanization of God, of which thus far only the beginnings have taken place'.[82] Indeed, this humanization of God, 'where the infinite will have become finite without impairing its infinitude',[83] could, for its part, be interpreted as the mirror of a man becoming man himself; this leads to the point where, in the shape of socialized humanity, the finite becomes infinite without impairing its finitude. That would be a Feuerbachian critique of historical idealism, but at the same dialectical level.

At first, the God of the *Ages of the World* has control over everything but cannot rule over anyone equal to him; he has so little dominance that he cannot renounce domination, even for the sake of love. This is why he begins creating the world, in order to bring forth an alter ego; but this alter ego stubbornly renounces God, and has to take over the creation of the world in God's stead, taking the lead up until 'the complete personalization of God',[84] the moment when the deified human race is allowed to bind itself in love to a God who has now become human. This God has been made to be deciphered as the alter ego of humanity. Of course, humanity lacks the very control that gives God such grief; God on the other hand does without the control over the uncontrollable that constitutes the substance of history: an autonomous being's domination over others, just like the precarious moments of the renunciation of domination in individual happiness. Interpreted in this way, the inversion of God's becoming man, namely the becoming man of the inverted God, can reveal its intention: to get rid of the mis-relation that has until now been found in the history of humanity between, on the one hand, the powerlessness to control what is controllable, and, on the other, the power to control what is uncontrollable. The intention would be to relinquish an atrophied domination in the midst of a humanity that has become self-assured and at peace.

THE THEORY OF POTENCIES OF THE LATE PHILOSOPHY: METAPHYSICAL LIFE INSURANCE AGAINST THE RISK OF A SELF-BETRAYAL OF GOD IN HISTORY

Considerations like this lead us far away from Schelling. After a brief, barely noticeable engagement with such ideas, he pulled back, claiming that the cleft between the inner and the outer could not remain as it is, 'for otherwise it would affect God's very existence. Yet how is this gap to be bridged? Certainly not by man in his present condition.'[85] Schelling saw that humanity would need to remember (*erinnern*) the outer and make it inner (*innerlich*).[86] With the help of intensified 'memory' (*Erinnerungskraft*), the appropriation of alienated nature can succeed only magically, never technically, in the sense that Schelling once expressed hypothetically in the following passage:

> I do not know whether we ought to accord such great significance to our present knowledge of the vital phenomena of the body, the electrical interplay of forces, and the chemical affinities; I do not consider it impossible that a whole new order of phenomena may arise for us if we could not only alter its exterior but immediately affect that inner living kernel. I do not know whether it is a delusion or the particular constitution of my kind that allows me to see this, but to me everything, even the most corporeal things, look as if they were ready to produce life signs completely different from the ones we now know.[87]

But if man cannot initiate this magical rapport himself, nature must come to *him*. The restoration of the human race would then be dependent on a restoration of nature: '(man) must wait for nature's complete existence to achieve his own. In the end, there must be a crisis of nature in which the long illness is decided. This is nature's last crisis, hence the "last judgement".'[88]

Nature's last decision is an apparent analogy to God's initial decision, which gave rise to the ideal world. But how could fallen man, or even a nature that he has thrown into the ground, still exercise control over such forces of moral crisis? Schelling only provisionally attempted to develop this version, and then he let it drop. Driven to the borders of idealism, the only solution offered by the speculative *Ages of the World* was to return to the other version, which was also suggested in the 1810 text: the salvation of the world by a revealed God:

> Only God *himself* can reestablish the bond between the spiritual and corporeal world, namely, by means of a second *revelation* ... the highest stage is that where the divine defines itself entirely, in short, where it becomes *man* and thus, as the second and divine man, comes to mediate between God and man in the same manner in which original man was meant to mediate between God and nature.[89]

The saving regression to the idea of revelation certainly requires the *Ages of the World* to adopt a fundamentally different construction. A humanity with an inalienable need for Christian revelation (and an ecclesiastical institutionalization of revealed truth) has its counterpart in a God who can never be wholly absorbed into history.[90] Accordingly, in the last and the only authorised version of the *Ages of the World*, contraction still only applies to nature in God, not to God himself; God, being utterly beyond question, always keeps himself outside of the 'circular motion' of forces. As the will that wills nothing, the nature-less divinity takes on (*annehmen*) the divine nature of restless being from above, as it were. 'Taking on being' means that in taking the other into itself, the divinity itself takes on or assumes (*annimmt*) another form; but at the same time, this is also an assumption (*Annahme*) in the hypothetical sense – assuming something in order to see what results from it, whilst remaining safe and unaffected. The assumption of being has something of the artistic freedom of being able to act one way as well as another. A God with this sort of reserve stays high enough above all risks and catastrophes to be able to help a fallen creation back onto its feet. It is no longer God's *contraction* but rather his *condescension* that is now the sign of creation.

After Schelling stopped working on the *Ages of the World*, he did not systematically take up the idea of the contraction of God again. The contractive dialectic of existence and ground of existence gives way to a quadrate of principles using the Aristotelian category pairs of matter and form, potency and act.[91] The first principle in which philosophy found its absolute beginning retains the name of matter. But it no longer indicates a contracting force of negation in the manner of a self-enclosure, a shrinking into itself; rather, it now means a force of unlimitedness (*Entgrenzung*), something posited outside itself, something without boundary or determination, being that resists all forms and rules, the Pythagorean-Platonic *apeiron*. The principle opposing this is no longer effusion and overflow (such as when love opposes egoism); it is, rather, limitation, limit-setting – *peras*. Certainly, matter retains some of its original meaning of a 'basis' because it also appears as potency, in opposition to act. In this sense, however, the relation of existence to ground of existence is not re-established either, because (as Schelling's Thomistic terminology already makes clear) Schelling left no doubt about the fact that actualization is completed in the potency as the *primum passivum*, and thus the potency neither releases it nor endangers it in any way. Indeed, there is a third principle that satisfies the need to have both God and the world-encompassing processes securely anchored in the principles, and this third thing is installed above the strife of the other two to watch over them:

> Because each of the other two has infinite desire for itself; the first wants only to maintain itself in being, the second only to lead it back into non-being; only the third (which is itself affectless) can determine the extent to which, at any time (i.e. for any moment of the process), being ought to be overcome; every becoming comes to a halt (i.e. is achieved) through this third thing alone; it both acts from within on everything purposive, and is itself a purpose.[92]

As *causa finalis*, the third cause is superior to the *causa materialis* or the *causa efficiens*; it is the ought-to-be opposed to the able-to-be and the must-be:[93]

The first, merely material cause is not really a cause; being an unde-termined nature which, for that reason requires determination, it is really only passion ... The second cause (which gives determinations and acts towards substance as determining cause) is a pure cause because it does not want anything for itself either. So: what can be thought above both, or rather, what must be thought above both in order to achieve a comprehensible conclusion? Obviously, something that is both substance and cause, determination and determining, which is to say a self-determining substance which, *qua* undetermined, entails ability, *but is raised above the associated danger through Being* ...[94]

The risk that God's self-disclosure entails to that other Absolute, his-torically acting humanity, is now ruled out in principle (literally, by a specially made-to-order principle), 'it is the ability that could never lose itself, which is eternally calm and always remains with itself.'[95] Schelling took out a sort of metaphysical life insurance against the danger of an absolute beginning out of matter: 'Thus the beginning is in that ability which could only become another through itself, and which is therefore originally subject to becoming.' This sentence is still a distant echo of the earlier insight that contraction is the beginning of all life – 'however, it is not left to itself, but is *provided with a guardian*, which protects it from its own limitlessness, and prevents its destruction.'[96]

The world loses the character of catastrophe in proportion to God's increasing security. Even the fall of man is interpreted according to the schemas of act and potency: the ideal world, which grows together out of the three principles, finds its unity in a fourth principle, in a final cause of a higher order, in mankind. This principle stands to the first three causes as act to potency. But as soon as man grasps himself as what God has become, then in order to exist *as* God, he actualizes the intelligible world into an exter-nally existing world: 'Man is the positing of the world, he has posited the world outside God, not merely *praeter deum* but *extra deum*; he can call this world his world.'[97]

The 'fall' that, as the perversion of principles and corruption of the world, was once viewed as the outer force seizing control over the inner, is now reinterpreted in a normal repetition of the first theogonical stage, according to the relation of act and potency:

Creation was complete, but it was placed on a moving ground – on a being mighty in itself. The final product was something absolutely mobile that could immediately change, and indeed *could not avoid change* in a certain respect ... God himself pushes irrevocably towards this world; it is through this world that he first distanced all being from himself, that he has a world free from himself, a creation existing outside himself. Every moment that has passed is thus a real, actual moment, but it is a merely conceptual moment to the extent that it could not be dwelled upon or stopped at until this world is born, the world in which we actually find ourselves.[98]

Schelling's late doctrine of potencies completes the development of potentializing through a continuing depotentialization. At every step, what was first an act is reduced to a potency – until God, as *actus purus*, purified of all potentiality, can finally step forth. Whilst the third cause, self-determining substance, was initially active in the space of the ideal world as the only actual principle, now it is superseded by a fourth cause and, together with the other two, reduced to a mere material cause. The formerly ideal world in its entirety now occupies the same position as the human spirit – it is just a potency of the higher act. As such, it has become the real world. Accordingly, the process of history completes itself by gradually overcoming even this actuality through an even higher act. Human spirit is ultimately depotentalized into soul and becomes effective by willingly subordinating itself to God, who is the single true *actus* of a fully developed world. The guarantee that comes with the third cause proves its power at every stage. God always preserves himself as the Lord of Being, as the effusive actuality of beginning and eternity. At the end of its process, the world is what God is, the essence of all being that God lets be, and thus owes to him the fact *that* it is what it is.

The category pair of essence and existence joins those of matter and form, and potency and act. This categorical apparatus reveals the priority of ontological questioning over any practical interest in overcoming a corrupt world; the corruption itself has lost its offensiveness. Each act that externalizes the ideal world into reality is no longer unique – it is just one more act in the process of the continuing actualization of the world. Catastrophe is ontologically normalized; philosophy no longer looks for the absolute beginning for the sake of an end to corruption, it looks for being as that which is certain and solid before and above all else, – 'we must first find . . . what truly endures'.[99] The late Schelling commits philosophy again to the task it has been traditionally and explicitly assigned ever since Aristotle; nevertheless, the interest that once determined the direction of the *Ages of the World* cannot simply be repressed. In the end, it maintains itself so successfully against even the theoretical interest that this conflict breaks the system into two parts: a negative and a positive philosophy.

THE DISCREPANCY BETWEEN ONTOLOGICAL INQUIRY AND PRACTICAL NEED: THE SPLIT IN THE SYSTEM

The doctrine of principles has a theogonical/cosmological meaning as well as a transcendental one. It concerns both the historical-developmental interconnectedness of being overall and the thorough comprehensibility of its laws.

The principles are first derived idealistically from reason thinking about itself; reason proceeds from its own immediate content. As such, it discovers 'the infinite potency of being', the indifference of subject and object that is neither being nor non-being, in short, that boundless capability to be that drives towards being and must always be presupposed – a sort of materially enriched 'Being' from the Hegel's *Logic*.

> The immediate potency is thus only materially, only by and large, which is to say only accidentally being. This means that it can fail to be what it is; it is only provisionally being, as it were, so long as it does not change, but as soon as it steps out of its capacity, it steps out of the sphere of that which is and into the sphere of becoming; and in so doing, it both is and is not what is ... Put in this position, reason indeed wants being itself; because it regards only being as its true content, on the grounds that it endures. But being itself, not what merely seems to be and yet is capable of becoming something else, something alien to reason, (nature, experience, etc.) – reason cannot attain being itself except by excluding the other, which is *not* being itself. But in the first, immediate thought, this other is not separable from that which is being itself; it is indisputably included in the first thought. Reason does not really want or posit this other: reason only fails to *not* posit what it only cannot exclude from the first thought. But how can reason exclude this other except by letting it step forth, actually letting it turn into its other, so that it can liberate true being, the *ontos on*, and present it in its purity.[100]

In the dialectical pursuit of the capacity to be, that which is, the act, is pressed down into a potency at each new stage, and at the end of the road, reason retains actualization as such, authorship as pure activity. Transcendental self-reflection attains the principles of every being (the four causes) by eliminating from being the capacity to be, eliminating non-being from that which allows everything with being to be.

Transcendental 'critique' claims to be the construction of this theogonical 'crisis'. In other words, in the process of depotentializing actualization, reason comprehends the world process as a whole. Certainly, Schelling can only equate the transcendental and theogonical meanings of the doctrine of principles if finite and divine reason are the same. But since Hegel's *Logic* had already had greater success with this presupposition, why would a 'purely rational philosophy' want to do it again, particularly with questionable recourse to Thomistic interpretations of Aristotelian categories? This is not what the aging Schelling had in mind. He had certainly not forgotten the triple insight derived from philosophizing on the basis of practical interest: first, the insight into the facticity of a world whose dark, incomprehensible remainder always escapes the ubiquity of reason; second, the insight into the undecidedness of a historical process that opens up at every moment and lets past and future arise together; and finally, the insight into the corruption of the relations that were originally accidental and continue to be unreconciled – as well as the fact that this corruption is, in principle, transient.

The finitude of the human spirit once proved to Schelling that evil is actual and that a solution, a redemption needs to be found. He could not deny it in practice, but neither was he able to acknowledge it in theory once he abandoned the standpoint of the *Ages of the World* in favour of the pure rational philosophy. The positive philosophy owes its existence to this dilemma, and it is now relativized as negative over and against the pure rational philosophy. Splitting the system solves the problem through a sort of trick: man is absolute spirit only with respect to knowledge of the essential interconnectedness of all existing things; he is finite with respect to the experience of existence itself. Existence, in the final instance, has an author; it derives from an irreducibly free act. God decides in favour of being, and there are no grounds for this decision; existence is the assumption of being.

Where the ground of existence once represented the principle of individuality, facticity and irrationality, these qualities are now ascribed to existence itself, to the pure act of a will above all being. But this being, matter, is simply identified with essence, what God is. What once resisted knowledge is now, as essence, considered absolutely knowable. In his later discourse *On the Sources of Eternal Truths*, Schelling says of matter that: 'only what is *toto caelo* different from God can be the *potentia universalis* to the extent that it must, according to its essence (which is to say merely logically) be independent of what all doctrines unanimously agree is pure actuality, actuality in which there is no potency',[101] and further:

> God contains nothing except the pure That of his own being; but the fact that he is would have no truth if he were not something ... if he did not have a relation to thought, a relation not to a concept, but to the concept of all concepts, to the Idea. Here is where the unity of being and thinking really takes place.[102]

Schelling refers to the notion that all things have a possibility that is independent of God's actuality but grounded in his essence, that *principium realitatis essentiarium*, which, according to Wolff, is to be thought as *distinctum* from God, but *coaeternum et connecessarium* with him. Schelling reverts to the level of pre-critical metaphysics so he can use the distinction between the two divine faculties to make plausible the claim that human spirit is God-like *qua* reason (it has the power of the embodiment of all essences), but *qua* person it remains subject to the divine will (it can experience existence, even represent it, but not think it). On the one hand, the theoretical need to have knowledge of the thorough interconnectedness of beings overall is possible only on the foundation of absolute idealism, on the other hand, the practical need for the historical concept of an unredeemed world can be satisfied only by suspending this foundation. Schelling wants to keep the one, and yet he cannot let the other go; he can only make the two philosophies compatible by a sort of sleight of hand. From a solidly idealist basis, Schelling wants to get beyond idealism; this is why he immediately falls backwards into pre-dialectical philosophy.

This backsliding is clearly visible in the peculiar way Schelling adopts Kant's doctrine of the transcendental ideal.[103] Kant advances from the Idea to the Ideal because the former, as the embodiment of all possible predicates, is insufficient to act as transcendental ground of the thorough determination of an individual essence. Consequently, any thought of objects in general must be led back to an Ideal as the concept of that individual essence which, of all possible, contradictory predicates, is determined by one, viz. that which belongs to being as such – ens entium. Schelling distorts this relation of Idea and Ideal into a relation of essence and existence:

> Kant thus shows that the Idea of the general possibility or embodiment of all predicates belongs to the determination of things in accordance with the understanding. Post-Kantian philosophy understands this when it speaks about the Idea as such without further determination. However this Idea itself does not exist, it is even, one must say, a mere Idea; nothing universal exists, only the singular, and the universal essence only exists when it is the absolutely singular being. The Idea is not the cause of being in the Ideal; rather, the Ideal is the cause of being in the Idea ... To say that God is the Idea does not mean that he is himself only an Idea, but rather ... he is the cause of being in the Idea, causing the idea to be.[104]

Kant had only authorized a regulative use of the Ideal of pure reason,[105] but with Schelling the concept of the absolutely singular being is not the result of transcendental investigation but a construction of being as a whole. This construction had been pushing the limits of subjective idealism all along, and does not reflect the conditions for the possibility of all objects so much as the necessary conditions for their actuality as possible. It is logic and ontology, transcendental and real philosophy in one. Schelling identifies the Ideal of pure reason with God's existence in the emphatic sense: the Ideal, which has un-prethinkable (unvordenklich) existence, is the cause of being of the Idea (as the embodiment of all possible predicates).

But once Schelling makes constitutive use of this regulative, limiting concept of subjective idealism, he becomes guilty of inconsistency, motivated as he is by that divergence of theoretical and practical need in a philosophy that did not pass unscathed through the project of the Ages of the World. His error lay in subjecting this highest category to criteria that, from the objective-idealist standpoint, were sublated long ago. He subsumes an Ideal that has already been ontologically re-interpreted under the distinction of existence and essence, as if the criteria of the Kantian critique of the ontological proof for the existence of God were still in effect for it as well. Schelling takes Kant's distinction between the hundred actual and hundred possible thalers and applies it once more to the Ideal of pure reason, although the latter had already secretly acquired the meaning of divine existence as the *actus purus*. The absolute concept of the Ideal, as the concept of the purely existing, is once again distinguished from existing itself.

> God is now outside the absolute Idea in which he was as if lost, and (as Ideal) is in *his* Idea, but for that reason only Idea, merely in a concept, not in actual Being ... But if that which is *essentiâ Actus* is *also* posited out of its concept, so that it is not merely the *essentiâ* or *naturâ* but is rather a being *actu Actus*, then the principle is no longer posited in the sense of a principle, as we have demanded for the goal of rational science ... rather is it then really posited as a principle, namely as a beginning, as the beginning of science, which has what being is as its principle, which means: as something it uses to derive everything else. So far, we have described this as that for the sake of which the principle was sought, and, in opposition to the first negative philosophy, we now call it the positive philosophy ... because it proceeds from existence, which is to say: from the *actu Actus*-Being of what, in the first science, was found necessarily existing in the concept (as being *naturâ Actus*).[106]

This transition from negative to positive philosophy does not stand up to Hegel's unwritten review of Schelling's late philosophy, which we can extrapolate from his *Logic*. There, Hegel repeatedly refers to Kant's critique of the ontological argument,[107] which he intends to rehabilitate.

> *Being*, as the *wholly abstract immediate relation to self* is nothing else than the abstract moment of the Notion, which moment is abstract universality. This universality also effects what one demands of being, namely, to be *outside* the Notion; for though this universality is a moment of the Notion, it is equally the difference, or abstract judgement, of the Notion in which it opposes itself to itself. The Notion, even as formal, already immediately contains *being* as a *truer* and *richer* form, in that, as self-related negativity, it is *individuality*.[108]

In each of the three spheres of logic, the categories of existence return as forms of immediacy: being and determinate being (*Dasein*), then existence and actuality, and finally objectivity. However, self-thinking reason also completes a corresponding movement in the 'logic' of the negative philosophy, which Schelling develops as his doctrine of principles. Even in the ponderous categories of the late doctrine of potencies, the categories of existence emerge and perish again from the process of actualizing the potencies with the actual being simultaneously de-potentalized. Expressed in Hegelian language, but just as valid for Schelling's self-understanding:

Existence, then, is not to be taken here as a *predicate* or as a *determination* of essence, the proposition of which would run: essence exists, or *has* existence; on the contrary, essence has passed over into Existence ... The proposition should therefore run: essence is Existence; it is not distinct from its Existence.[109]

The self-mediated immediacy that on every step lends a more determinate objectivity to being and determinate being, existence and actuality, is mediation itself. Under the title of the 'Method', it is separated from 'System' at the end of the *Logic*; correspondingly, it appears at the end of the negative philosophy as *actus purus*. Thus, only by way of a decision that the theory no longer excludes could all logical determinations taken together *once again* be reduced to an essence of all essentialities – an essence outside of existence, which is absolutely inconceivable. Either the relation of essence and existence in the negative philosophy is reconsidered at every step in the actualization and de-potentiation – in which case existence cannot seriously be pronounced inconceivable – or the relation of essence to existence has in fact withdrawn from thought – in which case the negative philosophy as a whole is invalid, unless it limits its epistemological claims to those of subjective idealism. But Schelling was never ready for that.

SEPARATION OF THEORY AND PRACTICE

If Schelling were serious about the 'crisis of the science of reason' that is sparked off by the 'un-prethinkable character [*Unvordenklichkeit*] of existence'; if he were serious about the insight that reason cannot be grounded in itself and cannot be realized through itself, that it must let even its self-mediation be mediated by something preceding it,[110] then reason would have needed to strike back against the science of reason as such. This consequence is clearly set out in Schelling's late philosophy: the approach of positive philosophy would really have had to be ratified by an abandonment of the negative. Schelling cleared the way for the 'existentialist' overcoming of idealism, which passed through Kierkegaard and Rosenkranz before finally being fulfilled by Heidegger. Heidegger first succeeded in doing what Schelling thought he had himself achieved in splitting the system: the unification of ontological questioning with the practical need to change the corrupted age of the world. The two intentions are forced together (at the price of an evacuated world, and in a sphere constricted into interiority) by the fact that reason (*Vernunft*) lets itself be mediated by something that it learns (*ein Vernommenes*), thought (*Denken*) lets itself be mediated by something intended for it (*ein ihm Zugedachtes*), whether it be kerygmatically, mythopoetically, or at least topologically. Theory and practice come together in a contemplative spiritual exercise. This, at least, is the promise of the stubborn, devoted pursuit of being, to overcome the state of emergency of time. With the conviction that the servile knowledge of being is in harmony with the evocation of the good (even if they are not exactly identical), idealism itself lives on in the overcoming of idealism. This dichotomy was Schelling's bequest to contemporary philosophy.[111]

Schelling *was* serious about the crisis of the science of reason, and gives a clear explanation of its theme:

> The science of reason leads beyond itself to a reversal; but it cannot take thought as its point of departure. Rather, it needs a practical impetus; but there is nothing practical in thought, the concept is merely contemplative and only deals with necessary, whilst here we are dealing with something that lies outside of necessity, something desired.[112]

The *Ages of the World* had put God at the mercy of history. The purely rational philosophy restores God to inviolability at the idealistic price of the identity of thinking and being; and as soon as this is apparent, the practical drive gains the upper hand. Which is to say that the purely rational philosophy leads back to Hegel, who had flattened out the *Ages of the World*, identified the present world with the real one, and in so doing had revealed the categories in which an end to corruption can be thought. Schelling believes that the two-part system of negative and positive philosophy can unite two complementary things: the logico-ontological convergence of reason and essence on the one side, and the ontological divergence of reason and existence on the other. In his own way, Schelling separates theoretical from practical philosophy, and once again perverts the attributes of the 'inverted God'. At the time of the *Ages of the World*, the fallen *alter deus* was equipped with a mode of knowing still unequal to the task of epic history; as such, he needed to make use of dialectics. Characterized by the finitude of his theoretical faculty and an infinite vocation for his practical faculty, he was confronted with the task of historically restoring the corrupted world. Now things are reversed. Man is absolute with respect to his knowledge, and finite in his practical dependence upon a redeeming act of God. This separation of theory and practice within theory finds its theoretically developed counterpart in a separation of practice and theory within practice itself.

In this sphere, the state appears as an institution that counteracts the fall of the human race. Schelling understands it as the 'Act of the eternal reason that become practical and which is effective against this factual world ... To this extent, the state even has a factual existence.'[113] Certainly, the essence of the state must be philosophically deducible; however, the power relation within which the state comes into existence and maintains its existence is itself totally inscrutable:

> Since reason thus has become factual power, it cannot exclude the accidental ... And so there is not much wisdom in famous claims which would have us believe that factual law must increasingly give way to rational law, and will continue in this manner until a purely

rational realm arrives, which (so they say) will make all personality superfluous, and do away with this thorn in the flesh of jealousy.[114]

Schelling's isolation of existence from essence here far exceeds the positivism of the Hegelian philosophy of right. Men remain subject to a law that 'is, as it were, scarred and engraved on their will' as an alienated power. The force that is recognized externally can only be overcome internally:

> For the I, there exists the possibility, not to sublate itself in its ungodly and unholy condition, but rather ... to pull itself back into itself ... In doing this, it has no other intention than to evade the misfortune of action, to take refuge in contemplative life in the face of the insistence of the law ... Without knowing God, it looks for a divine life in this ungodly world.[115]

The practical recommendation to separate contemplative life from political practice corresponds to the theoretical separation of reason and existence:

> Let yourselves be called an unpolitical people because most of you demand to be ruled rather ... than to rule, because you devote your leisure, spirit, and inclination to other things, and look for greater happiness than that of returning each year to political quarrels that only lead to conflict ... Let yourselves refuse the political spirit. [116]

The practically motivated contemplation in which reason at first remains wholly on its own leads only to the turning point in which it recognizes that not enough can happen in pure theory to satisfy practical needs. Philosophical thinking always finds itself overtaken by un-prethinkable (*unvordenklichen*) existence; the precedence of praxis over theory forces the transition from negative to positive philosophy:

> Because contemplative science leads only to a God who is end but not actual, it leads only to that which is God in his essence, not to the actual. If it could rest content with the contemplative life, the I would be able to reassure itself with this merely ideal God. But this is just what is impossible. Action cannot be given up; there must be action.[117]

On the other hand, a return from intermittent contemplation to active life would not be able to sublate the manifest unhappiness of action unless the human race were to challenge in practice the external force of the state, 'that last fact':

> It is disastrous enough to resolve to combat everything factual in the state, especially as it cannot be foreseen where this endeavour will come

to an end, since the moment it succeeds in excluding everything empirical and irrational, the state would have to dissolve, because it has its being and strength only in the empirical.[118]

This had in fact been the intention of the theory of the state developed in the context of the philosophical project of the *Ages of the World*: to break the seal of power that the outer has over the inner by sublating the state. Now, however, a God who is relieved of his world historical risk permits a 'freedom over and above the state, not one that works back on the state or in the state'.[119] The perverted world will not be overturned by political praxis but rather by a contemplation that surpasses itself practically in the contemplation of itself; positive philosophy directly paves the way for redemption.

THE SECRET MATERIALISM IN THE AGES OF THE WORLD: SCHELLING AND MARX

The Marxist tradition takes up the idea renounced by the later Schelling of radically abolishing political domination. Marx appropriates Hegel's dialectic as explicated by Schelling. Without getting into the question of intellectual historical continuity, we will only attempt to prove that Schelling anticipates certain intentions of historical materialism at the materialist turning point of his historical idealism

The structure of the present age of the world (conceived under the idea of the 'inverted God') contains three moments that recur in the speculative conception of the historical process found in the young Marx.

1. After the 'fall', the productivity of *natura naturans* retreated from nature and found an immediate arena for its activity only within the horizon of historical humanity. In late Schelling, this is confined to a mythological process within the collective consciousness of the human race. In Marx, on the other hand, productive life takes place in working on inorganic nature as well as in the practical production of an objective world in which 'man reproduces nature':[120]

> This production is his working species life. Through it, nature appears as his work and his actuality. The theme of work is thus the reification of the species life of mankind: this is because man sees himself doubled not only intellectually in consciousness but actually in work, and thus sees himself in a world of his own making.[121]

In Schelling as in Marx, the production of the human race offers a prospect for the resurrection of nature.

2. In the present state of things, the identity between nature and the human race has been broken. In a peculiar perversion of the 'true' relation, the outer has gained power over the inner, the lower over the higher. For Schelling as for Marx, this materialist perversion is summed up in the 'false unity' of the state, which institutionalizes the domination of man over man. For both of them, this perversion is only the expression of 'the domination of dead matter over man'.[122] But one of them diagnoses a theogony while the other undertakes a sociological analysis. Schelling and Marx both understand the corruption of this world 'materialistically': matter, which should merely underlie existence, has subjugated existence to itself. Of course Marx confines the material life-process to the reproduction of social life, where Schelling, the natural philosopher, still understood it as universal.

3. Finally, Schelling and Marx also agree that the corruption of the world should be attributed not to nature but to man: 'Not the gods, not nature, only man himself can be this alien power over man.'[123] Regardless of whether, as with Schelling, an original identity of man with nature is pre-supposed or, as with Marx, this question remains moot – in both cases, the particular form of 'materialism' to which human life is subject traces back to an 'egoistic' principle. In Schelling, this principle is as much physical as moral, and refers to the order of creation that was disorganized by the particular self-will of the first man. In Marx, it takes on an economic significance as the order of property defined by the private appropriation of social labour. Schelling's cosmological 'egoism' is deciphered as capitalism; the anthropologizing mode of expression of the *Paris Manuscripts* maintains its relationship to the physico-moral considerations of *On Human Freedom*, and translates the metaphysical categories into economic ones. The form of the private appropriation of social production requires that use values be produced and distributed under the economic law of an increase in exchange value that has become an end in itself. In this respect, private property appears, like the particular will in Schelling, as the capsule that contains the essential forces taken from man – 'love'. The devaluation (*Entwertung*) of the world of man increases along with the utilization (*Verwertung*) of the world of things. And although the reproduction of social life on the foundation of private property becomes independent from, and even opposed to, the will of the private property owner, it is nonetheless determined by the motives of the commodity owner. In this sense, Marx repeats what is anticipated mythologically in Schelling's doctrine of the fall: 'The alien nature to whom labour and the product of labour belong, in whose service the labour takes place ... and for whose benefit the product of labour exists, can only be man himself'[124] – and who, for that matter, will be overcome only by man. For Schelling as for Marx, the human species itself is the authorized subject of history who is nonetheless not in command of history – which is to say an 'inverted God'.

Viewed as such, the idea common to both the Schellingian and Marxist historical constructions of a contraction of God has several consequences for the philosophy of history. They share the practical need to trace the corruption of this world back to a historical origin; such an origin allows for the theoretical possibility that the corruption could be abolished, which is a practically necessary task. Because of this, they both agree on what could be called the dialectical framework of the materialist perversion. Schelling developed it ontologically as the perversion of an original relation of existence and the ground of existence. He makes the repeated overturning of the 'basis' (the restoration of the original relation) into the guiding principle for a philosophical interpretation of world history. Marx is also guided by the same idea of overcoming materialism: lowering matter to the basis of being after it has been falsely raised to being itself. Marx even shares Schelling's universal concept of matter that applies equally to nature and the historical productions of nature. Both also refer to that situation of the human species in which the spell of materialism will one day be broken as 'society' in the emphatic sense[125] and both make this dependent upon humanity's success in freeing nature (the nature of the universe as much as the nature of man) from its 'inorganic' form. 'The human essence of nature first exists for the social man; for only here does it exist as a bond with men, as existing for the other and the other for him; only here does it exist as the foundation of his own, human existence.'[126]

Marx ends this passage with that bold proposition which reads like a materialistic interpretation of the anticipated world age of the future from the end of the 'Stuttgart Seminars': 'Thus, society is the completed essential unity of man with nature, the true resurrection of nature, the realized naturalism of man and the realized humanism of nature.'[127]

Certainly the dialectical framework of the materialist perversion acquires its specific meaning in the context of a critique of political economy, where matter does not signify nature in general so much as the historical, natural productiveness of a material life process that has become independent over and against life itself. Matter, as the realm of nature, can only become the foundation of human existence when the economic realm of natural necessity is made into the basis of a social realm of freedom; in other words, when

> socialized man, the associated producers, regulate their exchange of materials with nature rationally and bring it under their social control instead of being ruled by it as if by a blind power ... But it always remains a realm of necessity. Beyond it begins the human development of forces, which counts as its own goal the true realm of freedom, *but that can only blossom forth out of that kingdom of necessity*.[128]

From a great, seemingly unbridgeable distance, Schelling had expressed the same relation in the mystically inspired language of Jakob Böhme: 'Only the conquered selfhood, that is, the selfhood brought back from activity to potentiality, is the good, and according to the potency which is overpowered by the good, it remains existing in the good for evermore.'[129]

The difficulty of bringing the two propositions together remains, in spite of the unity they enjoy in the context of the constructions of the philosophy of history. Marx drew the consequence that Schelling shied away from, taking his philosophy in another direction. If the human species can only break the power of the outer over the inner through an outer struggle against the outer, and can overcome it only through an effort that, in Schelling's words, is directed at the preservation of the outer foundations of life, then the objective possibility of a reversal of the materialist perversion can only be grasped out of the material life process of society itself. The moments of existence and the ground of existence can then be sufficiently grasped in a mutual relation that is certainly anthropologically essential, but not ontologically immutable; that is, they can be grasped 'fundamentally' only in the dimension of social labour. The foundation then becomes economic, not mythological. In this case, it is the maturity of the 'productive' forces rather than the ripeness of the 'moral' consciousness that indicates the world historical transformation central for overturning materialism. But this is better analysed using Hegel's dialectic of an externalization through reification rather than Schelling's dialectic of an externalization through contraction. Marx appropriates Hegel's dialectic within the secure framework of Schelling's, in order to historically relativise Hegel's overall dialectic *as* dialectic. Whether it is just an illusion or a deeper insight, this is the uncovered scaffolding of his materialist dialectic.

THE MATERIALIST SELF-SUBLATION OF THE DIALECTIC OF LABOUR – A SCHELLINGIAN PREPARATION FOR A RECEPTION OF HEGEL

Hegel develops the concept of labour in the *Logic* under the title of *teleology*. It is conceived as the result of the realization of subjective goals.[130] Hegel shows how subjective, purposeful activity must realize itself through means of its own making, while arising through the process of mediation itself. The famous passage states:

> That the end relates itself immediately to an object and makes it a means, as also that through this means it determines another object, may be regarded as *violence*, in so far as the end appears to be of quite another nature than the object and the two objects similarly are mutually independent totalities. But that the end posits itself in a *mediate* relation with the object and *interposes* another object *between* itself and it, may be regarded as the *cunning* of reason. The finitude of rationality has, as remarked, this side, that the end enters into relationship with the presupposition, that is, with the externality of the object ... [A]s it is, it puts forward an object as means, allows it to

wear itself out in its stead, exposes it to attrition and shields itself behind it from mechanical violence ... To this extent the *means* is *superior* to the *finite* ends of *external* purposefulness; the *plough* is more honourable than are immediately the enjoyments procured by it and which are ends. The *tool* lasts, while the immediate enjoyments pass away and are forgotten. In his tools man possesses power over external nature, even though in respect of his ends he is, on the contrary, subject to it.[131]

The whole point of the dialectic of labour is the fact that the subjective goals were ultimately only means for reason, which has itself become objective in the productive means. As such, the dialectic of reification first developed in the *Phenomenology of Spirit* finds its place in the *Logic*. Thus, Marx praises Hegel for having grasped the essence of labour and understood 'objective' man as the result of his own labour. But he immediately qualifies this by saying that Hegel sees only the positive side of labour, not the negative.[132] For Marx, in other words, the externalization of the worker in his product has the *double* meaning that labour power becomes both an object and an outer existence on the one hand, but also exists as independent and alien to him, and attains an autonomous power over and against him – 'the life he has given to the object confronts him as hostile and alien.'[133] To this extent, Marx joins Hegel in acknowledging a rationality inherent to labour, in that man is mediated with nature through his tools. But contra Hegel, Marx thought that the work man performs on nature remains under the spell of the productivity of nature as long as the mediation controls what is to be mediated – the plough remains nobler than the pleasures.

Hegel does not hesitate to turn the categories developed in the teleology of labour into determinations of the organic life process. In the life process, the reproductions of natural life are reduced to a common denominator with those of social life – a 'pure restless circle in itself'.[134] Marx polemically turns the same idea against itself. So long as humanity lives its life under the domination of 'dead' over 'living' labour, viz. in such a way that it does not consciously regulate its 'metabolic exchange with nature' but is instead subject to this exchange as if it were a foreign power; so long as in the sphere of the reproduction of social life the subjective activity has not assumed conscious control of the objective purposiveness of the 'realized end' – so long as all this remains in effect, society is limited to natural productiveness and its life process is in fact a natural process. Marx calls this the pre-history of humanity, because the materialist control of the means of life over life itself, the power of the 'base' in general, of the means over the ends, the lower over the higher, the outer over the inner – all this has yet to be broken.

In Hegel's *Logic*, the transition from 'organic life' to the 'absolute Idea' still takes place within the predetermined horizon of life itself. The transition from morality to ethical life, as central as it is awkward, only repeats the dialectic of labour in which subjective purposive activity is overtaken from behind by the objective purposiveness of its means. The acting subject must know and recognize that, in the relations institutionalized through its ends and their realization, the objective good has already become an actuality and a power over and against which the intended ends become merely subjective.[135] In absolute knowing 'the actuality found as given is at the same time determined as the realised absolute end.'[136] Only this double identification of technical labour with the organic life process, and in turn of the life process with the absolute life of the Idea, guarantees the pure unending circle, that is to say the history of humanity as natural history, which knows no redemption except the redemption from eternity through immortal death.

Schelling wanted to do justice to the exuberance of history by reducing the dialectic to a mere form of subjective spirit, one that is unavoidable and yet inadequate to its historical object. Marx conceives the same unavoidability *and* inadequacy of the dialectic from the materialist constitution of objective spirit itself. As long as men keep living in the forms of alienated labour, they remain caught in a cycle as natural as nature itself, and in which mediation has absolute power over what is to be mediated. In this cycle, externalization still controls the process of externalization and appropriation, reification still controls the process of reification and opposition. Dialectical logic is thus the 'currency of spirit'; it itself lives on the forced connection of a materialistically perverted reproduction of social life. Within this dialectic, the life of alienated labour appears as natural, eternal, and indeed the only sort of life there is. Dialectic, for its part, appears as the truth of this life:

> This movement in its abstract form as dialectic counts thereby as the truly human life, and because it is indeed an abstraction, an alienation of human life, it counts as a divine process, or as the divine process of man – a process which his abstract, pure, absolute essence [*Wesen*] (different from himself) works through.[137]

In the space of the dialectic of being and its basis as developed by Schelling, Marx grasps the possibility of a dialectical self-sublation of the Hegelian dialectic that, in its materialist guise, he both takes seriously and rejects. If the socially necessary labour under the control of the associated producers can ever be made into the basis of a realm of freedom, then it must be conceivable that that relation (of the subjective, purposive activity that is always superseded by the objective purposiveness of its means) can be historically sublated. Dialectic itself (as the objective power of a beginning-less, endless, circular mediation over the finite subject to be mediated) then forfeits its idealistic self-understanding. It sees itself clearly when it is arrested in a world that is materialistic and cannot, consequently, be sublated through dialectical thinking alone. Although it is already apparent in Schelling, it is only really in Marx that the critical project itself arises from the pre-theoretical need to overturn a perverse state of affairs that has been revealed through practical experience. Equally practical is the need to emancipate humanity from the power of matter, the need to make matter into the basis of a subject of history who has come of age, and thus the need for a society that, as a species, will control the controllable and respect the uncontrollable.

Of course, it would be an over-interpretation of Marx's Schellingian proclivities to follow Ernst Bloch in expanding the central natural-philosophical category of *natura naturans* into a historical materialist category, in order to add a guarantee of theoretical necessity to the already practical necessity of overcoming the corrupted world.[138] Bloch insists on matter as a principle, and meticulously follows the history of its concept:

> With respect to matter, certainly, the Idealists have not begun to create anything like a field of research; nevertheless, how many thoughtful attempts there have been in the history of idealist thought to confront the source of its embarrassment: matter. The Aristotelian attempt at a determination of being-possible is only the most important amongst them; it has successors. Apart from the Thomistic attempt (matter as principle of individuation), there is Averroes' attempt to determine matter in an almost immanent-creative manner (matter as *natura naturans*); there is the fantastical matter of Franz von Baader (matter as protection against the subterranean burrowing of chaos) ... Only the recognition of a matter to which life and human goals are not foreign but rather its own proper functions and further qualification of its mode of existence – only such a matter does justice to the dialectic of the real ... This would also make it possible for man to be understood as an objective material essence. In a world, that is, which holds not only a place but the highest place for a true and interactive con-sciousness; similarly, consciousness is true when it is the eye and theory-praxis organ of matter itself.[139]

In fact, Marx also confesses that 'the fact that the physical and mental life of mankind is connected to nature means nothing other than that nature is connected to itself, for man is a part of nature.'[140] But however nature may carry out its own creative process through human labour, from the finite standpoint of goal-directed man it is impossible to achieve certainty about an identity of nature and society, organic life and historical process – an identity grounded in matter as its principle.[141] Materialism is not an ontological principle, but rather the historical indication of a social constitution; and mankind living under this constitution has not yet succeeded in eliminating the control of the outer over the inner that it experiences in practice. Nor, on the other hand, does materialism guarantee that subjective, purposive activity will someday *necessarily* harmonize with the objective purposiveness of a compliant nature. If the *Paris Manuscripts* still reveal the intention of providing a materialistic anchor for a world historical goal – that is, if they

are still trying to theoretically deduce the emancipation of society, the resurrection of nature, and the complete realization of both in the naturalization
of man and humanization of nature from a dialectic inherent in the material
life process in the manner of identity philosophy – then certainly Marx the
economist later characterized such a 'goal' at best negatively, as the practical
attempt to eliminate the 'non-sense' of the economic and political crises that
are always produced anew and in new forms in the materialist state of the
world. But it remains to be seen whether nature (as people understand the
term) would not still remain alien and external, even if a critically
enlightened praxis were to make a rationally controlled life process into the
basis of an emancipated society – into its *matter* in the way Schelling uses the
term in *Ages of the World*.

Notes

1   Schelling, F., *System of Transcendental Idealism*, trans. Peter Heath (Charlottesville: University Press of Virginia, 1978). *System des transzendentalen Idealismus*
(1800), in *Werke, Münchner Jubilaumsausgabe II*, 327ff. Subsequent references to
Schelling's works (*Werke*) will refer to this edition. [Translator's note: when
possible, references will be given to the standard English translations of German texts, followed in parentheses by the page reference to the German edition
cited by Habermas.]
2   Ibid., p. 195 (p. 582).
3   Ibid., p. 195 (p. 583).
4   Ibid., p. 202 (p. 591).
5   Ibid., p. 207 (p. 598).
6   Ibid., p. 210 (p. 602).
7   Schelling, F., 'Stuttgart Seminars' (1810) in *Idealism and the Endgame of Theory,
Three Essays by Schelling*, trans. Thomas Pfau (Albany: SUNY Press, 1994), 195.
Stuttgarter Privatvorlesungen (1810), in Schelling, F., *Werke*, IV, 354.
8   Ibid., p. 227 (p. 353).
9   Ibid., p. 227 (p. 353).
10 Ibid., p. 227 (p. 353).
11 Ibid., p. 229 (p. 356f.). A similar thesis can already be found in the plan for the
System of 1795 discovered by Rosenkranz; last reprinted by H. Zeltner,
Schelling (Stuttgart: Frommann, 1954).
12 Schelling, F., *Philosophische Einleitung in die Philosophie der Mythologie oder Darstellung der rein rationalen Philosophie*, bes. 23. Vorlesung, in *Werke* V, 716ff.
13 Ibid., p. 729.
14 Ibid., p. 730.
15 Ibid., p. 715.
16 Ibid., p. 732.
17 Schelling, 'Stuttgart Seminars', 228 (*Werke* IV, 354).
18 Translator's note: *Bruno, or On the Natural and Divine Principle of Things* (1802),
trans. Michael Vater (Albany: SUNY, 1984).
19 Hegel, G. W. F., *Phenomenology of Spirit*, trans. A. V. Miller (Oxford University
Press, 1977), §19.
20 It is a knowledge, 'which forms the essence of the soul itself, and is only called
intuition because the essence of the soul, which is one and the same as the
Absolute, can have only an immediate relation with the Absolute.' Schelling,
F., *Werke* IV, 13.

21 Hegel, G. W. F., *Science of Logic*, trans. A. V. Miller (London: Allen & Unwin, 1969), 67. (*Wissenschaft der Logik*, ed. I. Lasson, 51.)

22 Hegel, *Phenomenology of Spirit*, trans. A. V. Miller (Oxford: Oxford University Press, 1977), §4.

23 The excellent work by Fulda, H., *Das Problem einer Einleitung in Hegels Wissenschaft der Logik* (Klostermann, Vittorio, 1965) devotes itself to this problem.

24 Hegel, *Science of Logic*, 70 (*Wissenschaft der Logik*, ed. I. Lasson, 54).

25 Ibid., p. 73 (p. 58).

26 Ibid., p. 586 (II, p. 224).

27 Hegel, G. W. F., *Berliner Schriften*, ed. J. Hoffmeister (Hamburg: Meiner, 1956), 9.

28 Hegel, G. W. F., *Logic*, trans. W. Wallace (New York: Oxford, 1975), §17. *Enzyklopädie* (1830), ed. F. Nicolin and O. Pöggeler (Hamburg: Meiner, 1975), 50.

29 'Historical' ('*historisch*') still has the Greek meaning of empirical discovery here.

30 Hegel, G. W. F., *Science of Logic* (*Wissenschaft der Logik*, ed. I. Lasson, II, 252).

31 Hegel, G. W. F., *Science of Logic*, 770. (*Wissenschaft der Logik*, ed. I. Lasson, II, 424).

32 Ibid., p. 759 (p. 412).

33 Schelling, *Werke*, V, 751.

34 Schelling, F., *Weltalter*, ed. M. Schröter (Munich: Biederstein & Leibniz, 1946), 211.

35 Ibid., p. 211.

36 Ibid., p. 202 (modified by the author).

37 Schelling no longer puts forward this worldview; the expression is unchanged in *Philosophie der Offenbarung*.

38 Kant, I., *Religion Within the Bounds of Reason Alone. Die Religion innerhalb der Grenzen der bloßen Vernunft*, in *Werke*, ed. W. Weischedel (Darmstad: Insel, 1956), bd. IV, 680.

39 Schelling, *Weltalter*, 230. [Translator's note: Schelling wrote three versions of *The Ages of the World*, Habermas refers exclusively to the first version (1811) – unfortunately only the second (1813) and third (1815) versions have been translated into English (Schelling, F., 'The Ages of the World' (1813 draft), trans. J. Norman, in *The Abyss of Freedom/Ages of the World* (Ann Arbor: University of Michigan Press, 1997); Schelling, F., *The Ages of the World* (1815 draft), trans. J. M. Wirth, (Albany: SUNY Press, 2000).)

40 Schelling, *Werke* V, 328.

41 Hegel, *Science of Logic*, 50 (*Wissenschaft der Logik*, ed. I. Lasson, 31).

42 Benz, E., 'Schellings theologische Geistesahnen' *Abh. d. Ak. d. Wiss. u. d. Lit. in Mainz*, geistes- u. sozialwiss. Klasse. 1955, Nr. 3. Benz, E., *Die christliche Kabbala*, (Zürich: Rhein, 1958). Schulz, W., 'Jakob Böhme und die Kabbala' in *Zeitschrift für philosophische Forschung* X, 1955, 447ff. Schulz, W., 'Schelling und die Kabbala' in *Judaica* XIII, 1957, 65ff., 143ff. Scholem, G., *Major Trends in Jewish Mysticism* (New York: Schocken Books, 1974). *Die jüdische Mystik in ihren Hauptströmungen* (Frankfurt: Suhrkamp, 1967).

43 Scholem, G., 'Schöpfung aus Nichts und Selbstverchränkung Gottes' in *Ueber einige Begriffe des Judentums* (Frankfurt: Suhrkamp, 1970), 53–89.

44 Böhme, J., *Schriften*, ed. W. Schulze (Leipzig, 1938), 96.

45 K. Jaspers gives a biographical interpretation of Schelling's philosophy in *Schelling* (Munich: Piper, 1955).

46 Schelling, F., *Werke*, IV, Erg. Bd., 135.

47 Schelling, F., 'Stuttgart Seminars', 226 (*Werke*, IV, 351f).

48 Appearances that arouse a universal natural repugnance, even without consideration of their dangerousness to man. Schelling, *Werke*, IV, 260.

49 Schelling, F., 'Stuttgart Seminars', 228 (*Werke*, IV, 354).
50 Ibid., p. 292f.
51 Schelling, F., *Weltalter*, 51.
52 Schelling, F., 'Stuttgart Seminars', 210 (*Werke*, IV, 331). [Translator's note: the translation given above corrects a mistake in Pfau's Schelling translation, which has 'self-love' for 'Liebe für sich', thus confusing the stark opposition Schelling is expounding between outreaching love and contracting egoism.]
53 Scholem, G., *Grundbegriffe* explains the talk of the 'abyss in God': among the Kabbalists, Asriel of Gerona is indeed the first who explains the place where every essence remains in formless indifference as 'the infinite, boundless and unfathomable abyss, which reaches right into pure night'. This symbol is later connected with the idea of the ZimZum or of contraction, so that in the mystical tradition the Aristotelian doctrine of *steresis* could be reinterpreted to the effect that every Something comes with an abyss.
54 Schelling, *Werke*, IV, 258.
55 Ibid., p. 29.
56 Schelling, *Weltalter*, 19.
57 Ibid., p. 23.
58 Ibid., p. 25f.
59 Ibid. p. 35.
60 Ibid. p. 77f.
61 Ibid. p. 75.
62 Schelling, *Werke*, IV, 250.
63 Schelling, *Weltalter*, 59.
64 Ibid., p. 230.
65 On the temporal structure of the God of the *Ages of the World*, see Wieland, W., *Schellings Lehre von der Zeit* (Heidelberg: Winter, 1956); and Habermas, J., *Das Absolute und die Geschichte, Von der Zweispältigkeit in Schellings Denken* (Bonn: Dissertation, 1954) especially 323ff.
66 Schelling, *Weltalter*, 99.
67 Schelling, *Werke*, IV, 300.
68 Ibid., p. 108.
69 Ibid., p. 291.
70 Schelling, *Weltalter*, 5.
71 Ibid., p. 193.
72 Ibid., p. 9.
73 Hegel, *Science of Logic*, 588 (*Wissenschaft der Logik*, II, 226).
74 Ibid., pp. 441–2 (p. 61).
75 Hegel, *Phenomenology of Spirit* (*Phänomenologie des Geistes*, 558).
76 Hegel, *Science of Logic*, 440 (*Wissenschaft der Logik*, II, 59).
77 Schelling, *Werke*, IV, 263.
78 Hegel, *Logic*, §6 (*Enzyklopädie*, 38).
79 Schelling, 'Stuttgart Seminars', 232 (*Werke*, IV, 360).
80 Scholem, *Major Trends of Jewish Mysticism*, p. 304 (*Hauptströmungen*, p. 333); Scholem, G., *Judaica* 1 and 2 (Frankfurt: Suhrkamp, 1967 and 1970); see also my investigations into the German Idealism of Jewish philosophers in *Philosophisch-politische Profile* (Frankfurt: Suhrkamp, 1971), 37ff.
81 Schelling, 'Stuttgart Seminars', 226 (*Werke*, IV, 352).
82 Ibid., p. 241 (p. 373).
83 Ibid., p. 243 [translation amended] (p. 376).
84 Ibid., p. 206 (p. 325).
85 Ibid., p. 228 (p. 355).
86 Ibid., p. 239 (p. 370).
87 Schelling, *Werke*, IV, supplemental volume 156f.

88 Schelling, 'Stuttgart Seminars', 242 (*Werke*, IV, 374f).
89 Ibid., p. 228 (p. 355).
90 [Translator's note: endnote number missing from original German text.] I have proved this in detail in my dissertation *Das Absolute und die Geschichte*, p. 344ff.
91 On the doctrine of principles of the late Schelling cf. *Werke*, V, 437ff. (*Darstellung der rein rationalen Philosophie*); and *Werke*, IV, supplemental volume, 3ff. (*Einleitung in die Philosophie d. Offenbarung*).
92 Schelling, *Werke*, V, 578f.
93 Ibid., p. 577.
94 Ibid., p. 576f.
95 Ibid., p. 572.
96 Ibid., p. 580.
97 Schelling, *Werke*, IV, supplemental volume, 352.
98 Ibid., p. 359.
99 Ibid., p. 67.
100 Ibid., p. 69f.
101 Schelling, *Werke*, V, 767.
102 Ibid., p. 769.
103 Kant, *Critique of Pure Reason*, trans. Norman Kemp Smith (New York: St. Martin's Press, 1965), 573 ff. The central proposition in the Kantian deduction states: 'Although this idea of the *sum-total of all possibility*, in so far as it serves as the condition of the complete determination of each and every thing, is itself undetermined in respect of the predicates which may constitute it, and is thought by us as being nothing more than the sum-total of all predicates, we yet find, on closer scrutiny, that this idea, as a primordial concept, excludes a number of predicates which as derivative are already given through other predicates or which are incompatible with others; and that it does, indeed, define itself as a concept that is completely determinate *a priori*. It thus becomes the concept of an individual object which is completely determined through the mere idea, and must therefore be entitled an *ideal* of pure reason.'
104 Schelling, *Werke*, V, 767f.
105 Kant, *Critique of Pure Reason*, A 639.
106 Schelling, *Werke*, V, 744ff.
107 Hegel, *Science of Logic, passim* (*Wissenschaft der Logik* I, 71ff, 99f.; II, 61f., 103ff., 353ff.).
108 Ibid., pp. 706–7 (p. 355).
109 Ibid., p. 483 (p. 105).
110 Walter Schulz has brought out this feature of the late philosophy with great precision: *Die Vollendung des deutschen Idealismus in der Spätphilosophie Schellings* (Stuttgart: Kohlhammer, 1955).
111 See Habermas, J., *Theorie und Praxis* (Berlin: Luchterhand, 1969), 363f.
112 Schelling, *Werke*, V, 747.
113 Ibid., p. 720.
114 Ibid., p. 720f.
115 Ibid., p. 738.
116 Ibid., p. 731.
117 Ibid., p. 741f.
118 Ibid., p. 732 n. 2.
119 Ibid., p. 733.
120 Marx, K./Engels, F., *Kleine ökonomische Schriften* (Berlin: Dietz, 1955), 105.
121 Ibid., p. 105.
122 Ibid., p. 93.
123 Ibid., p. 107.
124 Ibid.

125 Schelling, *Werke*, V, 723.
126 Marx/Engels, *Kleine ökonomische Schriften*, 129.
127 Ibid., p. 116.
128 Marx, K. *Das Kapital*, Bd. III, Berlin 1949, 873f.
129 Marx/Engels, *Werke*, Bd. 4, Berlin 1969, 292. [sic.]
130 Hegel, *Science of Logic*, 734ff (*Wissenschaft der Logik* II, 311ff.).
131 Ibid., p. 746f. (397f.).
132 Marx, K., *Frühschriften*, (Stuttgart: Kröner, 1971), 269f.
133 Marx/Engels, *Kleine ökonomische Schriften*, 99.
134 Marx, *Frühschriften*, 282, cf. Hegel, *Science of Logic*. 761ff. (*Wissenschaft der Logik* II, 432ff.).
135 Hegel, *Science of Logic*, 821ff. (*Wissenschaft der Logik* II, 481ff.)
136 Ibid., p. 823 (p. 483).
137 Marx, *Frühschriften*, 282f.
138 See my essay: 'Ernst Bloch, A Marxist Schelling', in *Philosophisch-politische Profile*, 147ff.
139 Bloch, E., *Subject – Object*, (Berlin: Aufbau, 1951), 415ff; expanded edition, Frankfurt, 1962.
140 Marx/Engels, *Kleine ökonomische Schriften*, 103.
141 For a critique of the presuppositions in Bloch's materialism drawn from identity philosophy see Schmidt, A., *Der Begriff der Natur in der Lehre von Marx* (Frankfurt: Europäische Verlagsanstalt, 1962).

4

SCHELLING AND NIETZSCHE: WILLING AND TIME

Judith Norman

INTRODUCTION

On the face of it, Nietzsche and Schelling do not seem to have much in common. Nietzsche is content to poke gentle fun at Schelling, painting him as a naïve romantic Idealist with a basically theological agenda. Schelling does not even rise to the level of an 'antipode' for Nietzsche; rather, Nietzsche treats him with what we might call (borrowing from Schelling) *Indifferenz*. Nor has there been a tradition in the scholarship of reconstructing any sort of conversation between the two,[1] as there has been of exploring Nietzsche's complex relationships with Schopenhauer and Hegel. Nietzsche and Schelling seem, by contrast, to be mutually indifferent historical neighbours in nineteenth-century Germany.

That said, Nietzsche (and, until quite recently, most scholars of the history of philosophy) was familiar only with Schelling's earlier works, the period when Schelling still maintained close intellectual connections with idealism and romanticism. But Schelling's middle-period philosophy of will is quite distinctive, and there are grounds for suspecting there might be important affinities between this philosophy and Nietzsche's thought. Those grounds are given by Nietzsche himself who, in *Twilight of the Idols*, lists what he considers to be the fundamental errors of traditional philosophers. These can be used as a sort of elementary (negative) compatibility test for him and Schelling. Nietzsche castigates traditional philosophers for (1) rejecting history and hating becoming; (2) distrusting the senses and devaluing the body; (3) confusing the first things with the last, deducing the lower from the higher rather than vice versa, and holding that the highest principle must be a *causa sui*; and (4) dividing the true world from the apparent and underrating appearances.[2]

In his middle-period writings, from 1809 to 1815, Schelling is in fact acquitted on all of these counts, even the first and fourth where Schopenhauer fails. As to the first, Schelling was an eager advocate of becoming, writing: 'the concept of becoming is the only one adequate to the nature of things.'[3] He was enthusiastic about history and argued that philosophy should adapt a historical rather than dialectical method.[4] On the second, we can point to the fact that Schelling had himself been an experimental scientist, albeit of a peculiar kind ('transcendental physics' couldn't have sounded good to Nietzsche). But he went out of his way to valorize materiality and the material world ('what leads people to slander matter as they do?' he wondered, WA II, 150). As for confusing the first and the last, Schelling explicitly affirmed the genesis of the highest things from out of the lowest, and criticizes people who would rather 'bedazzle from the very start with spiritual concepts and cliches than descend to the natural beginnings of every life' (WA II, 148). Schelling is accordingly hostile to the notion of a *causa sui*, theorizing that even God required a material ground. And finally, Schelling makes no distinction between the true world and the apparent one. He has passed Nietzsche's first round of tests, at least.

Nietzsche's list of grievances is not a random one, of course; he considers them to be particular symptoms of philosophy's inability to affirm life, the material world and the present moment in its full, temporal glory. And here is an even greater measure of affinity; not only does Schelling make a point of affirming life and the present, but, like Nietzsche, he develops a conception of will specifically geared towards such an affirmation. This confirms their similarities over and against Schopenhauer, whose notion of will is neither affirmative nor in any sort of contact with history or even temporality. But the similarity is more striking than this: both Nietzsche and Schelling constructed the notion of a will capable of *creating* the past as a way of affirming the present. Which is to say that for both of them, the will not only intervenes creatively in time, it constitutes temporality in the first place by willing the past. And in both cases, this willing of the past functions within a project of affirmation, as a way of embracing and valorizing the present. The task for this paper will be to explore this startling similarity.

GREAT HEROIC POEMS

The most fundamental point of comparison between Schelling and Nietzsche is that they both developed philosophies of the will. Schelling says: 'in the final and highest instance there is no other Being than Will. Will is primordial Being ...' (HF, 24). And Nietzsche claimed: *'This world is the will to power – and nothing besides!'*[5] Schelling described his conception of material will in a well-known passage:

> the unruly lies ever in the depths as though it might again break through, and order and form nowhere appear to have been original, but it seems as though what had initially been unruly had been brought to order. This is the incomprehensible basis of reality in things, the irreducible remainder which cannot be resolved into reason by the greatest exertion but always remains in the depths. Out of this which is unreasonable, reason in the true sense is born. (HF, 34)

Several aspects of this description of the will are striking with respect to a comparison with Nietzsche. First, as I will discuss in this section, Schelling considers the will to lie outside of the typical categories of rational thought: it escapes the sort of analysis that we apply to experience. And second, as I will discuss in the next section, Schelling stresses its ontological primacy, its generative and grounding function in producing the seemingly tame and reasonable structures of reality.

The question of the 'irrationality' of the will provides a point of positive comparison between Nietzsche and Schelling from which Schopenhauer is excluded. All three stressed the fact that the will lies outside the accustomed structures of intelligibility. With Schopenhauer, however, this is really decisive; we formulate concepts guided by the principle of sufficient reason, and as the noumenal will does not obey this principle, it cannot be conceived. But since Schelling and Nietzsche largely broke free from an epistemological dualism of phenomena and noumena, they were not similarly constrained by the Kantian representational problematic. Nietzsche agrees that his own conception of will lies outside of traditional structures of intelligibility – but his business is to subject these structures to rigorous critique and to invent/discover new concepts for conceptualizing the will. And Schelling too took the will's irrationality as a challenge to thought more than anything else, experimenting with different ways of expression and representation. 'Will is primal being ...' Schelling writes: 'All philosophy strives only to find this highest expression ...' (HF, 24).

However, Nietzsche does believe that our ability to think the will is hindered by the reactive forces of consciousness that have little affinity for its overflowing nature.[6] Schelling expresses the same thought in a different way – that consciousness (the ideal, in his vocabulary) has a hard time comprehending the will, which is by nature more closely related to the unconscious, the body, and so forth. So they both recognize a structural incongruity between consciousness and the will. Unlike Schopenhauer, though, this is not a disabling obstacle. Schelling writes: 'the Real is, precisely on account of [its problematic relation to comprehension], all the less easy to comprehend and harder to penetrate. It requires diligence and mental effort to become comprehensible ...' (WA II, 142).

How can we think the will, in light of these obstacles? Again, we see similar strategies in Nietzsche and Schelling's approaches. For one thing, they both try to enhance the repertory of philosophical method by combining it with art. Schelling thinks the task of 'recounting' the working of the will is best rendered in the form of a 'great heroic poem' (WA II, 119) of which he claims only to be the harbinger. Nietzsche puts forward his *Zarathustra* in the same way, with the same ostensibly humble claim to be only a harbinger.[7] This reliance on artistic presentation does not strictly speaking distinguish Schelling and Nietzsche from Schopenhauer, who thought music could accomplish the sort of presentation (or expression) that philosophy could not. Still, in contrast to Schopenhauer, Schelling and

Nietzsche did not make the sharp disjunction between art and philosophy that Schopenhauer did. Schelling and Nietzsche (notwithstanding *Zarathustra*) generally prefer to work within rather than outside philosophy, and extend rather than police its boundaries.

MATERIALIST NARRATIVES OF SELF-CREATION

As I mentioned above, Schelling avoided all four of the errors that Nietzsche thinks traditional philosophers have committed. Of these four, the most significant in terms of their philosophies of will is the error of deducing the lowest from the highest rather than the other way around. Schelling was particularly insistent that his philosophy of will began from the bottom, and he makes a point of contrasting his bottom-up genetic model of development with a Neo-Platonic top-down model of production:

> The system that, descending from on high wants to explain the origin of things, comes almost necessarily to the thought that the products of the highest original force must finally lose themselves in a certain exteriority, where only a shadow of essence, a smallest scrap of reality remained, a something that can be said to be but really is not ... Following the opposite direction, we also claim an exteriority under which nothing is; for us it is not the last, the product, but the first, from which everything begins, not mere lack or near total deprivation of reality, but active denial.[8]

But what Schelling proposes is not just a 'reversal' of the top-down model. The lowest element in the Neo-Platonist scheme is an inert, desiccated concept of matter, an 'exteriority' characterized by lack (of reality, actuality, power). A bottom-up genetic model requires a more robust starting point, which Schelling characterizes here as active denial. He elsewhere theorizes it as a primal spiritual quality of matter (WA II, 150). His fundamental point is that a system that tries to reverse the tradition by starting with matter rather than spirit cannot buy into the traditional conception of matter as inert, or indeed the traditional opposition between active spirit and passive matter. Schelling proposes a new conception of matter with his actively negating, spiritualized conception of material will, and criticizes philosophy for propagating an inert materialism: 'the whole of modern European philosophy ... has this common deficiency – that nature does not exist for it and it lacks a living basis ...' (HF, 30).

This last comment offers another a new compatibility test, this time one that Schelling can use to test his affinities with Nietzsche. And it is clear that Nietzsche, with his notion of the will to power in nature, would certainly pass Schelling's test. But we can note a second similarity in that Nietzsche also described his philosophical revolution as a type of reversal of the highest and lowest. In his famous discussion of 'How the "true world" finally became a fable', he sketches the inversion, not of Neo-Platonist ontology, but rather of Platonic epistemology; the priority Plato gives to a transcendent 'true' world of essences is reversed, and philosophy comes to give sensuous appearances the highest value instead. And like Schelling, this revaluation does not entail a strict reversal, but rather calls into question the whole problematic dichotomy between the highest and the lowest. Getting rid of Plato's top-down model is not a matter of asserting the rights of the illusory world over the 'true' one. Rather, Nietzsche insists, *we got rid of the illusory world along with the true one!*'; (TI, 'How the true world finally became a fable'). Nietzsche contests the Platonic hierarchy not by reversing it, but rather by rejecting the oppositional thinking it is predicated on. A genuinely non-Platonic philosophy does not just mean starting from the other end, it requires a counter-traditional conception of what counts as 'lowest'. Instead of describing his alternative conception, Nietzsche writes: 'INCIPIT ZARATHUSTRA'; in place of the deposed Plato, Zarathustra will arrive as the representative of active, affirmative, creative will to power.[9]

Nietzsche and Schelling are in agreement that oppositional thinking and top-down models of production prevented traditional philosophy from developing a generative concept of material will. Further, not only is it false to say that the lowest is opposed to the highest; for both of them, the lowest and the highest are in some sense the same. Nietzsche tentatively proposes this idea:

It could even be possible that whatever gives value to ... good and honorable things has an incriminating link, bond or tie to the very things that look like their evil opposites; perhaps they are even essentially the same. Perhaps! – But who is willing to take charge of such a dangerous Perhaps! (BGE 2)

One answer, it seems, is Schelling, who writes, for instance: 'Good and evil are the same, only regarded from different aspects; or evil in itself, that is regarded at the root of its identity, is goodness, on the other hand, regarded in its division or non-identity, is evil' (HF, 80). Elsewhere Schelling makes clear the ontological relation here, that the 'lowest' is the ground of the highest.

... it is the irrational itself that constitutes the very foundation of our understanding. Consequently, madness is a necessary element, albeit one that is not supposed to manifest itself or become an actuality. What we call the understanding, if it is to be an actual, living, and active understanding, is therefore, properly nothing than a coordinated madness.[10]

Nietzsche and Schelling give different values to this idea, of course. Nietzsche is a champion of the 'evil' and 'irrational' (in this restricted sense) and Schelling most certainly is not. The key difference is that Schelling grants only respect and ontological priority to the 'lowest', while maintaining a valuative priority for the 'highest'. He writes: 'priority stands in an inverse relation to superiority' (WA II, 179). Nietzsche, on the other hand, wants to cast general aspersions on the highest, which he calls 'the last wisps of smoke from the evaporating end of reality' (TI, 'Reason in Philosophy', 4). But it is important to note that Nietzsche mobilizes this well-honed sense of contempt only in the service of debunking the spirit-seeing aspirations of traditional metaphysics with its notion of *causa sui*, believing that 'things of the highest value must have another, separate origin *of their own* – they cannot be derived from this ephemeral, seductive, deceptive, lowly world, from this mad chaos of confusion and desire' (BGE, 2). In a different context, one in which the material world is affirmed rather than denied, Nietzsche has a much more positive take on such derivatives. That is, he lauds cultural products that have their genesis in 'this mad chaos of confusion and desire' if they celebrate rather than disavow their origin. For instance he applauds various spiritual*izations*, such as the spiritualization of sensuality into love (TI, 'Morality as Anti-Nature', 3). And he approves of the elevation of reality into appearance in art 'because "appearance" here means reality *once again*, only selected, strengthened, corrected ...' (TI, 'Reason in Philosophy', 6).

The key phrase here is 'once again', which suggests that for Nietzsche, the productivity of the will lies in its iterative function. And this is key to understanding the fundamental difference between Nietzsche's and Schelling's notions of creative will: where Schelling thinks the productivity of the will lies in its *grounding* function, Nietzsche thinks it comes from the will's ability to generate *repetition*. So for Schelling, matter is the ground of spirit while for Nietzsche, spirit is matter 'once again'. Yet both see this genetic relation as expressing identity or sameness. Schelling believes ground and grounded stand in a relation of identity (HF, 14). Identity for him is productive in the case where the ground is identical with the grounded. (Schelling takes this as the true meaning of Spinoza's equation of God and nature – that nature is the ground of God.) Nietzsche, on the other hand, thinks that the creative power of the material principle lies in its ability to generate repetition, and in the highest instance to will a return of the same:[11] Zarathustra teaches that 'all things recur eternally, and we ourselves too'.[12]

It is striking that in both these accounts of materialist production, whether the mechanism is grounding or repetition, the producer is the same (or identical) with its product. This enables both Schelling and Nietzsche to develop accounts of self-creation. The idea of self-creation features prominently in their writings: Nietzsche has a famous injunction to 'become what you are', and Schelling describes the will as 'the longing of the One to give birth to itself ...' (HF, 74). (Nietzsche even uses a slogan similar to Schelling's stating: 'the world is a work of art that gives birth to itself'; WP, 796). For Schelling, it is God's self-creation that is at issue, while for Nietzsche it is the self-creation of the individual. But the primary model for self-creation is the very *causa sui* against which Nietzsche and Schelling are supposedly united. Understanding how Nietzsche and Schelling give genuinely materialist (not *causa sui*) accounts of self-creation puts us at the heart of their engagement with temporality.

The main factor distinguishing Schelling's and Nietzsche's principles of self-creation from a notion of the *causa sui* is that they lack any element of spontaneity; the self (or, in Schelling's case, God) does *not* emerge from nothing, but rather has a past. What makes this a self-creation is that the self (or God) creates its own past. For both Nietzsche and Schelling, the self (God) is a product of a past that it has itself created. Which is to say self-creation is not spontaneous, but *circular*. So both of these materialist models of production – grounding and repetition – lead Schelling and Nietzsche to develop theories of reverse or circular causation. In order to explain this, I will need to turn to the details of their particular philosophical accounts, and how each thinks that the past has been produced.

SCHELLING

In his *Philosophical Inquiries into the Nature of Human Freedom* (1809), Schelling explores the idea that the will functions as the natural ground of God's existence. In the drafts he wrote for his uncompleted *Ages of the World*, he theorizes this notion of will further, explaining how it both constitutes and creates the past, which is to say the temporal ground of God's existence. The story takes the form of a creation myth, explaining the origin of the dimensions of time. Schelling famously never progressed further than the past before abandoning work on the project. (This has a nice, though accidental parallel in Nietzsche, who focused largely on a genealogical uncovering of origins, and only hinted broadly that he saw a new age arriving.)

Schelling describes the grounding relation in both ontological and moral terms. Ontologically, Schelling believes the ground must be a contractive, inward force, 'All development presupposes envelopment. In attraction there is beginning, and the fundamental force of contraction is in fact the original force, the root force of nature. All life begins with contraction ...' (WA II, 179). This quickly acquires a moral dimension: 'The negating, enclosing will must precede ... Wrath must come before love, severity before mildness, strength before gentleness.' Schelling's idea is that contraction grounds and makes possible an anti-contractive force of freely flowing expansion, an act of affirmation in which God says yes to existence.

According to Schelling, every thing in nature is composed of forces in a relation of a grounding contraction and a grounded expansion. The negating contraction gives things a corporeality and the expansive force gives them a spiritual essence. But nature as a whole also acts as a negating contraction with respect to God, providing the ground for God's existence, the nature in God. Schelling argues that if we take seriously the idea that God has created himself, we will be forced to conclude that God has a material ground. If God is his own ground, the argument runs, and the ground cannot have the properties we attribute to what it grounds, the ground of God cannot have the qualities we normally attribute to God. So if God is spiritual, the ground must be natural. Which means that if God is his own ground, there must be a physical side to God (which is identical to the spiritual side, as we saw in the previous section) (WA II, 149).

But God not only needs the spatial ground of nature, he needs a temporal ground as well; the grounding relation is chronological as well as onto-logical. And indeed we find within the notion of God both jealousy and forgiveness, which is to say both an exophobic contraction and generous expansiveness. When God decided to create himself, he did so by positing the negative force as the ground of his existence, which is his positive, expansive presence. In this case, the negative force is the past, which serves as the ground of the positive force of the present. God effects a synthesis of these forces; specifically, he tucks a past under his present in order that he can exist. Schelling calls this backward willing a 'repression' of the negative force into the base of God's existence.

This is an odd conception of the past: the past is not just the chronological but the transcendental ground of the present, the condition of its possibility. This means that the past is not a past present, it was never a 'now'. Rather, it is always already past; it is a unique dimension separated from the present by ontological difference. We experience the present as an outward expansion, driving us forward; but, Schelling argues, we also feel the presence of this past as a permanent heaviness or undertow, a constant though subliminal sense of the melancholy that infuses all things.

The past was created when God decided to create himself. This is an affirmative notion; God's affirmation of the value of existence and of the present entails a production of temporality and a creation of the past as past. But this also involves a paradoxical sort of backwards willing (which Schelling describes as repression, as God puts the past behind him). Schelling discusses the consequences of this non-linear notion.

> In the cycle whence all things come, it is no contradiction to say that that which gives birth to the one is, in its turn, produced by it. There is here no first and no last, since everything mutually implies every-thing else ... God contains himself in an inner basis of his existence, which, to this extent, precedes him as to his existence, but similarly God is prior to the basis as this basis, as such, could not be if God did not exist in actuality. (HF, 33)

Or, as Schelling puts it elsewhere, 'The subsequent cooperates in what precedes it ...' (HF, 65). The circle is Schelling's image of inextricable, mutual implication. Schelling writes: 'we recognize ... that the concept of becoming is the only one adequate to the nature of things' (HF, 33). God's affirmation of existence produces a cycle of becoming, which is a cycle of time.

This theory has many obvious similarities to Nietzsche's idea of eternal return, and I will turn to the details of Nietzsche's theory next. But first it must be said that the theological context of Schelling's theory is not in itself enough to mark a strong distinction from the resolutely anti-theological Nietzsche. For Schelling, God does not play the sort of decadent role that Nietzsche criticizes. Nietzsche's critique is not of God *per se* (Nietzsche can imagine gods he would like) but of the impulse to create a transcendent notion of God that devalorizes life and the body. Schelling's God does not play this role, largely for the reason that it is still conceived along fundamentally Spinozistic lines, as a God who is not distinct from life and the body. In affirming himself, God affirms nature and the present (indeed, the affirmation functions to create them) and, most significantly, becoming.

This last point does mark a distinction from Spinoza, but it is a modification of Spinoza along decidedly Nietzschean lines. Where Spinoza introduces God's productive activity into nature (space), Schelling introduces it into time as well. Just as Spinoza spreads God across space, Schelling spreads him across time. Schelling corrects Spinoza by providing a temporal notion of immanence, which acknowledges the centrality of becoming and believes in a constant becoming-God, a spiritualization of all things.

NIETZSCHE

Nietzsche's conception of the will to power, the constitutive material drive that informs all natural and psychological process, is directly tied to his theory of time, because in Nietzsche's mind, the highest task for the affirmative will is to will eternal return.

Eternal return is linked to the thought of the interconnection of things: 'are not all things knotted together so firmly that this moment draws after it all that is to come?' (Z III, 270). Or: 'Have you ever said Yes to a single joy? O my friends, then you said Yes to all woe. All things are entangled, ensnared, enamored ...' (Z IV, 435). Our lives and world do not come in discrete pieces – and eternal return is the thought that we are not free to pick and choose. To be able to affirm eternal return means being able to affirm the totality of life and history; it makes willing whole. Nietzsche writes: 'oh that you would reject all halfhearted willing ...' (Z III, 284).

This sort of global affirmation needs to be rigorously distinguished from a quietist resignation, however. Nietzsche is not celebrating a will capable of enduring or accepting life. This is clear in his treatment of the ass in *Zarathustra* – the ass is a Christ-like figure that takes on all burdens. This attitude lacks the sort of creativity that is the hallmark of affirmative will, whose remit is not to take account of what exists and then affirm it, but rather to express its affirmation through creativity, to posit values rather than accept existing values.

The sort of creative affirmation championed by Nietzsche finds its greatest challenge when confronted with the past, which is set and unalterable:

> To redeem those who lived in the past and to recreate all 'it was' into a 'thus I willed it' – that alone should I call redemption. Will – that is the name of the liberator and joy-bringer; thus I taught you, my friends. But now learn this too: the will itself is still a prisoner. Willing liberates; but what is it that puts even the liberator himself in fetters? 'It was' – that is the name of the will's gnashing of teeth and most secret melancholy. Powerless against what has been done, he is an angry spectator of all that is past. The will cannot will backwards; and that he cannot break time and time's covetousness, that is the will's loneliest melancholy. (Z II, 251)

As with Schelling, the relation to the past is a source of melancholy, and has the quality of a weight or anchor on the present. But Nietzsche makes clear that a rejection of the past is a rejection of time itself. 'This, indeed this alone is what *revenge* is: the will's ill will against time and its "it was" '(Z II, 252).

So what would a good will towards time be? Clearly, it will be one that affirms the past. But this does not mean being glad that the past is past. Rather, Zarathustra makes clear that an affirmative will is one that can actually *will backwards*: ' "The will is a creator." All "it was" is a fragment, a riddle, a dreadful accident – until the creative will says to it ... "But thus I willed it; thus shall I will it" '(Z II, 253). The project of learning to 'will backwards' is key to *Zarathustra*; and Nietzsche's 'redemptive' idea that changes 'it was' into a 'thus I willed it' is eternal return.

But the thought of eternal return is stronger than this: it does not just transform the 'it was' into a 'thus I willed it' – it transforms the 'it was' into a 'thus *shall* I will it'. Eternal return is an affirmation that has as a project the creation of the past: '... [T]he knot of causes in which I am entangled recurs and will create me again. I myself belong to the causes of the eternal recurrence ... I come back eternally to this same, selfsame life, in what is greatest as in what is smallest, to teach again the eternal recurrence of all things ...' (Z III, 333). Here, the past is not only the cause but the effect of my willing the eternal return of all things. ('I myself belong to the causes of the eternal recurrence.')

When describing eternal return, Nietzsche makes ample use of the image of the circle or the ring: 'the nuptial ring of rings, the ring of recurrence ...' (Z III, 340). And indeed, the will that wills eternal return brings together the past and future into an interconnected whole.

> O my soul, I taught you to say 'today' and 'one day' and 'formerly' and to dance away over all Here and There and Yonder ... O my soul, now there is not a soul anywhere that would be more loving and compre-

hending and comprehensive. Where would future and past dwell closer together than in you? (Z III, 333–5)

In willing eternal return and linking the past, present and future, the 'soul' is creative in terms very familiar to Kantian philosophy: it functions as a principle of synthesis. In fact, both Nietzsche and Schelling exhibit a striking and unexpected fidelity to Kant, not only by construing production as a synthesis, but by making temporality the principle of that synthesis. In Nietzsche, the individual creates itself by synthesizing the dimensions of time; in Schelling, God creates himself in the same way. But we can also note the unsettling nature of this synthesis for both Schelling and Nietzsche, the fact that it is a diffuse, polychromatic creature that results. Which is to say, synthesis does not work in the service of stability and identity, but rather the opposite. We see this in the heterodox notion of God that Schelling introduces, a historical God rooted in nature and possessing a sort of transcendental unconscious in the form of his repressed past. For Nietzsche too, synthesis is unsettling: eternal return does not stabilize the subject through repetition, but rather spreads it across time, and across things in time. 'The fatality of human existence cannot be extricated from the fatality of everything that was and will be . . . a person belongs to the whole, a person only *is* in the context of the whole . . .' (TI, 'The Four Great Errors', 8). The diffuse nature of the individual that results from Nietzsche's temporal synthesis can be understood with reference to the sort of temporal Spinozism we saw in Schelling, applied to the individual rather than to God. Like Schelling's God, Nietzsche's individual is spread across time, and eternal return expresses a will for the dissolution of the subject into the circular nexus of becoming.[13]

MYTH AND PROPHECY

There are many and obvious similarities between Schelling's theory and that of Nietzsche. Both develop the concept of a will capable of willing its own past, a notion that entails reverse causality. In both cases, the will has a synthetic function of unifying the present with the past; in creating the past, it creates itself by spreading itself across time. Perhaps the most significant similarity from a Nietzschean perspective is the affirmative nature of both notions of creating the past. For Nietzsche, eternal return is a way of affirming the present moment by willing the entire chain of past events that cannot be unlinked from the present. For Schelling, God's creation of the past is part of the primal act of repression through which God decides in favour of existence over non-existence. For both, then, the past is created through an act of self-affirmation and an affirmation of the present.

One key difference should not be overlooked. The creation of the past functions primarily as an origin myth for Schelling, a story of the foundational constitution of temporality; for Nietzsche, on the other hand, willing backwards is a project to be achieved, Zarathustra's most difficult thought. In other words, Schelling buries the act in the inaccessible past, while Nietzsche postpones it into the indeterminate future. As such, neither one makes a straightforward ontological claim about reverse causation; it is not a present possibility for either of them, but is rather deferred: backwards for Schelling and forwards for Nietzsche. For Schelling, the notion is a transcendental one, an event that is a condition for the possibility of our present experience of time, and has thus always already occurred. And Nietzsche is not concerned to establish the metaphysical viability of the idea of eternal return, but would rather analyse the selective function the thought plays in distinguishing between those who are capable of a truly affirmative will and those who are not. His distinctive questions are: where is the will capable of willing eternal return? And when will the world be ready for this most difficult thought?

More to the point, both philosophers deploy literary forms at this very juncture, where they need to explain the creation of the past. Nietzsche puts the doctrine into the mouth of his fictional Zarathustra, and alludes to it only in fables, riddles, parables and poems. (Zarathustra's animals make the doctrine into 'a hurdy-gurdy song', Z III, 330.) Schelling makes a methodological point of explaining that the story of the past should be *recounted*, and calls for a 'great heroic poem' that would do so. The science of history will finally be uncovered 'when truth becomes fable and fable truth . . .' (WA II, 114). For Schelling, backwards willing is myth and for Nietzsche it is prophecy. And for each of them, this literary turn is a testimony to the rigour of their engagement with the issue of willing and time.[14] For Nietzsche, the thought of a will capable of willing return is so new an idea that he cannot refer it to conventional philosophical tools. For Schelling, it is the notion of an authentic past (that is not just a previous present) that cannot be comprehended by traditional means. They are both at work crafting new modes of expression; the mythic or prophetic registers testify, in these cases, to the depth and novelty of the ideas they are trying to express.

WILLING BACKWARDS: SCHELLING AND NIETZSCHE CONTRA FREUD

Another key difference between Nietzsche and Schelling's ideas of a will capable of creating the past is that, while Schelling saw the production of the past as a form of repression, Nietzsche wanted to reproduce the past in the mode of a return. If we want judge the proximity of these conceptions we should look to Freudian psychoanalysis, which both brings together the ideas of repression and return and marks, in many ways, a culmination of the tradition of nineteenth-century philosophies of will. Freud even offers a thought of reverse causality in the notion of *Nachträglichkeit*, which can be translated as 'deferred action' (or, following Jean Laplanche, 'afterwardsness').

Nachträglichkeit offers a model of psychic temporality distinct from somatic, linear temporality. It describes an act that is only constituted as a trauma by subsequent events. A patient will manifest traumatic symptoms due to a cause that was not traumatic when it occurred; and so the event will only retroactively acquire the character of a trauma. Central to this notion is the thought of return, that a traumatic event is only manifested in a returning symptom – its *recurrence* in the present first determines its *occurrence* in the past. As Jean Laplanche writes: 'it always takes two traumas to make a trauma'.[15] As such, Freud's notion neatly mirrors the ontological deferral we saw in both Nietzsche and Schelling's notions of the act of creating the past, the fact that this act of creation is not a present one. For Freud, the trauma is never present, never happens the first time – it has either been (always already) repressed into the past or returning from the future.

Freud's theory proposes a rapprochement between Schelling and Nietzsche. But does it succeed? That is: to what extent do either Schelling's or Nietzsche's theories really conform to this Freudian structure? Significantly, Nietzsche and Schelling had very different conceptions of the relation between the past and the present. For Nietzsche, the past flows into the present and future (and then back into the past), while for Schelling the past remains outside of the frame of the present, as its ground; that is, for Schelling, the past was never itself present. For both thinkers, the past is an essential and inseparable component of the present, but for Schelling this intimacy is due to the position of the past as transcendental ground – while for Nietzsche, there is absolutely no ontological difference. This means that what the will wills in creating the past is essentially different for the two of them. For Schelling, the will wills that the past be *past*, while for Nietzsche the will wills that the past *return*. But this means that neither theory conforms to the Freudian structure; for Schelling the past is repressed but it does not return – for Nietzsche it returns but it was not repressed.

These differences are significant. Although Schelling theorizes a circular causation, it is not the thought of return. In the creation of the dimensions of time, the past is put at the ground and it remains there; it does not break the surface of the present. Which is to say this primal negation or repression is not something that happens *in* the past but rather *to* the past – repression is what makes the past past. Schelling repeatedly stresses the extent to which this repression cannot be taken back:

> ... it is a permanent deed, a never-ending deed, and consequently it can never again be brought before consciousness. For man to know of this deed, consciousness itself would have to return into nothing ... and would cease to be consciousness. This deed occurs once, and then immediately sinks back into the unfathomable depths; and nature acquires permanence precisely thereby. Likewise that will, posited once at the beginning and then led to the outside, must immediately sink into unconsciousness. Only in this way is a beginning possible, a

beginning that does not stop being a beginning, a truly eternal beginning. For here as well, it is true that the beginning cannot know itself.

As we have said, that deed is done for eternity; that is, it is eternally what is done, and is consequently what has past. We thus see that by sinking into unconsciousness, the negating will is actually already acting as past – namely for us. (WA II, 181–2)

The repression cannot be taken back which is to say the repressed cannot return.

With Nietzsche, on the other hand, we find the thought of return without repression. In fact, he clearly rejects the notion of repression. The will of eternal return does not push the past into the past but rather thrusts it out into the future. This is why Zarathustra is admonished to become a child, and told 'whoever would become as a child must overcome his youth too' (Z II, 259). As a condition for willing eternal recurrence, Zarathustra needs to overcome any tendency to repression. He confronts his 'abysmal thought' saying:

up, abysmal thought, out of my depth! I am your cock and dawn, sleepy worm ... And once you are awake, you shall remain awake eternally ... Zarathustra, the godless, summons you! I, Zarathustra, the advocate of life, the advocate of suffering, the advocate of the circle; I summon you, my most abysmal thought! (Z III, 327–28)

Nietzsche's point is not that the repressed thought is returning, but that Zarathustra cannot become the advocate of return until he has overcome repression and pulled all thoughts onto the same plane, the open light of the eternally awake ('Oh my soul, I ... persuaded you to stand naked before the eyes of the sun' Z III, 333–4). The idea Zarathustra would prefer not to confront is that even the smallest things will return: 'the eternal recurrence even of the smallest – that was my disgust with all existence' (Z III, 331). Which is to say that Zarathustra needs to learn to affirm even his worst thought, that the lowest returns along with the highest. The thought of return is incompatible with any reluctance or holding back – any partial willing. It is a universal affirmation that runs contrary to the notion of a repressed trauma.

Reading Nietzsche and Schelling through Freud enables us to see precisely how wide a distance there is between them, how far myth can be from prophecy, repression from return (and it also enables us to appreciate the system that can unite them). But at the same time, Nietzsche and Schelling's theories, different as they are, both differ from the Freudian conception in that they are affirmative. For Schelling, the past is created as part of an act in which God decides to exist – God affirms his present and presence. For Nietzsche, eternal return emerges from a love of life that wills that it happen again and again. Freud is not moved by an affirmative gesture. The repetition compulsion is a function of the death drive, and the symptom of the repressed trauma mars rather than celebrates life. When Freud reaches this conclusion he reports: 'we have unwittingly steered our course into the harbour of Schopenhauer's philosophy'.[16] Nietzsche also likes comparing his philosophical project to a ship sailing out to sea; but however divergent their courses, both he and Schelling steer well clear of Freud's pessimistic return to Schopenhauer.

Notes

1   A typical instance is Robert Pippin who, in his discussion of the German roots of Nietzsche's will to power, discusses Kant, Fichte and Hegel (and Hobbes, Rousseau and Spinoza for good measure) but never mentions Schelling. See 'Commentary: Notes on Nietzsche's Modernism' in *Independent Journal of Philosophy*, vol. IV, 14–19. A notable exception is John Elbert Wilson's fine monograph, *Schelling und Nietzsche: Zur Auslegung der frühen Werke Friedrich Nietzsches* (New York: Walter de Gruyter, 1996). As the title suggests, Wilson focuses almost exclusively on the influence of the later Schelling (the doctrine of potences, and so forth) on the early Nietzsche (of the *Birth of Tragedy*).
2   *Twilight of the Idols*, trans. Judith Norman (New York: Cambridge University Press, forthcoming), 'The Four Great Errors'. Citations of this work will appear as 'TI' and refer to this edition.
3   *Philosophical Inquiries into the Nature of Human Freedom*, trans. James Gutmann (La Salle, IL: Open Court, 1992), 33. Citations of this work will appear as 'HF' and refer to.
4   *The Abyss of Freedom/Ages of the World* (Ann Arbor MI: University of Michigan, 1997), 114 (essay by Slavoj Žižek with a translation of Schelling's 1813 *Ages of the World* by Judith Norman). Citations of this work will appear as 'WA II' and refer to this edition.
5   *The Will to Power*, trans. Walter Kaufmann and R. J. Hollingdale (New York: Vintage, 1968) § 1067. Citations of this work will appear as 'WP' and refer to section numbers in this edition.
6   For a discussion of this see: Gilles Deleuze, *Nietzsche and Philosophy*, trans. Hugh Tomlinson (London: Athlone, 1983), 39–45.
7   For Schelling, the aesthetic element affects only the form of presentation – unlike Nietzsche, he does not go so far as to suggest the text be judged according to aesthetic rather than epistemological criteria.
8   Schelling, *Die Weltalter. Fragmente in den Urauffassungen von 1811 und 1813*, ed. Manfred Schröter (Munich: Biederstein & Leibniz, 1946), 230.
9   See for instance *Beyond Good and Evil*, trans. Judith Norman (New York: Cambridge University Press, 2002), 36. Citations of this work will appear as 'BGE' and refer to section numbers in this edition.
10 'Stuttgart Seminars' (1810) in *Idealism and the Endgame of Theory*, trans. Thomas Pfau (Albany NY: SUNY, 1994), 223.
11 Schelling is critical of the notion of sameness but approves of the notion of identity (HF, p. 14 n 1); Nietzsche, on the other hand, affirms the return of the same while being sharply critical of all forms of identity.
12 *Thus Spoke Zarathustra*, trans. Walter Kaufmann in *The Portable Nietzsche* (New York: Viking, 1954) Bk. III, 332. Citations of this work will appear as 'Z' and refer to book and page numbers in this edition.

13 For a discussion of this idea see Pierre Klossowski, *Nietzsche and the Vicious Circle*, trans. Daniel W. Smith (London: Athlone, 1997).

14 Heidegger's *Being and Time* is the classical locus for this line of analysis.

15 *New Foundations of Psychoanalysis*, trans. David Macey (London: Blackwell, 1989), 88.

16 *Beyond the Pleasure Principle* in *The Pelican Freud*, vol. 11 (London: Penguin, 1985), 322.

5

PHILOSOPHY AND THE EXPERIENCE OF CONSTRUCTION

Alberto Toscano

AN EPISODE IN THE GENEALOGY OF MATERIALISM (ANTI-SCHELLING)

In 1841, with the blessing of the Prussian state, the aged Schelling climbed the rostrum of the University of Berlin to denounce the errors and short-comings of the Hegelian dialectic and reveal the contents of his own positive philosophy.[1] This intellectual episode has gone down in the annals of the history of philosophy principally on account of the audience that came to listen to this last survivor of the golden age of idealism, speaking from the post that once belonged to his philosophical nemesis, Hegel. Kierkegaard, Bakunin, Feuerbach, Marx's friend Arnold Ruge, and Friedrich Engels were amongst them. Engels, writing under the pseudonym of Friedrich Oswald for the *Telegraph für Deutschland*, gave a summary of these lectures, which soon thereafter developed into the anonymous polemical tract *Schelling and Revelation. Critique of the Latest Attempt of Reaction against the Free Philosophy*, a veritable *Anti-Schelling*. On the basis of Engels' account, these lectures appear both as momentous, functioning to crystallize a philosophical camp, and anti-climactic, because Schelling cut a reactionary figure much at odds with his former, radical self. The first of Engels' two articles for the *Telegraph* begins thus:

> Ask anybody in Berlin today on what field the battle for dominion over German public opinion in politics and religion, that is, over Germany itself, is being fought, and if he has any idea of the power of the mind over the world he will reply that this battlefield is the University, in particular Lecture-hall No. 6, where Schelling is giving his lectures on the philosophy of revelation.[2]

The tract itself leaves no doubt as to the nature of Engels' own engage-ment within this battle. In its unsparing invective, barbed sarcasm, and insistent demolition of Schelling's philosophy of revelation, it provides a testament to the thoroughly negative perception of the figure of the late Schelling on the part of the Young, or Left, Hegelians. This perception, as we can glean from the following passage – taken from the conclusion, and steeped in the language of bathos and euphoria – is made all the more acute by the perception of Schelling as a philosophical traitor of sorts, once an irreverent innovator, now, at the end of his odyssey, the agent of Reaction. These lines should perhaps be read in counterpoint to the beginning of the Transcendental Doctrine of Judgement of Kant's *Critique of Pure Reason* (B295/A236), where the stable land of critique is juxtaposed with the delirious sea of speculation:

> So we have come to the end of Schelling's philosophy and can only regret that such a man should have become so caught in the snares of faith and unfreedom. He was different when he was still young. Then there arose from the ferment of his brain forms as radiant as Pallas, of which many a one forged to the front also in later struggles; then freely and boldly he sailed into the open sea of thought to discover Atlantis, the absolute, whose image he had so often seen rising from the distant horizon of the sea like a dreamily shimmering *fata morgana*; then all the fire of youth broke from him in flames of enthusiasm; a prophet drunk with God, he foretold a new era; carried away by the spirit which came over him, he often did not know himself the meaning of his words. He tore wide open the doors to philosophising so that the breath of nature wafted freshly through the chambers of abstract thought and the warm rays of spring fell on the seed of the categories and awakened all slumbering forces. But the fire burnt itself out, the courage vanished, the fermenting new wine turned into sour vinegar before it could become clear wine. The old ship dancing joyfully through the waves turned back and entered the shallow haven of faith, ran its keel so fast into the sand that it is still stuck there. There it lies, and nobody recognises in the old, frail wreck the old ship which went out with all sails spread and flags flying. The sails have long since rotted, the masts are broken, the waves pour in through the gaping planks, and every day the tides pile up more sand around the keel. Let us turn away from this waste of time. There are finer things for us to contemplate.

In the agonistic genealogy of philosophical orientations, Schelling, as the reports of Engels, Kierkegaard and others attest, did not, as some seem to argue, provide the tools for the critique of Hegel that is still played out today. On the contrary, if we are to trust Engels' reaction, his return to Berlin merely served to exacerbate the attempt to *realize* the Hegelian project, that is, to force the logical concatenation of the vicissitudes of reason into the real articulation of material relations. The thesis about the philosophical conjuncture of the time that transpires from the testimony of Engels is this: Schelling is the new that failed, Hegel is the old that bears the promise of the new. The new, in this instance, is the material appropriation for human ends of the rationality of the concept, no longer the speculative identity of the real and the rational, but the forcing of rationality into the real, the Idea incarnate. Such a forcing was mortally inimical to the Schellingian introduction of the 'thatness' of positive revelation into the 'whatness' of a merely abstract, or negative, determination of the rational. Reason's need of Revelation was, to say the least, an inopportune theme at a time when the base foundations of the essence of Christianity had just begun to be 'revealed' to Germany's young radicals. Marx's own appraisal was even more damning, and its polemical urgency such as to lead him to make his first contact with Feuerbach, in a letter dated 3 October 1843. This brief and combative epistle adds two elements to our understanding of the response of Schelling's contemporaries to the old man's grand return onto the philosophical scene. The first is the explicit definition of the philosophy of the future as both a reversal of Schelling and a sublating return to the first Schelling, the Schelling that introduced, through *Naturphilosophie*, the themes of construction and production into the narrow territory of transcendental philosophy. This is Marx's entreaty to Feuerbach:

> You would therefore be doing a great service to our enterprise [the journal that Marx was planning at the time, A.T.], but even more to truth, if you were to contribute a characterisation of Schelling to the very first issue. You are just the man for this because you are Schelling in reverse. The sincere thought – we may believe the best of our opponent – of the young Schelling for the realisation of which however he did not possess the necessary qualities except imagination, he had no energy but vanity, no driving force but opium, no organ but the irritability of a feminine perceptivity, this sincere thought of his youth, which in his case remained a fantastic youthful dream, has become truth, reality, manly seriousness in your case. Schelling is therefore an anticipated caricature of you, and as soon as reality confronts the caricature the latter must dissolve into thin air. I therefore regard you as the necessary, natural – that is, nominated by Their Majesties Nature and History – opponent of Schelling. Your struggle with him is the struggle of the imagination of philosophy with philosophy itself.[3]

We will return to this implicit recognition of Schelling's early philosophy as the introduction of a certain materialism into the field of the transcendental. Let us simply note that the current that shook, first through Feuerbach and then Marx, the very foundations of the image of philosophy that bound speculation to State and Church, found its negative inspiration in the Berlin lectures. Materialist dialectics appears to have begun with this opposition to Schelling, an opposition that, as both Engels and Marx did not fail to emphasize, was almost immediately political, and all the more so when the struggle in theory was an explicit anticipation of a struggle in practice. In Marx's eyes Schelling was not only the provider *supplement d'âme* for the regime but was indeed part and parcel of it. This much he communicated to Feuerbach:

> Schelling, as you know, is the 38th member of the [German] Confederation. The entire German police is at his disposal as I myself once experienced when I was editor of the *Rheinische Zeitung*. That is, a censorship order can prevent anything against the holy Schelling from getting through.[4]

This role was only aggravated by Schelling's perceived ability to be all things to all people outside of the German theatre of philosophical warfare. In this regard Marx's remarks to Feuerbach should be kept in mind as we assess the virtuality and function of a Schellingian resurgence in the current philosophical debate: 'To the French romantics and mystics he cries: "I, the union of philosophy and theology," to the French materialists: "I, the union of flesh and idea," to the French sceptics: "I, the destroyer of dogmatism," in a word, "I . . . Schelling!" '[5]

I think this entire episode is not to be ignored if we ourselves wish to confront the stakes of a return to Schelling, especially insofar as such a return inevitably entails some consideration of philosophy's relation to its own history. From the remarks by Marx and Engels, we can glean that their view of Schelling's role, whilst tempered by a recognition of the interest and radicality of his youthful work, ultimately comes down to that of an obstacle in the path of the expansion and refinement of a materialist philosophy. Yet, what is at stake in the responses of Engels and Marx is not an Olympian struggle of concepts but a question of intervening in a conjuncture which extends (or rather, *must* extend) far beyond the narrow frontiers of academic debate. In this light, and regardless of the many pages spent by Engels in refuting (but also in dismissing, mocking and reviling) Schelling's lectures, we must acknowledge that the disruptive force of the encounter between the old Schelling and the new guard of aspiring materialists is carried, not by words such as 'Absolute', 'positive philosophy', 'revelation', but by rather more immediate ones: 'police', 'university', 'State'. Or, to put it less bluntly and more technically, the political affect at work in the political terms seems to thoroughly over-determine the status of the philosophical ones. In this genealogical scenario Schelling's return is a negative catalyst, his reactive appearance serves to accelerate, to precipitate the constitution of a materialist camp. He is the *éminence grise* in the conflicted and conflictual inception of materialist dialectics.

Fully acknowledging this negative, albeit catalysing, role played by Schelling in the development of the Marxist materialist tradition, I would nevertheless wish to uphold in a rather circumscribed sense the proposition of a return to Schelling, in order to delineate what I would call a *materialism of the concept*, a position encapsulated in the theses of Deleuze-Guattari's *What is Philosophy?* In an encounter that could only take place in the *stratigraphic time* that this book describes as the time of philosophy,[6] let us ask, through the work of Kant, Schelling and Deleuze-Guattari, a question that seems to go to the heart of any consideration of materialism in philosophy: *What is Construction?* The paradox here is that it is only by asking a question of this order, which belongs to the problematic, dys-chronic, time of the concept that, if such a thing ever be allowed to a philosophy, the name of Schelling can be regarded as *new*. This novelty is not, as in Engels, of the kind that would allow philosophy to find itself finally realized in the world, in the here and now of a historical conjuncture; it is not a novelty that would be indexed to a worldly transformation, but rather one occurring within the bounds of philosophy, as the (re-)emergence of a new configuration for thought. The link between such a configuration and political actuality, or between the time of philosophy and the kind of time that saw Marx hounded by Schelling's police, does not disappear as such, but it must be reframed, according to a new articulation of philosophy and its outside, in other words, a new figure of materialism.

In centring the discussion on the theme of construction, moving from its critical matrix in Kant to its assumption as the organon of philosophy in Schelling, and then to the formulation of philosophy as constructivism by Deleuze-Guattari, I am consciously operating a *restriction* of the question of materialism. Rather than establishing the philosophical rights of materialism as a generative ontology, as a philosophy of production, in a line that might run from Schelling's *Naturphilosophie* to Marx's *Grundrisse* and to Deleuze-Guattari's *Capitalism and Schizophrenia*, my concern here is with materialism *in* philosophy, materialism as a determination of philosophical *practice*. It is precisely this theme of practice that allows us to grasp the discontinuity between materialism before and after Marx, and not to fall into a misconception (admittedly, one sustained by texts such as Engels' own *Dialectics of Nature*) that would consider materialism simply as a philosophy *of* matter. To maintain the singularity and radical force of materialism 'after Marx', the primacy of practice, which in philosophy takes the guise of an 'experience of construction', must be both assumed and investigated. This is not to dismiss the question of a thinking of matter, and of matter as production, but to assert that an inquiry into the practice and production in and of philosophy should precede a determination of a philosophy *of* practice and production. Whilst, as should be evident from what follows, we do not intend to rehash the depleted and simplistic debate regarding the precedence of epistemology over ontology, or vice versa, we can regard this as one way of defending the importance of the legacy of critique for a definition of contemporary materialism. It is in this light that Schelling's radical transformation of the Kantian theme of construction can be viewed as a vital contribution to the definition of a materialist philosophy.

THE TRANSCENDENTAL ARTIFICE

In philosophy, the stakes of conflict and novelty often appear to revolve around the issue of demarcation, no more so than in the history of materialism, whose mutations can be traced in terms of the disputed articulation of philosophy and its outside (whose many guises include the natural world, the senses, the domain of economic production, praxis, or, as we shall see, the Outside as such). Inevitably, demarcation is, at one and the same time, a demarcation of philosophy with respect to other practices of thought, or realms of being, and a demarcation of a philosophy from those rivals with which it vies for hegemony. Far from constituting a purely negative gesture this task of demarcation functions as a sort of propedeutic to the systematic articulation of a philosophical camp, to the constitution of an image of philosophy.

In this regard the formidable apparatus erected by Kantian critique is perhaps the modern paragon of the strategy of demarcation. A key textual *locus* in this demarcation is the first section of the first chapter of the Transcendental Doctrine of Method, The Discipline of Pure Reason, entitled 'The Discipline of Pure Reason in its Dogmatic Employment' (A709/B737). This text, concerned with the place of the concept in philosophy and mathematics, is a fine example of the 'positive' function of prohibition and censorship within philosophical discourse. If the late Schelling could be seen as a negative catalyst for the development of modern materialism within the genealogical time of philosophical confrontation, then the whole of critique can be presented as the most elaborate and, in spite of itself, productive system of 'negative instruction', to borrow Kant's own words. Arguably, it can be said to constitute a sort of instruction manual for the theoretical insurrections whose rhythm punctuates philosophical modernity.

The discipline of pure reason presents itself as a sort of pedagogical corollary to the elements of critique. Its aim, a 'training by constraint', aimed at the suppression and extirpation of 'the constant tendency to disobey certain rules' (A709/ B737).[7] Yet this discipline of the concept does not, as is to be expected, simply give rise to a whole host of transgressions; it thoroughly determines the specific terms and gestures that transgression will adopt. The production of resistance, elicited by the apparatus of critique, could not be more clearly displayed.

If, as we will see with Deleuze-Guattari's *What is Philosophy?*, the question of materialism in philosophy remains so deeply bound to certain aspects of Kant, it is because the Kantian project provides one of the most thorough delineations of the relationship between the concept and (its) production, as well as between the concept and its non-philosophical outside. The 'censorship function' of the discipline of pure reason – the determination of certain questions as beyond the pale of speculation – is altogether inseparable from the positive determination of the *problem* of the production of concepts and the conceptualization of production (the twofold problem of materialism in philosophy). Kant's role as a privileged referent for the *materialism of the concept*, which we will encounter in the next section of this essay, is crystallized in his discussion of the place of *construction* in philosophy. It is only through the displacements undergone by philosophical construction, in which Schelling plays a key role, that we might come to understand how the materialism propounded by Deleuze-Guattari is still wedded to the question of the transcendental, a transcendental that Schelling had already appropriated to the problematic of a generative ontology, in his early speculations on the productivity of nature, but which is considered here strictly in terms of its intra-philosophical function.

Returning now to Kant's discipline of pure reason, we can see that the errant use of reason that demands to be curtailed takes the name of dogmatism. Behind this, there lingers the threat, or the temptation, of a Spinozist ontology. The *more geometrico* is to be shown up in the illegality of its pretence. Mathematics and philosophy are once again to be assigned their rightful places and all contamination prevented. The demarcation is commanded by the articulation of the fourfold: universal/particular, intuition/concept. At stake are the respective rights of philosophical speculation and empirical experience.

In the critical image of philosophy, at least as concerns knowledge, these two domains are never to fuse, their distance marked by the separation between the discursive universality of the concept and the contingent particularity of sensation. Yet mathematics appears to display a significant difference within the economy of reason. This difference takes the name of construction. As Kant writes:

> *Philosophical* knowledge is the *knowledge gained by reason from concepts*; mathematical knowledge is the knowledge gained by reason from the *construction* of concepts. To *construct* a concept means to exhibit *a priori* the intuition that corresponds to the concept. For the construction of a concept we therefore need a *non-empirical* intuition ... Thus philosophical knowledge considers the particular only in the universal, mathematical knowledge the universal in the particular, or even in the single instance, though still *a priori* and by means of reason. (A713/ B741)

There are therefore two uses of the concept: the philosophical one, which maintains the concept in the element of a universality that awaits its determination by experience; the mathematical one, which in the realm of pure intuition, that is, in the element of space and time and by means of the imagination alone, produces a particular – for example, a triangle – which is at one and the same time its concept, its 'universal representation'. Whilst philosophical knowledge prepares the capture of particular intuition within the universal concepts of the understanding, mathematics immediately
. expresses the universality of its concepts in the construction of its figures.

Construction names this capacity to forego the receptivity presupposed by the understanding in favour of a *singularization of the concept*. Construction introduces reason's capacity to manipulate and exhibit intuitions into concepts that are at once concrete and non-empirical, whilst at the same time short-circuiting the modal either-or between possible and actual. Thus, a mathematical figure, be it a triangle or an algorithm, is neither a concept whose empty universality awaits the determination of experience, nor a merely actual instance bound by its contingency and facticity. This command over intuition allows mathematics, 'by means of the construction of concepts in the intuition of the object' (A733/B761), to be both *a priori* and *immediate*, insofar as its axioms, definitions and demonstrations have no need to call on the determining function of actual experience.

The discipline of pure reason demands that philosophy, whose discursive use of the concept does not permit the use of construction, refrain from venturing into the realm of pure and, to use Schelling's terminology, *productive* intuition. Its fidelity to perceptual, sensible experience consists in establishing the synthetic unity of the domain of experience, not in extracting from it, or instilling into it, its own fanciful inventions. These inventions, concrete particulars derived from the empty universality of concepts, are what Kant calls *dogmata*. Dogmatism is founded on just such an illegitimate derivation, a forgetting of intuition as the intimate, sensible passivity that checks the spontaneous efforts of the understanding. It turns determinability into determinacy, possibility into ontology, receptivity into thoroughgoing constitution. Only the *mathemata*, whose being is founded on a construction woven from pure intuition into axioms, definitions and demonstrations, possess apodeictic legitimacy. Only they can, *outside experience*, decide upon the certain existence of their objects.

Though the philosophical effects of its formulation can be registered to this very day, Kant's 'discipline' fared disastrously in its intention to train the thinkers of his time into an ascesis of constraint. This ideal of philosophical continence was undone almost as soon as it was stated. From Fichte onwards, the fate of intellectual intuition is a testimony to this. Schelling himself, while still under Fichte's influence, exuberantly pronounced the emancipation from the fetters of critique in his *System of Transcendental Idealism*. In §4 of this work, entitled 'The Organ of Transcendental Philosophy', he makes explicit reference to Kant's demarcation of philosophy and mathematics precisely in order to invert it and to crown philosophy *the art of construction*. This newly attained, creative eminence of philosophy is founded on the radical redefinition of intuition itself. No longer bound to the receptivity of sensation, intuition takes place in an inner sense characterized, with Fichte, by its centrifugal activity. Spontaneity unbound, emerging out of the unconscious depths of production. Intuition thus becomes the torsion of subjective production (the inner sense) upon itself, in the play of activity and limitation that makes the transcendental into the element of the genesis, and no longer simply of the possibility, of actual determinations. This genetic transformation of the transcendental entails the reversal of roles between the philosopher and the mathematician:

> The mathematician is never concerned directly with intuition (the art of construction) itself, but only with the construct which can certainly be presented externally, whereas the philosopher looks solely to the *act of construction itself*, which is an absolutely internal thing. Moreover, the objects of the transcendental philosopher exist not at all, save insofar as they are freely produced.[8]

If, as Schelling states, 'all philosophy is productive', it is because the transcendental itself, no longer conceived as empty universality, as analytical and descriptive, has become the domain of inner experience, intuiting itself as the genetic activity that gives rise to the individuated products of external experience; in other words, as the activity that accounts for the entire field of representation and objectivity.

Soon after the *System of Transcendental Idealism*, Schelling's identity philosophy was to discard this Fichtean framework, thus decoupling the productivity of the transcendental from the interiority of a subject. It is to this phase of Schelling's career that belongs a review article entitled 'On Construction in Philosophy' (1803).[9] Nominally concerned with a book on philosophy and construction by the Swedish philosopher Höyer, it is for the most part a sustained attack on Kant's discipline of pure reason, aimed at presenting construction as the cornerstone of philosophical method. It is no accident then that it is introduced by an interrogation of the relation between the matter and the form of philosophical speculation and a qualified defence of Spinoza and his *more geometrico*. Swimming against the polemical current of the pantheism controversy, Schelling dares to suggest that Spinozism is the 'system situated at the antipodes of the dogmatic system'. This reconsideration of the Spinozist system, which marks the entirety of the phase known as identity-philosophy, signals a considerable transformation in the role of the concept of construction.

The charge of dogmatism, in Kant as well as in the pantheism controversy, was always linked to the condemnation of ontology as the uncritical and illegitimate sovereignty of the objective. The epithet of Spinozism stood for the philosophical foreclosure of subjective constitution, for a necessitarian denial of the function of the transcendental. Dogmatism versus criticism, this was the struggle that Schelling himself had so acutely defined in his *Philosophical Letters* of 1797.[10] Having experimented, in the period immediately preceding the identity-philosophy, with the parallelism of transcendental philosophy and nature-philosophy – the first as the subjective history of self-consciousness, the second as the objective *pre*-history of consciousness – Schelling's return to Spinoza entails a dissolution of this methodological complementarity into a full-blown monism, into a philosophy that *begins* with the Absolute. This development, whose germs lay in the earlier formulation of the concept of the 'point of indifference', or subject-object, radically transforms the meta-philosophical question of construction.

Whilst the overt terms of the 'Discipline of Pure Reason', the textual matrix for the philosophy of construction, remain standing, the pre-suppositions that shored up its argument are washed away in the tide of Spinozism. In his 1803 review, Schelling is no longer arguing, in a Fichtean vein, for the extension of the scope of the constitutive function of the subject. Having taken from Fichte the primacy of activity, the transformation of a descriptive transcendental into a fully genetic one, Schelling, who had prepared this shift through the work undertaken in his philosophy of nature, appears to sever the production of experience from reference to either the intuitive interiority of a subject or the mechanical exteriority of objectivity. This escape from the practical and epistemological binds inherited from Kantianism is at the source of the new perception of Spinoza as a philosopher of absolute production, a production that is located at the point of indif-ference of subject and object. As he writes in the second edition of the *Ideas for a Philosophy of Nature*, also published in 1803:

> Spinoza has lain unrecognised for over a hundred years. The view of his philosophy as a mere theory of objectivity did not allow for the true absolute to be perceived in it. The definitiveness with which he recognised subject-objectivity as the necessary and eternal character of absoluteness shows the high destiny implicit in his philosophy, whose full development was reserved to a later age.[11]

This reappraisal, in which Schelling explicitly portrays himself as the heir of the *princips atheorum*, is accompanied by the ideal of a philosophy which, no longer bound to the discipline of reason, is integrally traversed by the work of the Absolute. To philosophize is to think 'from the point of view of production'.[12] Within the terms of the Kantian demarcation this turn in the philosophy of Schelling appears as a capitulation to the temptation of the *mathema*. In a sense, this is precisely the case. With the abandonment of subjectivity as the principled *locus* of the transcendental, the problem of the constitution and intelligibility of the real is removed from the domain of cognitive experience, now demoted to the status of product, and shifted to the relationship between philosophy and the Absolute. *The construction of experience is replaced by the experience of construction.* Kant's effort to maintain the distance between the determinable universality of the concept and its 'filling out' by the sensible intuition of the particular collapses.

In light of these remarks, let us turn again to the 1803 review. Having given Kant his due for establishing the dignity of the concept of construc-tion, Schelling proceeds to question the validity of the Kantian demarcation. The claim is simple. The introduction of the concept of non-empirical intuition cannot serve to adjudicate the concept of construction between mathematics and philosophy. *Either* all intuition is sensible – which is after all the claim that in Kant supports the denial of intellectual intuition for the human subject – *or* a different form of intuition is possible, one that would entail the immediate, pure unity of the universal and particular. Kant surreptitiously relies on the possibility of an empirical support, a trace, for mathematics to differentiate it from philosophy as the art of construction. As he had already remarked in the *System of Transcendental Idealism*, Schelling sees the supposed privilege of mathematics as based on its capacity to *reflect* its own intuition in an empirical trace. Yet, Schelling remarks, philosophy is in this by no means opposed to mathematics, especially as it is even less needy of what he terms the 'aleatory support of sensible intuition'. Its capacity for construction, for the singularization of the concept in the indifference of the universal and the particular is simply more radical. Thus, the demarcation is only relative.

The attack on Kant continues. Not only is it illegitimate to bind philosophy to the vacuity of transiting between the empty universality of the understanding and the manifold of sensibility, the real issue is the genesis of the understanding itself, the construction of the concepts out of which the transcendental domain is built. As Schelling remarks, it is certainly true that *a priori* concepts cannot be constructed, but this is so precisely to the extent that they themselves must be subject to construction. The alternative posed by Schelling is stark. Either what pertains to the level of transcendental constitution is itself constructed or it is merely extracted from experience by analogy. Construction versus analogy, these are the stakes of the Kantian legacy.

The insufficiency of the concept gives way to the *idea*. It is here that what I termed the singularization of the concept takes place. The task of construction lies in the philosophical identification, the *indifferentiation*, of the universal and the particular. This indifferentiation takes place in the element of the absolute, itself conceived as the unconditioned ground of indifference, the coincidence of producer and product, affirmation and affirmed, intuition and intuited, *natura naturans* and *natura naturata*. From the point of view of the absolute, 'fanatically' attained only by the philosopher that allows it to think through him, the subject is itself merely a construct, a derivation or differentiation of absolute unity.

In the *System of Transcendental Idealism* Schelling had defined the transcendental artifice as the philosopher's capacity to follow the articulation of production and product within his own inner sense. Intuiter and intuited at once, the philosopher-subject experienced, by way of a recapitulation, the production of objectivity out of the sequential limitation of the activity of self, from its unconscious bases to its moral peaks. In the identity-philosophy, the artifice has changed. The philosopher is no longer a subject in the sense of a subject of experience, he is no longer in the business of bridging, or even of producing, the gap between the inner self and the outer world. These are nothing but constructs, results. The artifice of construction calls for the philosopher to abdicate his subjective status, and, in a manner prefigured by Schelling's experiments in *Naturphilosophie*, to immerse himself in the element of the absolute, to produce the coincidence of universal and particular; in other words, to articulate the differentiated expression of the absolute through the construction of ideas. This construction or idea is nothing other than the immediate, non-empirical intuition of a concept. Schelling reduces the universals of reflection to the status of derivatives of the constructions that emerge from the point of indifference of thinker and thought: the Absolute, also referred to as *the principle of construction*. Each and every idea is an archetypal crystallization of this principle, a figure of the Absolute that expresses a singular degree of its infinite activity. As Valerio Verra writes:

> Each idea incarnates all the others, not in an indifferent and inter-changeable way, but following an ascending order of 'potentialisation' which culminates in absolute identity, an identity that is nevertheless not empty, but rich in articulations, tensions, differences. ... [The] idea is the unitary principle of the infinite and the finite, the universal and the particular, of the organisation of the parts in the whole and the articulation of the whole in the parts.[13]

Having radicalized the genetic turn initiated by Fichte within transcendental philosophy, Schelling's identity philosophy undoes the universality of the concept in favour of what could be termed a monism of construction. The highest aim of philosophy is to suspend the subject-object dichotomy, together with all of its by-products (the separations of the infinite and the finite, the universal and the particular, the whole and its parts), in order to truly re-construct (or recapitulate) the dynamic unity of the absolute. For Schelling, philosophy's status as science is wholly bound to this capacity for constructive 'ideation', which allows it to sustain the immanence of thought to the self-differentiation of the Absolute. Schelling's unique appropriation of Kant's concept of 'construction' is based on the conviction that this immanence can only be attained through the detour of a certain artifice; that the production of ideas in philosophy is the necessary medium for the full deployment of the dynamic unity of the Absolute, of the real movement of productivity itself.

A MATERIALISM OF THE CONCEPT

Besides any traces of direct filiation that we may glean from Deleuze's and Guattari's footnotes and passing references, the philosophies of Schelling and Deleuze(-Guattari) are brought together by the way in which both antag-onistically inhabit a philosophical universe of Kantian extraction, incor-porating several of the problems laid out by critique and gnawing away at the speculative prohibitions that the discipline of pure method has bequeathed to philosophical modernity. There are several indexes of this post-Kantian convergence, all of which play determining roles in each philosopher's project: the entire thematic of production – overcoming the Kantian limitation of life to the subject's power of desire and of nature to the exteriority of representation; the concept of organization – which is rendered a constitutive and not just a regulative notion for both philosophers; the critique of hylomorphism – which opposes the Kantian capture of the matter of sensation by the formal universality of the concept; the use of intensity – a radicalization of the Kantian notion of a *mathesis intensorum*, which extracts it from the realm of sensation, in order to erect it into a fundamental concept within a theory of individuation that turns the transcendental into a field of impersonal production;[14] intuition as a philosophical method – the denial of its restriction to the realm of sensibility alone and its expansion into a defining trait of the speculative of philosophy.[15] And – verifying the pertinence of Deleuze's apostolic vision of the philosophy of immanence – Spinoza's presence as the timeless operator behind this desire of philosophy to elude the fetters of discipline. All of these are components in the appropriation of transcendental philosophy to the problematic of a generative ontology, binding Schelling and Deleuze – as diachronically 'mediated' by the lineage of French 'spiritualism' (Maine de Biran – Victor Cousin – Félix Ravaisson – Henri Bergson).

Yet for all the weight of the family resemblance, the genetic transformation of the transcendental that couples the philosophies of Schelling and Deleuze should not hide a distance that is all the more significant to the very extent that it is articulated on a background of considerable philosophical affinity. It is precisely around the concept of construction that this distance makes itself most acutely felt. As Schelling had noted, it is the privilege of philosophy not to find its constructions bound or limited by axioms or definitions. Thus it comes to be that, as he puts it, philosophy 'also constructs anew construction itself'. It is to just such a new construction of construction, the one found in Deleuze-Guattari's *What is Philosophy?*, that we now turn. The transformations that it brings to the concept of construction will allow us to discern what effects its Kantian origin and its Schellingian transformation can still produce, as well as what reconfigurations this concept incurs when situated within a new philosophical problematic.

The vitality of 'The Discipline of Pure Reason' as a textual matrix for the conceptualization of construction could not be more evident than in Deleuze-Guattari's final collaborative work. In returning to the immemorial task of demarcation, the authors provide a negative trace of the Kantian text which appears to repeat Schelling's 1803 'On Construction in Philosophy'. Immediately following an attack on that legacy of the transcendental that would see philosophy's task as one that revolved around a discourse on universals – punctuated by the programmatic motto: 'The first principle of philosophy is that Universals explain nothing but must themselves be explained' – Deleuze-Guattari introduce their definition of philosophy as a constructivism by way of an overt reference to Kant's text:

> To know oneself, to learn to think, to act as if nothing were self-evident – wondering, 'wondering that there is being' – these, and many other determinations of philosophy create interesting attitudes, however tiresome they may be in the long run, but even from a pedagogical point of view they do not constitute a well-defined occupation or precise activity. On the other hand, the following definition can be taken as being decisive: knowledge through pure concepts. But there is no reason to oppose knowledge through concepts and the construction of concepts within possible experience on the one hand and through intuition on the other. For, according to the Nietzschean verdict, you will know nothing through concepts unless you have first created them – that is, constructed them in an intuition specific to them: a field, a plane, and a ground that must not be confused with them but that shelters their seeds and the personae who cultivate them. Constructivism requires every creation to be a construction on a plane that gives it an autonomous existence. To create concepts is, at the very least, to make something.[16]

The Nietzschean verdict was of course prefigured by Kant himself, in a key passage wherein he gives mathematics the capacity for invention, only to deny it to a philosophy that remains bound to the discursivity of the concept and the constraint of receptivity:

> Since, then, neither empirical concepts nor concepts given *a priori* allow of definition, the only remaining kind of concepts, upon which this mental operation can be tried, are arbitrarily invented concepts. A concept which I have invented I can always define; for since it is not given to me either by the nature of the understanding or by experience, but is such as I have myself deliberately made it to be, I must know what I have intended in using it ... There remain, therefore, no concepts which allow of definition, except only those which contain an arbitrary synthesis that admits of *a priori* construction. Consequently, mathematics is the only science that has definitions. For the object which it thinks it exhibits *a priori* in intuition, and this object certainly cannot contain either more or less than the concept, since it is through the definition that the object of the concept is given – and given originally, that is, without its being necessary to derive the definition from any other source. (A729 /B757)

It is from formulations such as these that Schelling himself drew the speculative ammunition needed to attack Kant's own demarcational verdicts, and to affirm a productive capacity proper to philosophy itself, conceived as the art of construction. Likewise, by defining philosophical activity in terms of the creation of concepts, Deleuze-Guattari seem to draw on the delineation of the *mathemata* in the first Critique in order to undo the limitations that Kant himself imposed upon the being and function of the concept. In both instances, we could say that the notion of construction is enlisted to maintain the requirement of immanence which belongs to the very project of critique, whilst at the same time disjoining it from any subordination to the complementary claims of knowledge and faith, claims that would make immanence into a synonym of limitation. It is not enough, in other words, to sing the praises of production, to breathe new life into Spinozism through the consideration of the cutting-edge sciences of dynamics – the very function of thinking, of speculation, must itself be understood as a variety of production if critique is to be truly radicalized, rather than merely side-stepped. Considered in terms of this intimate confrontation with Kant, the touchstone of any philosophy of production is therefore not so much the richness of its ontology as its capacity to bring production into the concept.

In the overall lineaments of their project, Deleuze-Guattari seem to be treading the path cut by Schelling very closely indeed.[17] Yet it is in their phenomenology of the concept, in their account of its a-subjective intuition and composition, that a different vision of construction begins to emerge. In order to make this difference evident it is necessary to flesh out the components of philosophical constructivism: intra-, pre-, and non-philosophical. The interaction of these levels of constructivism not only transforms the terms of the Schellingian formulation but provides a materialist and anti-foundationalist slant to the philosophy of construction, as well as articulating a set of rather different requirements for the constitution of a post-Kantian generative ontology.

Remaining within the terminology inaugurated by 'The Discipline of Pure Reason', the key transformation brought about by Deleuze-Guattari's 'construction of construction' is to be found in their displacement of the relationship of concept and intuition. On closer inspection, the definition of philosophical practice is no longer founded on a provocative reversal of Kant's definition of the *mathema* and its attendant demarcation. Construction is not to be understood the immediate and reciprocal union of the particularity of intuition and the universality of the concept in the idea. For Deleuze-Guattari, philosophical intuition becomes indiscernible from the constitution of a transcendental or problematic field on the edge of philosophy itself, at the point of its 'extimate' contact (to borrow a term from Lacan) with the pre- and the non-philosophical. Constructivism has two complementary faces, or aspects, whose confusion signals the demise of philosophical productivity and the resurgence of the imaginary discourse of universals. The first, of course, is the creation of concepts, the second relates precisely to the modality of intuition within constructivism, which Deleuze-Guattari identify as the construction and experience of a plane of immanence.

Concepts, which for Deleuze-Guattari are multiplicities whose components are held together by intensive connections, compenetrations and adjacencies, are themselves not intuitions. As multiplicities that are self-positioning and self-surveying, concepts can only communicate or cohere within a consistent field. The entire question of immanence, whose insistence in the work of Deleuze-Guattari is unrelenting, is elicited by this demand that creations (concepts) connect without the mediation of supposedly universal forms or categories. Transcendence names precisely this operation, which reinscribes intensively individuated, singularized concepts into a static, supplementary dimension. This capture of the creative profligacy of thought can of course take numerous guises, all of which however return us to the sedentary, hylomorphic dichotomy of universals and particulars (remember the motto above: 'The first principle of philosophy is that Universals explain nothing but must themselves be explained'). The only consistency afforded to a constellation of concepts is in the infinite movement of a thought that envelops them in one problematic field, a field whose monadic solutions they constitute. The plane of immanence is thus not a concept above those created by a philosophy, it is the zone wherein they communicate, a single zone which is simply defined by the movements that may come to pass within it. It is what Deleuze-Guattari call a diagram, which is not a container or envelope, but the co-determination of the topology and dromology, of the spaces and the speeds of thought. In this regard, the plane of immanence is, like the Schellingian absolute, indifferent to an over-determination by the concept. As Deleuze-Guattari write, once again with Kant in their sights:

To 'orientate oneself in thought' implies neither objective reference point nor moving object that experiences itself as subject and that, as such, strives for or needs the infinite. Movement takes in everything, and there is no place for a subject and an object that can only be concepts.[18]

Yet it is here that the separation from Schellingian construction is most evident. For the plane is not the *principle of construction*; instead it is both the element of construction (the One-All that affords the consistency of a conceptual constellation) and itself a construct. Intuition is not the immediate material of construction; it is the result of its artifice. Immanence, together with the intuitions that traverse it, is not a source naturally differentiating itself into conceptual constructions; it must itself be attained or, in the Deleuze-Guattari lexicon, traced. The intuitions of immanence are not contemplations compressing the gap between the universal and the particular into the unity of the idea, they are themselves determined by the singular construction of a plane.

I would like to argue that this separation of concept and intuition provides the key to what I would call Deleuze-Guattari's *materialism of the concept*.

Tracing the plane is at once the unique construction of the convergence of thought and being ('movement is not the image of thought without also being the material of being', they write)[19] and the relationship of the thought of philosophy to its non-philosophical outside. The distinction of plane and concept, together with the identification of the operators (conceptual personae) that make their correlation effective, constitutes the double articulation of materialism in philosophy. In this regard materialism in the field philosophy (as distinguished from a philosophy *of* materialism) is, somewhat perversely perhaps, faithful to the Kantian dualism of receptivity and spontaneity, as well as to Schelling's own early parallelism of *Naturphilosophie* and transcendental philosophy. This is especially clear if we take into account the introduction into Deleuze-Guattari's constructivism of the notion of a non-philosophical infinity, or *chaos*. The plane is traced upon this chaos, it is the extraction of a sort of space-time of the concept from a non-philosophical material of evanescent determinations and infinitely divergent directions. Philosophy, and thought in general, is drawn by the unliveable, or inconceivable, intensities of the non-philosophical. Chaos is both its ever present danger (inanity, delirium . . .) and its ownmost promise, its ou-topia.

Without this outside, without this originary *passion* for chaos, which is the counterpart of philosophy's desire of construction, the creation of concepts would be no more than a passing fancy or a mere procedure. Materialism in philosophy is thus twofold. On the one hand, it singularizes philosophy in terms of the traits of its *practice*: philosophy does not 'discover' the universals that draw the particularity of non-philosophical production into the nets of the intelligible. On the other, it keeps the construction of immanence suspended in an encounter with the outside of philosophy; precisely because it scorns the sovereignty of universals, philosophy does not pretend to the integral deduction or derivation of the non-conceptual; it does not correspond to its outside, it responds to it, or counter-actualizes it. The genetic transformation of the transcendental attains its greatest force and consistency when it no longer poses as a conditioning of experience, but instead fully assumes its own constructive character, becoming an experience of construction – the experience of a practice, *not* the experience of a subject – which foregoes its monopoly on the productivity of the non-philosophical.

* * *

Where then can we locate the divergence from Schelling? In my view, it is around two key issues, those of *immanence* and of *necessity*.

As we saw in the previous section, the philosophy of identity achieves its immanence – which is to say, its 'scientific' character – by conceiving of every idea as a re-construction of the Absolute's process of self-differentiation. The archetypal or monadic singularity of the idea, as a finite configuration of the infinite activity of production, is immanent to the living unity of the Absolute. This is Schelling's antidote to the nefarious dominance of the subject-object distinction, which, as he remarked in the 1804 *Würzburg System*, constitutes the fundamental error in all knowledge. The price of this immanence, which demands that we always begin from the principle of construction – that the philosopher abdicate his subjectivity so as to be at one with the productions of the Absolute – is that philosophical experience take place in an element of complete interiority. Through the construction of ideas, philosophy configures the Absolute into an 'organism of knowledge',[20] that is, a living system in which the many figures, degrees and powers of genesis are necessary expressions of the unified being of production. The Kantian separation between the universality of the concept and the particularity of intuitions, which had sustained the original formulation of the problematic of construction, is undone by the conviction that ideas permit philosophy to produce the coincidence of – that is, to 'indifferentiate' – these poles of being, to demonstrate that all manifestations of the Absolute are the expressive parts of a dynamic whole. In this regard construction for Schelling is of the order of totalization; it shows that – rather than demanding mediation and subsumption under universals – beings are the products of the self-differentiation of the Absolute. Construction is thus always a re-construction, a repetition that immerses itself in the inner life of the Absolute to draw out the necessary concatenations of its productivity, the different stages of its unfolding. To construct is to establish the place of an idea (be it aesthetic, scientific, historical, and so forth) in the seamless unity of the Absolute. In construction, philosophy experiences its immanence *to* the Absolute by demonstrating the necessity *of* the Absolute.

I think we are justified, in considering this link of immanence and necessity within a totalizing unity, to point out the insistence in Schelling of something like an *organic image of thought*.[21] This is in fact the most obstinate counterpart, the intimate nemesis perhaps, of Deleuze-Guattari's own conception, according to which the image of thought as a plane of immanence is itself an object of construction; in other words, that far from providing a principle out of which the philosopher may repeat the real articulations of being, immanence is itself to be produced. It is important here to recall the properly materialist requirement, in Deleuze-Guattari, to maintain the distance between the plane of philosophical intuition and the concepts that populate it, and between this pre-philosophical plane and a properly non-philosophical chaos. By conceiving construction as the repetition and systematic totalization of the productivity of being – a conception answering to the project of establishing philosophy as the highest of sciences – Schelling effectively eliminates the contingency of artifice from philosophical production. This is evidenced by the *telos* of Schellingian construction, that of establishing an organism of knowledge in which, as Verra writes, 'each idea incarnates all the others'. To use Deleuze-Guattari's terminology, non-philosophical chaos and the pre-philosophical plane are collapsed into a totalizing unity – the Absolute as organism of knowledge – which is not the element but the principle of construction; the pre-philosophical plane and the philosophical concept are fused in such a way that the latter becomes the simple expression of the former, that is, it becomes an intuition that is *immediately* a creation.

In the end, the crucial differend that sets these two philosophies of construction apart is that, for Schelling, the convergence or in-difference of thought and being is ultimately not something to be constructed, to be experimented in the movements of the plane of immanence; it is posited unconditionally. We construct from the point of view of the Absolute. Yet, once the principle is no longer itself to be constructed, once philosophy is always already immanent to the Absolute, any non-philosophical exteriority vanishes. Construction in Schelling has no outside. Constituting itself as interior to the Absolute, and guaranteed in its operations by an immanence *to* the latter's organic unity, philosophy is no longer able to assume its own specificity as a mode of production. To consider philosophy as a practice, to introduce into it what I have referred to as a materialism of the concept, two things are required. First, philosophical construction is to be conceived not simply as a repetition or expression of productivity as such, but as an instance of production *sui generis*. Second, and following from this, rather than standing in a privileged and internal relation to the source of production – that is, rather than issuing from the principle of construction – philosophy is to be suspended to an encounter with a non-philosophical outside.

It is in this regard that Deleuze-Guattari's materialism, which interposes the tracing of a plane of immanence between the construction of the concept and the savage multiplicity of a non-philosophical chaos, breaks the reflexive circle that characterizes the organic image of thought. Its insistence on heterogenesis is aimed precisely at uncoupling immanence from necessity, and construction from interiority. Even if the concept is defined by its auto-position, it is an auto-position that emerges as a *result* of philosophical construction and as a response to an encounter with the non-philosophical, and not auto-position as the unified *source* of philosophical experience. Heterogenesis, both in the intra-philosophical articulation of constructivism (separation of plane, concept, and conceptual personae) and in its 'transactions' with its non-philosophical outside, is a determining trait of materialism in philosophy.

It remains the case that Schelling's transformation of the Kantian concept of construction, especially when situated in the wider scope of a genetic transformation of the transcendental, is of immense importance. The 'awakening', to borrow Engels' words, effected by Schelling's philosophy consisted in turning philosophy away from the products that populate the domain of everyday cognition and common sense towards the acts of production that traverse, constitute and exceed experience. What must not be overlooked, as I have tried to argue, is the possible consequences of this awakening when fully applied to philosophy itself. By reversing the terms of Kant's demarcation of philosophy and mathematics, it opened the way for a consideration of philosophy as a productive discipline, as a form of thought that, far from being of the order of a reflection of reality, of judgement or categorization, can be considered as a creative practice in its own right, with its own criteria and its own products.

In this light, the weakness of Schelling's thought, rather than deriving from an idealization of production – as Marx and Engels might have been seen to argue – should perhaps be sought in the insufficient radicality with which it considers the productivity of thought itself, the operations of philosophy as a specific practice. The ultimate index of idealism is thus represented by an incapacity to think the construction of construction – which Schelling had the immense merit of introducing as the defining trait of philosophical activity – without the guarantee provided by its interiority to the Absolute. It is only once shorn of its reliance on a pre-given systematicity, on an organic immanence *to* production, that materialism truly separates itself from dogmatism, that it enacts the critical appropriation of philosophy as a determinate artifice. Materialism in philosophy is in this sense nothing but the affirmation of a productivity proper to philosophy itself. Admittedly, by doing without the transcendence of principle or the totalization afforded by a unitary *system* of production, this constructivism makes the very idea of a philosophy *of* production, of a full-blown generative ontology, far more problematic than Schelling's own philosophy, or the many incarnations of materialist dialectics, would ever allow. The *experience of construction*, the materialist assumption of philosophy as a practice, tells us that the *construction of experience* is not something that philosophy can simply repeat or reveal; it tells us, in brief, that philosophy cannot be content to inhabit immanence – it must produce it, each and every time, by constructing construction anew.

Notes

1   Or, as Engels quipped: 'the Philosophical Messiah mounted his wooden, very poorly upholstered throne in the *Auditorium Maximum* . . .' Marx, K., Engels, F., *Collected Works*, vol. 2 (London: Lawrence & Wishart, 1975), 192.
2   Marx, Engels, *Collected Works*, vol. 2, 181.
3   Ibid., vol. 3, 349–50.
4   Ibid.
5   Ibid.
6   Deleuze and Guattari organize their stance around the conceptual distinction of history and becoming: 'Philosophical time is thus a grandiose time of coexistence that does not exclude the before and after but *superimposes* them in a stratigraphic order. It is an infinite becoming of philosophy that crosscuts its history without being confused with it . . . Philosophy is becoming, not history; it is the coexistence of planes, not the succession of systems' in *What is Philosophy* (New York: Columbia University Press, 1994), 58. Whilst remaining sympathetic to this paradoxically atemporal, or *aionic*, time of philosophical innovation, of the event(s) of philosophy, I would like 'at the same time' to affirm the impure temporalities of the movements of thought that allow us to pass from the brusque time of polemic, to the *longue durée* of certain discursive

matrixes, to the pure becoming of concepts which, for D-G, identifies the
singularity of the philosophical. This essay is nothing but an attempt at such an
impure, composite movement.

7   Kant, I., *Critique of Pure Reason*, trans. N. Kemp Smith (London: Macmillan,
     1929).
8   Schelling, F., *System of Transcendental Idealism* (1800) trans. P. Heath (Char-
     lottesville: University of Virginia, 1978), 13.
9   Originally published in Schelling's own *Kritisches Journal der Philosophie*. Col-
     lected in Schelling, F., *Sämtliche Werke*, ed. K.F.A. Schelling (Stuttgart and
     Augsburg: Cotta, 1856), vol. V. A French translation appeared in the journal
     Philosophie, 19 (1988), 31–55, with a helpful introductory note by Christian
     Bonnet. A fine overview of Schelling's philosophy of construction is provided
     by Valerio Verra's 'La "construction" dans la philosophie de Schelling' in
     Planty-Bonjour, G. (ed.), *Actualité de Schelling* (Paris: Vrin, 1979), 26–47.
10   I have discussed the *Philosophical Letters on Dogmatism and Criticism* at length,
     together with the question of Schelling's Spinozism, and his metaphysics of
     production in my 'Fanaticism and Production: On Schelling's Philosophy of
     Indifference', *Pli* 8 (1999), 46–70.
11   F.W.J. Schelling, *Ideas for a Philosophy of Nature*, trans. E. E. Harris and P.
     Heath (Cambridge: Cambridge University Press, 1988), 53–4.
12   Quoted in Fichte, J.G., 'Correspondence and polemical writings', F.W.J.
     Schelling, *Carteggio e Scritti Polemici*, ed. F. Moiso (Naples: Prismi, 1986), 143,
     n. 10.
13   Verra, 'La "construction" dans la philosophie de Schelling', 38.
14   On Schelling's use of intensity see Riccardo Martinelli's admirable history of
     the concept, *Misurare l'Anima. Filosofia e Psicofisica da Kant a Carnap* (Macerata:
     Quodlibet, 1999). For Deleuze on intensity, see *Difference and Repetition*
     (London: Athlone, 1994), ch. 5, 'The Asymmetrical Synthesis of the Sensible'.
15   See Badiou, A., *Deleuze*, as well as all of Deleuze's writings on Bergson, in
     particular his 1956 essay on 'The concept of difference in Bergson'.
16   Deleuze-Guattari, *Difference and Repetition*, 7.
17   Just as they do not fail to pay homage to their precursors, by means of a
     remarkable nod to the appropriation of the themes of the *Critique of Judgement*
     by German Idealism:

> Creation and self-positing mutually imply each other because what is truly created,
> from the living being to the work of art, thereby enjoys a self-positing of itself, or an
> autopoietic characteristic by which it is recognised. The concept posits itself to the
> same extent that it is created. What depends on a free creativity is also that which,
> independently and necessarily, posits itself in itself: the most subjective will be the
> most objective. The post-Kantians, and notably Schelling and Hegel, are the phil-
> osophers who paid most attention to the concept as philosophical reality in this sense.
> (*What is Philosophy*, p. 11)

However, Hegel's uncompromising condemnation of construction in the
preface to the *Phenomenology* points us to the crucial differend of a construction
based on intuition with production as its motor, and a dialectics founded on
reflection, with negation as its motor. This difference, which in our eyes
accounts for some of the affinities between Schelling and Deleuze-Guattari on
the issue of construction, is closely investigated in the second chapter of Werner
Marx's *The Philosophy of F. W. J. Schelling* (Bloomington: Indiana University
Press, 1984). Unlike the author we do not think however that it is the systematic usage of *self*-intuition which accounts for Schelling's relevance to the
contemporary philosophical debate. Rather, we have chosen to look towards the

artifice in construction, to the concept, for the site wherein, to put it with W. Marx, 'intuition is fulfilled in a form that is the expression of the utmost productivity' (p. 39).

18 Deleuze-Guattari, *Difference and Repetition*, 37.

19 Deleuze-Guattari, *What is Philosophy*, 38.

20 As Verra writes, 'The intrinsically organic and necessary character of philosophical knowledge, in brief, the scientific character of philosophy, is in effect exclusively guaranteed by the concrete and organic character of ideas.' Verra, 38.

21 A brilliant account of the many and apparently contradictory manifestations, together with the ultimately homogenizing discursive function of this image of thought, grounded on the notion and practice of *totalization*, can be found in Judith Schlanger's *Les Métaphores de l'Organisme* (Paris: Vrin, 1971). This book is especially useful in tracking the movements of this metaphor (neither a concept nor a state of affairs) between the realms of politics, science, and philosophy throughout the nineteenth century. Once again, the source of the organic image of thought is to be located in Kant, and specifically in the realization of the problematic convergence, within Kant's *Critique of Judgement*, of intellectual intuition, on the one hand, and the organized being as the symbol of self-production, on the other. In Schelling's philosophy of construction, both organic being and the systematicity of knowledge, rather than remaining of the order of the regulative, become entirely constitutive.

6

'PHILOSOPHY BECOME GENETIC': THE PHYSICS OF THE WORLD SOUL

Iain Hamilton Grant

The whole of modern European philosophy since its inception (through Descartes) has this common deficiency – that nature does not exist for it.   (Schelling: VII, 356; HF, 30)[1]

The present chapter has two principal purposes. Firstly, to establish some key components of speculative physics or *Naturphilosophie* as Schelling constructed it. Secondly, as physicists too are calling for it,[2] to present a philosophical impetus to pursue speculative physics in the present. The core of this case is the relation between thought and nature – which, since Schelling tells us Descartes is responsible for the abolition of *nature from thought*, or of *phusis* from metaphysics, does not reduce to 'mind and body'. And the means for its vehiculation are provided by the *physical history of the concept of the World Soul*.

THE PHYSICS OF THE WORLD SOUL

I certainly agree there is no World Soul.

(Leibniz)[3]

'Without a doubt there is a world soul', counters Deleuze;[4] the question is, *what is its nature?* While Gode von Aesch, echoing the traditional accounts of the world soul in the *Timaeus*, typically considers it 'a mythical concept',[5] Esposito grants it an ideal *essence*, making it an early sketch of Schelling's 'ahistorical, eternal and essentially changeless' Absolute.[6] Thereby, however, he not only deprives the World Soul, but also the Absolute, of a *nature*, entirely eliminating the express physicalism of Schelling's *World Soul*, 'the two struggling forces condensed and recapitulated ... Perhaps this is what the Ancients wished to indicate by the *world soul*' (III, 382).[7]

Plato develops a complex theory of the World Soul, as 'the original principle of movement, movement itself [*arche kineseos, autokinesis*]' without which 'the universe would collapse' (*Phaedrus* 245e and *Laws* 896a: 'self-generating motion'); as 'pilot [*kybernetes*]' (*Statesman* 273d–e), after the model of a thermodynamic governor.[8] Aside from Plato's 'phoronomy' of the World Soul he also discusses its matter, generation, and organization, considering it as living metal[9] ('are metals the bones of an ancient world – or the preface to the new?' wonders Ritter),[10] and as cosmic animal (*Timaeus* 36b–c), whose organism metabolizes the substantial mathematics of the Same and the Different that generate the world-body (Plotinus, Oken).[11] The 'universal animal' appears in Schelling's *Bruno* (IV, 278; *Bruno*, 176).[12] Bruno himself described the World Soul as the internal artificer of matter that animates everything, an animator that Ritter identifies with galvanism, the 'pulse of the cosmic animal'.[13]

The cosmic animal or 'great animal totality' has recently resurfaced in Alain Badiou's account of Deleuze's 'philosophy "of" or ... as nature'.[14] 'There have never been,' Badiou notes, 'but two schemes, or paradigms, of the Multiple: the mathematic and the organicist, Plato or Aristotle ... The animal or the number? This is the cross of metaphysics.'[15] But it is not the Multiple that concerns us here; rather the *antithesis* of animal and number, and the disjunction of the two as a deliberate scission of Plato's *Timaeus*, the source text for the World Soul and the repeated beginning of Schelling's researches in the philosophy of nature.[16] The *Timaeus* starts with number – 'One, two, three, but where is the fourth ...?' (17a) – and ends with the 'cosmos ... being itself a visible Living Creature embracing all the visible creatures' (92c). In presenting himself as a Platonist, Badiou extracts number from the 'physics of the all' (*Timaeus* 27a, 47a) and argues instead for the received Platonism of the sort known in mathematics, so that, in presenting Deleuze and the animal as Aristotelian, he excises the animal from Platonism. But, crucially, Badiou also *Aristotelianizes* Platonic physics, insofar as, along with the excision of the animal from the cosmos, number too ceases to be part of *phusis*, and becomes instead something approached by intellect alone. In other words, there is a distribution of bodies (animal) and events (number) in relation to 'sense' ('worldly multiplicities')[17] and 'intellect' (the 'perforation' of being by the event of truth), which reverses Aristotle's determination of intellect by sense (*Physics* 184a), such that a discontinuous 'generaticity of truth' takes a stand against the philosophers and mathematicians of the organo-mathematical continuum.[18]

The introduction of the antithesis presents the 'cross of metaphysics' as the intersection of two barriers: between number and animal, but also between thought and nature. For Badiou, a 'physics of the all' is impossible ('give up the all', he argues, 'and generate discontinuities'), which impossibility he contrasts with Deleuze's project of 'a philosophy "of" ... or as nature'.[19] At stake, then, in this angular redistribution of the World Soul is the nature of this physics, that is, the *physics of this metaphysics* of 'the cross', that is, the *chiasmus*, 'of metaphysics'. But this has a tradition: the Kantian transcendental confronts an insuperable gulf between nature and freedom, which is precisely a means to allow the causality of freedom to perforate inanimate nature and animal inertia. When, in the *Transition* project,[20] the interaction of subjective-bodily and ethereal forces provides a physical-transcendental means to overcome this gulf, Kant almost ceases to be Kantian and, in a certain manner, reverts to Leibniz, whose own 'transition between metaphysics and physics' was similarly accomplished by way of the actions of a *potentia agendi*, an active force within the monads.[21]

Another problem is the related one of the *solutions of continuity* by which physics and mathematics sought to ground the matter and nature of the continuum: the *hypokeimenon*, substrate, *ousia* or *protes hules*. In physics, matter cannot be susceptible of infinite division, for otherwise there would be no simples, matter would not be composed of anything, and research could no longer pursue the infinite divisibility of matter and the exponentiality of abstraction, both of which find place in speculative physics. In mathematics, meanwhile, the differential relation of infinitely small distances takes the place of the positive construction of the continuum, just as Leibniz says, there is no World Soul, but every natural machine contains within itself an 'infinite number of organisms'.[22] Continuity is assembled from innumerable number-animals, like links in an extended metabolism, or cells in an infinite galvanic chain. As we shall see, Schelling's solution to this problem consists of three elements: material individuation, or the identity of matter and the absolute (II, 60; *Ideas*, 47), Kielmeyer's transphyletic extension of the theory of recapitulation, and the 'dynamic process'.

Continuum or discontinuity? The introduction, in Badiou's critical *Auseinandersetzung* with Deleuze, of the discontinuity into Platonic physics makes Badiou's text a phylogenetic recapitulation of the ontogenesis of its set-theoretic base. Here too, Badiou belongs to a tradition most clearly encapsulated in Lorenz Oken's *Lehrbuch der Naturphilosophie*. That work presents *Naturphilosophie* as 'mathematics endowed with substance' (*Lehrbuch*, § 26), and nature itself as the resultant 'mathematical multiplicity' which 'must have proceeded ... out of zero' (*Lehrbuch*, § 35). But Oken is also the most fervent of organicists, so that the substantialization of the matheme becomes the algorithm of an absolute organicism, yielding a (highly linear) account of the recapitulation thesis where the *terminii ad quo* and *ad quem* are fixed: 'Animals are only the persistent foetal stages or conditions of man' (*Lehrbuch*, § 3048), so that all of organic nature becomes a single megaorganism with a human head.

Naturphilosophie is infamous for its organicism; it is found throughout Ritter's works, from the *Proof of a Continual Galvanism*: 'Nature is ... the All-Animal';[23] to the *Fragments* of 1810: 'The Earth is there for the sake of Man. It is only his organ.'[24] As for Oken, nature mathematizes: 'Vegetation is natural algebra'. More contemporarily too, philosophers of nature recapitulate these recapitulations. René Thom, for example, following D'Arcy Wentworth Thomson in pursuing a mathematicization of organic morphogenesis, articulates the 'hope that scientists ... take up the torch of the quest for a synthetic knowledge in the manner of the eighteenth century *Natur-philosophen*';[25] Deleuze and Guattari demonstrate a residual organicism even while insisting that their 'material vitalism' is 'nonorganic . . . a vital state of matter as such', when they stipulate that life is not possible with silicon, albeit for *a posteriori*, or 'machinic' reasons[26] – which is at least odd, since many argue that life is not only possible, but actual, precisely due to silicon machines.[27]

Wherever we look, the vital is opposed to the inorganic. It is as though Kant's barrier between reflective and constitutive judgment has been maintained at the level of the thinkable: thought can become organic, but not inorganic. Fichte, for example, is similar to Badiou in his rejection of 'worldly multiplicities', even nature itself, according to Schelling. It is well known that Fichte reduces Kantianism to the 'pure act'. Accordingly, organism was as far down the *evolutive* ladder as he could go, before activity dissolved into the inorganic, the non-metabolic and the inert, far enough into nature only to act as a counterposition against the inevitable consequence of the absolutizing of the *Ich* that 'nature did not exist' for it. Nature exists therefore, only insofar as it remains *Ich*-able, that is, only insofar as the *Ich* can metabolize its thinkability into potential action, Leibniz's *potentia agendi* in things, 'a force or power of action by which the transition is made between metaphysics and physics'.[28] Yet, to take the *Science of Knowledge* at its word, what sort of philosophy of the infinite acts of an unconditioned subject needs to bother with physiological particulars at all? Doesn't the Fichtean philosophy of the animal entail the admission into the unconditioned of the conditions of organic life? And these must surely themselves arise in the inorganic.

As a result of claims such as: 'Things are therefore not principles of the organism, but rather conversely, the *organism is the principle of things*' (II, 500), Schelling's *On the World Soul* is often held to be precisely such an organicist philosophy, an impression strengthened by the presence of the 'cosmic animal' thesis in the *Bruno* (IV, 278; *Bruno*, 176). Already in the *World Soul*, Schelling, following Kielmeyer's 'Ich, DIE NATUR',[29] concedes the consequence of confronting deep time with 'natural kinds' lenses borrowed only from the present. Just as Kielmeyer's *Rede* – from which 'coming ages will no doubt date the advent of a new era in natural history' (II, 565) – brought deep time into service as a critique of uniformitarianism in natural history, on the one hand, and *against the entire framework of the transcendental* a priori *forms of intuition based on physiologically contingent particulars* on the other,[30] so Schelling realized the implications for the philosophy of nature:

That our experience has known no reorganization [*Umgestaltung*] of nature, no transition of one form or type into the other . . . is no proof against this possibility; for, if an advocate of this could answer, the changes to which organic as much as anorgic [*anorgische*] nature is subjected, could (until a universal standstill of the organic world comes to pass), have happened over ever longer periods, for which our small periods (which are determined by the cycles of the earth round the sun) provides no measure, and that are so large that until now yet no experience of the course [*Ablauf*] of one of them has been undergone. (II, 348–9)

Schelling's philosophy is not like Kant's: he does not see in an organism the occasion for a lawful projection of subjective purposes into nature *for reflection*, since the organic kinds for which reflection is as it is at the moment of the transcendental deduction of the *a priori* forms of intuition, is itself manifestly contingent according to natural history. Accordingly, the universality of the *a prioris* is undermined, as well as the sequence of carefully crafted conditions, culminating in the unconditioned. Therefore, as the *First Outline* puts it, 'empiricism extended to the unconditioned is indeed naturephilosophy' (III, 24):

> In every organization *individuality* (of the parts) goes on to infinity; (this proposition, even if it cannot also be shown to be a constitutive principle from experience, must at least be established as a regulative principle of every investigation ...). The essence of the process of organization must therefore consist in the *individuation of matter to infinity*. (II, 520)

This is not only to extend the concept of organization, it also, literally, *unconditions the subject of the organization*. In other words, infinitely individuated parts never turn back on themselves to be sealed up into *an* organization, but proliferate unrestrictedly, as the 'positive force' of nature: 'All individual things have the positive *in common*; the multiplicity of different things only develops from the determinations and restrictions of the positive' (II, 408). These determinations are the effect of the 'negative force'. There is no basis for analogy, since connectivity fills all available conceptual space, leaving no 'gulfs'. This is why both *Ich* 'has no predicates and is no *thing*' (III, 372; STI, 29),[31] and why '*matter* has no inwardness' (III, 368; STI, 26); in the 'self-construction of matter' (IV, 4), there is no *self*, no 'subject' or 'auto', but only the infinite externality of matter. In Schelling, there never was a 'struggle against subjectivism' (Beiser, *German Idealism*), but only 'an excess of objectivity'.[32] In fact, there is no struggle at all, only a tension in the 'common principle ... fluctuating between inorganic and organic nature' (II, 347), between, that is, force and organization. Thus, in the *First Outline of a System of Naturephilosophy* and the *Introduction to the Outline*, Schelling resolves this tension by opting for a Boscovite-Priestleyan 'dynamic atomism' (III, 23n.). While these here remain 'ideal explanatory grounds', the *Universal Deduction of the Dynamic Process* (1800) opens decisively with the 'self-construction of matter' (IV, 4), by which time, to equip the *World Soul* with a later vocabulary, *animal is insufficiently evolved* to serve as the basis of speculative physics, having not yet *involved* the infinite individuality of its parts *as matter*.

That the World Soul is a conflict of forces, that deep time is phenomenologically inscrutable, means that *there can be no* a priori *finality in nature*. All that is certain is the conflict – although, again following Kielmeyer, not the *proportions* – of these forces.[33] This is why a Schellingian philosophy of nature works not with the continuity or discontinuity of organization and matheme, but with the tension of the infinite individuation of matter and the un-conditioning of experience as it moves from recording to producing further individuation. Finally, therefore, since 'organization is the principle of things', and since individuation is infinite, the World Soul cannot be approached as though it were a body. Rather, the investigation of the World Soul feeds back on itself (eventually giving rise to the theory of the involution and evolution of the powers, or *Potenzen*), since it is the axis of the composition of natural things, or rather, as Kielmeyer put it 'all variations in dead, material nature ... derive ... from a striving in the soul of nature ... for heterogenesis.' Kielmeyer's account, of course, has a naturalistic basis: his 'physics of the animal kingdom'[34] developed the theory of recapitulation[35] from one relating solely to the organic world, as Oken understood it, for example, to a 'developmental history' that included inorganic elements, and that gave these latter elements a causal role in the 'changes that the animal kingdom and its groups have suffered on the earth ... and those probable in the solar system.'[36] Thus, due to the identity of the forces involved, *all* matter was subject to recapitulation, that is, to parallel development, regardless of the resulting product. From this aspect of Kielmeyer's *Rede*, Schelling derived the hypothesis of a higher physics – one of the *dynamic core of nature*. However, Kielmeyer went further. At the end of the *Rede*, he suggests that 'the human mind also manifests the proportion of forces that are combined in it',[37] and again, Schelling will follow suit, confirming in 1797 that 'philosophy is the natural history of mind', in pursuit of which 'philosophy becomes genetic' (II, 39; *Ideas*, 30), and postulating in 1800 'the identity of dynamics and the transcendental' (III, 452; STI, 91). While Deleuze has remarked on the 'autopositing' of the concept 'as a philosophical reality' in the post-Kantians, 'particularly Schelling and Hegel',[38] Schelling goes further: since '*Naturphilosophie* gives a material explication of idealism' as the latter 'erupts at the threshold of nature' (IV, 76), it necessarily entails a physics of the idea, or 'physical concept formation' (the Stoic and Neoplatonist *phusike ennoia*),[39] no different than the actions of gravitation in the formation of 'stones and rubble' (VI, 279). Thus, there are two aspects to Schelling's *Naturphilosophie*: the dynamics of nature, and of the idea. To explore this further, following Kielmeyer's extension of the concept of recapitulation to cover everything from rocks to ideation, we now move from the World Soul to the world body.

THE ABYSS OF FORCES

The abyss [Abgrund] of forces into whose depths we peer, already
introduces this question: what ground or reason might there be in the
first construction of our Earth, that no generation of new individuals
is possible on it otherwise than under the condition of opposing
powers?   (*Schelling: III, 324n.*)

Thus naturephilosophy must follow the 'infinite individuation' of matter
into the inorganic rather than remaining with the animal or plant. 'In the
first construction of our Earth': Schelling's response to the hyper-tellurianism
of second natures and analogical gulfs – and, implicitly, to the 'transcendental or volcanic spatium'[40] – is to physicalize the analogy and make matter
active. In identifying the dynamic core of natural production, however,
Schelling asks after the contingency of individuals currently available to
scrutiny, and the determinacy of their ground in the forces. Thus, chemically
speaking, he writes: 'the earth-principle, i.e., only the symbol [*Sinnbild*] of
things irreducible, or rather the irreducible itself' (III, 245). Is the chemical
earth then an unconditioned body, or merely the 'sensible image' of it? Are
chemical bodies the phenomenal output of unstable forces, or are they permanent material artifacts? Peering into the abyss of forces means: retro-
specting the natural history of the earth, much as Steffens did in his
'physiology of the universe'.[41] Where Schelling saw an abyss, Steffens saw
The Inner Natural History of the Earth (1801) as demanding an equivalence of
human and natural history:

> It became steadily clearer to me that just as the natural sciences
> themselves had ushered in an absolutely new historical element,
> through which our own time was cut off entirely from the past, so
> the most important of the sciences [i.e., geology, the natural history
> of the earth] must become the basis of the entire intellectual future
> of the species. History must itself become nature through and through,
> if it wants to assert itself as nature; that is, in every aspect of its being.[42]

Ritter says this too: 'Not history *of* physics; rather: history = physics =
history.'[43] If history is not natural history, it is not history at all: the only
possible means to preserve the 'entire intellectual future of the species' is that
it be accounted for as natural history. Why, however, would a natural history
guarantee the future of any species, or its exclusive maintenance of intellect?
Who can tell that no generation of species is possible except under currently
observable conditions (uniformitarianism)? As a buttress against natural
historical contingency, Steffens' geology places man at the summit of the
earth's creations. But the fact that a natural history will thus guarantee the
species' future at all rests, for Schelling, on certain key assumptions.
According to 'natural history in the strict sense of the term' . . .

...we would think nature in its freedom as it develops along all possible trajectories in accordance with an original organization (which for that very reason cannot now exist anywhere), as now one force, at the cost of suppressing the others, has here a lower and there a higher intensity, and thus an equilibrium is attained amongst these same organic forces; this would even have the advantage ... of being able to reduce the external variations amongst the Earth's creatures as regards the number, magnitude, structure and function of the organs to an original, inner variation in the proportions of organic forces[44] (of which these were only the outward phenomenon). (I, 469)

Natural history and the history of freedom can only coincide if nature rests on an 'original organization': a little determinacy of the ground alone can guarantee freedom. If, on the other hand, this organization no longer exists, then existing organizations, differing from the original, cannot be it – and this only by assuming that it *did* once exist. Otherwise, the ground of the determinacy is to be sought in the proportions of the forces; if these change, then so too do the resultant organizations, thus accounting for the successive eradications of species throughout natural history. Steffens has followed Kielmeyer's injunction to carry recapitulation beyond the animal and vegetable, and into the geological realm, but at the cost of constituting Earth and Man as permanent, unchanging bodies, against all the evidence of natural history itself. The question Schelling poses to this is remarkably transcendental: the fact that the Earth's creatures are merely the 'outward phenomenon' of the proportions of the forces, poses the challenge: *if the ground cannot be sought in bodies*, and if all bodies are accessible to sense, then the forces themselves are unintuitable; 'matter is the darkest of all things' (II, 359) says Schelling, repeatedly echoing Plato. Ground, Earth and Body therefore establish a polarity between the planomenon and the phenomenon. The abyss of forces is therefore an abyss for our 'peering' (sensuous intuition), but also a physical abyss, insofar as premising our guarantees against extinction events on observable bodies has no ground other than these bodies. Since, according to the evidence of natural history, these are necessarily contingent, the abyss of forces is the chaos logically and materially prior to 'the first construction of our earth'.

When, therefore, Schelling provides a 'geology of morals' in the *Philosophical Inquiries*, it begins with 'the self-operation of the ground' and ends with 'the crisis of the *turba gentium*' (VII, 379–80; HF, 56–8), global turbulence and storms of species. Within this naturalistic 'ages of the world', the 'will of the deep' realizes particularization in organic bodies,[45] establishing a series of bodies repeatedly swept away by this periodic recapitulation of primal forces. Just as

we record the eruptions of volcanic mountains; if we could only glimpse the rule of their recurrence and finally establish it, we could dispense with recording them. Therefore: *what must be judged* a priori *and happens according to necessary laws, is not an object of history; and conversely, what is an object of history cannot be assessed* a priori ... (I, 467)

So the periodic recapitulation of the self-operation of the ground in created nature sweeps its forms aside. Thus, not only is the circuit of creation and destruction not history because it is periodic, but also because it cannot be said to follow any chronological sequence; this is because the conditions for accounting a phenomenon recurrent depend crucially on non-recurrent elements: but the only non-recurrent elements are the bodies established and eliminated periodically, so that, 'our small time-frame provides no measure' of the recurrence. Once again, the antithesis of the geo-planomenal and the phenomenal establishes the abyss as inaccessible to sense (Kant's *das Übersinnliche*), since it exceeds the physiologically contingent forms of intuition available to specific organizations that would enable the specification of difference between the recapitulated and the recapitulating. Thus the ground is ungrounding: 'in the unground [*Ungrund*] or indifference there is admittedly no personality [no individuality]; but is the point of origin the whole?' (VII, 423; HF, 93). In other words, given the 'will of the depths' that 'excites the self-will of the creature' – that produces individuality,[46] there are two foci for *naturphilosophische* inquiries: the whole (Absolute, Unconditioned) and the individual.

The upshot is that the forces are unavailable both for intuition and for reflection. Schelling maps two escape routes from the dilemma of the inscrutability of the self-construction of the earth. The first is to seek an articulation of those forces that is the archetype of nature's activity without being subject to the terminal contingency of organic forms (the 'universal categories of physics' (IV, 1–78); while the second is that the '*Naturphilosoph* puts himself in the place of nature'.[47] The first is the route opened by intellect becoming productive, the second by 'empiricism extended to the unconditioned' (III, 24).

Given, however, the ungrounding of the ground, the errancy of the planomenon, the merely symbolic irreducibility of the Earths or Elements, and the contingency of organization, how is an articulation of the forces to be found in nature? How, in other words, is the 'deduction of the dynamic process' possible? While the *Ideas for a Philosophy of Nature* are busy physicalizing the transcendental apparatus ('chemistry is nothing other than sensory dynamics': II, 343; *Ideas*, 257), the *World Soul* says that the duality or conflict of positive and negative force is basic; the *First Outline* and the *Introduction* posit a 'dynamic atomism', embedding a *potentia agendi* into atoms, although mediated by the idea, as we have seen. In the *Universal Deduction of the Dynamic Process*, however, there is no hesitation concerning the transcendental or ideal status of the 'primitives of nature':

the same phenomena that we conceive under the term 'dynamic process,' and which are the only primitives of nature, are nothing other than a consistent self-construction of matter, simply recapitulated at different stages. A deduction of the dynamic process also therefore counts as a complete construction of matter itself, and therefore one and the same with the highest task of natural science as a whole. (IV, 4)

Here Schelling gives his solution to the continuity problem: forces before bodies. At one level, this is already well known from innumerable narratives of the demise of mechanism and the rise of organicism. But the dimensions of the problem extend beyond the cliché of its accepted solution. In particular, we have already elucidated the problem of the identity of the primitive forces, since they are inaccessible to sense or reflection. Facing this same problem in his 'inner natural history of the earth', Steffens announces he will 'establish magnetism as the first step in the evolution of all the developments on our earth and even thereby elevate the theory of evolution to a principle'.[48] Thus, the magnet would embody the polarity of whole and individual, insofar as, being a body, and thus individual, it is also one of the 'universal categories of physics' Schelling 'deduces' along with electricity and the chemical process (IV, 4). While in terms of physics, this is either a successful explanation or not (the earth's magnetic field and its causes in the iron core at the planet's centre; the consequent retention of atmosphere and shielding from cosmic radiation, and so forth – but in what sense 'consequent'?), the process by which such primitives are to be 'deduced' is far from clear.

Negotiating precisely this task, Schelling opens his *Universal Deduction* thus: 'The sole problem of natural science is: *to construct matter*. This problem can be resolved, although the applications to be made of this general solution will never be complete' (IV, 3). The categories of physics thus to be deduced are equally the categories of the 'self-construction of matter', that is, they are to be unconditioned with respect both to the ideal and the physical. Since 'it is the nature of philosophy to consider things as they are in themselves' (IV, 120), while *Naturphilosophie* 'knows only the purely *productive* in nature' (III, 101), nature and philosophy move in contrary directions; naturephilosophy, however, moves in both trajectories at once: 'to philosophize about nature is to produce it' (III, 13). This is one (formal) reason why the *Universal Deduction* can affirm that 'the deduction of the dynamic process is at the same time the complete construction of matter' (IV, 4). In the later Schellingian lexis of the powers (*Potenzen*), these trajectories will be known as the *evolutive* and the *involutive*, respectively. This is why the 'Introduction' to the *Ideas for a Philosophy of Nature* (1797) affirms of that work that it 'does not begin *from above* ... but *from below* ...' (II, 56; *Ideas,* 42), not with hypotheses, but with bodies. This is not simply to comply with empiricism in the norms of the 'experimental arts,' but rather for fully philosophical reasons, namely, as the ground of an '*unconditioned* empiricism' (IV, 82; III, 24) which, in turn, is the only method by which to *involve* the 'unthinged' (*dem Unbedingten*), 'the absolute in the natural sciences' (III, 283).

Of course, anything unconditioned must be identical; there could not be two unconditioned things, since 'things' are, by definition, conditioned particulars. It is in this *evolutionary*[49] sense that the absolute is to be understood: for *Naturphilosophie*, the unconditioned is not arrived at by simply *positing* it (as does Fichte), but rather by successive 'un-conditionings' of particulars. The so-called 'identity philosophy' – really a continuation of *Naturphilosophie* – will articulate this in terms of the *Potenzen*, which are maximally potentiated when *involved* into the particular, and maximally depotentiated when *evolved* into the unconditioned. Simply put, involution is like cubing a number (VII, 449) and cubing its product again (no product is without *Potenzen*); evolution is like cube-rooting it. The absolute, or identity, is therefore 'devoid of all powers' (VI, 212), while differentiation is 'an intensification of the unity' or a 'doubling of the essence' (VII, 424–5). While Schelling's powers function mathematically, their basis lies in the structure of polarity. Hence the 'magnetic' diagrams (VII, 416) that litter the identity philosophy:

$$
\begin{array}{cc}
+ & + \\
\mathbf{A=B} & \mathbf{A=B} \\
\end{array}
$$
$$
\mathbf{A=A}
$$

(IV, 137)

Or, as the raw schema of magnetic polarity:[50]

$$
\begin{array}{c}
\longleftarrow 1^{+} \qquad 1^{-} \longrightarrow \\
1^{+\infty} \quad /3 \quad /2 \quad /1 \qquad -1/ \;\; -2/ \qquad -3/ \;\; 1^{-\infty} \\
1^{0}
\end{array}
$$

Châtelet writes, 'We know that the patient exposition of the absolute was one of the major ambitions of the philosophy of nature,'[51] an 'exposition' that had to progress, phenomenon by phenomenon, through the infinitely reca-pitulating categories of physics. While in Eschenmayer's diagram, the potentiation of the unity becomes visible as differentiation, as does the depotentiation of the differentia into unity, what Schelling's own magnetic diagram additionally shows is the polar reciprocity that exponentiates the involution of differentia. The second remains susceptible of linear inter-pretation, while the first is itself dynamic, exchanging poles not on the basis of particular identities, attributes or species, but by virtue of the identity into which they are depotentiated. Polarity is both a schematizing and a physical apparatus: it is like Buffon's 'primitive general outline'[52] of nature, naturalized, 'the basal form [for the construction] of our entire system' (IV, 138 [Schelling's addition]). 'Philosophy becomes genetic' (II, 39; *Ideas*, 30) because it is articulated by the same polarities that articulate nature. This is, Schelling remarks, 'the very ancient doctrine ... that "like is known [*erkannt*] by like"' (VII, 337; *Ideas*, 8), and its starting point is *physics*.

THE 'PHYSICS OF THE ALL' AND 'THE PHYSICS OF ALL THINGS'

Merely reflective humanity has no idea of an *objective* reason, of an Idea that as such is utterly real and objective; all reason is something subjective to them, as equally is everything ideal, and the idea itself has for them only the meaning of a subjectivity, so that they therefore know only two worlds, the one consisting of stone and rubble, the other of intuitions and the thinking thereupon.

(Schelling: VI, 279)

At the core of Platonic physics lies the theory of matter. Matter is a 'difficult and dark *idea*' (49a) since it cannot be sensibly intuited but can be thought; unlike the other ideas, however, matter cannot be thought clearly, but only with difficulty. Or, matter is not a clear thought. It is as if, when Parmenides asks Socrates: 'is there a form of hair, or mud, or dirt or any of these things' (*Parmenides* 130c–d), he is asking *is the form of dirt itself dirty* (and if not, in what way is it the form of dirt)? No one takes this thought of matter further than Plotinus: 'We utterly eliminate every kind of form; and the object in which there is none whatever we call Matter: if we are to see Matter we must so completely abolish Form that we take shapelessness into our very selves' (*Enniads* I.8.ix).

Plotinus gives a material theory of the idea of matter on the grounds that a non-material theory of matter would not be a theory of matter. This does not depend on capturing its attributes or making an inventory of our knowledge of it; rather, *physics is immediate and chancy*, especially as regards matter, because its difficulty and darkness must necessarily be part of its idea. Moreover, this idea must, like Parmenides' hypothetical question, be itself material. What would later be seen (and particularly for Schelling: 'What after all can work upon the mind other than itself, or that which is akin to its nature?' II, 222; *Ideas*, 157) as a principle of identity *that must itself be identity*, becomes casually glossed, in Plato's *Timaeus*, as 'eikota muthon*, likely story' (29d2). In this casual sideline, Platonic physics replicates the principle 'like is known by like' in the *Timaeus'* 'eikota muthon'. This provides commentators with all they need to package this work – which 'embraces the whole of physiology and . . . pertains to the theory of the universe', as Proclus began his *Commentaries on the Timaeus of Plato*[53] – as a 'myth' or a 'discourse on discourse',[54] or indeed as a lesson in the epistemic status of generated things.[55] The *eikota muthon*, however, is closer to Parmenides than to the myth of Er. That is, just as Parmenides' One makes mere semblance out of the many, so Plato, conjoining the two, gets the cycles of the Same and the Different from which the World Soul is fabricated. Against this, Cornford particularly reinforces why the very idea of a Platonic physics seems self-defeating: a world of becoming, and one of being; what becomes is not, and what is does not become. Divest it of its physics, therefore, and its

metaphysics assumes the same old laughable two-worlds variety; it is not
Plato however, but Kant and particularly Fichte who say, 'intellect and thing
inhabit two worlds, between which there is no bridge.'[56] Thus, when Krings
writes that Schelling 'Platonizes Kant' and 'Kantianizes Plato',[57] this is true
only insofar as the *'productive nature'* (*Philebus* 26a6) of Plato is pitted against
the purely practical 'second nature' of Kant,[58] which becomes so extreme a
gulf as to form precisely a two-worlds antiphysics in Fichte, the target of
Schelling's invective.

The *Timaeus* is not a two-worlds metaphysics, however, because it has a
one-world physics, embracing, if not the *ideai* themselves, then certainly
genesis eis ousian, 'the becoming of being' (*Philebus* 26d9). When this component is overlooked, because the story is a myth, or because its little
positive theoretical content is outmoded – who today would say matter was
'difficult and dark'? – little is lost for physics, but everything is lost as
regards the nature of metaphysics. As Kant uncharacteristically put it,
leaving aside his doctrinal somatism, 'meta-physics is physics beyond the
empirical cognition of nature'.[59] Schelling's own writing on the *Timaeus* of
1794 therefore develops what the *Philebus* (26d8) calls 'the becoming of
being [*genesis eis ousian*]' alongside 'productive nature [*e tou poiountas phusis*]'
(26e6), as the basic principle of Plato's 'physics of the all [*tou pantos phuseos*]'
(47a9 and 27a5). Moreover, the 'difficult and dark' (*Timaeus* 49a5) idea of
matter is discussed, as well as the *matter of the ideas*, the 'substance of the
Forms in general' (Plotinus *Enniads* VI.6.vi). This last stems from Aristotle's
account, in the *Physics* (209b15), of the connections between the *Timaeus* and
Plato's 'unwritten teachings', and it becomes a steady theme in Plotinus not
only to investigate whether the ideas are material, but whether there is
'matter in the intelligible universe [*kosmos noetos*].'[60]

The physics of becoming and of productive nature, alongside the theory of
Platonic matter – the fact that this is not a physics for those of us who come
later means that we are, as Proclus[61] says of those who do not see the stated
topics treated seriously therein, 'illiterate'.[62] To put it briefly: for Schelling,
Plato's physics is an early synthetic account of matter as developing from the
unlimited (productive nature), the limit (*idea*), their conjunction (*to koinon*)
and causation (*aitiai*);[63] in a phrase – ideating productive nature causes their
own conjunction in creating material things, with no need of a substrate.
This theory satisfies two of Schelling's later demands:

1. Whoever cannot philosophize without a substrate, cannot philosophize
   at all (III, 308n.);
2. The concept of matter is itself, by origin, synthetic; a purely logical
   concept of matter is meaningless (II, 235; *Ideas*, 188).

Matter is not a substrate but a product. This means that nature's dynamics
(its synthetic productivity) encompass the construction of matter (which
Schelling calls 'infinite individuation'). Since, moreover, matter is a 'difficult

and dark idea' (*Timaeus* 49a), it is, as in Schelling's use of the Platonic term,[64] non-intuitable; that is, the origin of matter is not empirically accessible, although, crucially, it is thinkable. This is due to the principle that like knows like, insofar as the mixture of matter and idea is common to all *phusis*.

This alters the post-Nietzschean acceptance of Platonism considerably. Despite his weariness at contemporary philosophy's 'not having done with overturning Platonism', and in spite of his disparagement of the 'anti-Platonism' of the modernists and postmodernists, Badiou excises the dimension of physics from metaphysics somewhat prematurely.[65] That matter is non-intuitable but thinkable, that it is synthetic substance, that it is generated, alters all the relations of Platonism as received: there is thought, and there are changeable bodies, but their conjunction, as the becoming of being, yields productive nature. This allows the becoming that besets the world of appearances as phenomena to result from the interplay of the syntheses in nature's productivity *through which the idea moves*, as through the 'sea of unlikeness' Plotinus mentions (*Enniads* I.8.xiii). Thus Plato too has his floods and earthquakes, as nature's productivity enters a phase of metabecoming, undoing its own works through its excess of dynamics in a 'universal ruin' (*Statesman* 273–4), until the *kybernetes* regains control. The identity of the World Soul is therefore thought, in Plato, not as a particular material body (Cornford's copper), but as precisely a polarity of the Same and the Different. When the World Soul is functioning optimally, there is a dynamic identity between the Parmenidean One (thought-being) and Many (nature); when erratically, either 'too much' or 'too little' – to use the 'indefinite dyad' that is said to define Platonic matter (Aristotle, *Metaphysics* 987b–988a, 1090, *Physics* 187a)[66] – then *turba gentium* ensues, 'the world turns with a sudden shock' (*Statesman* 273a).

Following all this reciprocity between the like and the unlike, the becoming like and the becoming different that we find in the Platonic physicists, the Aristotelian reduces the 'physics of the all' to that of 'all the things of nature', and ties likeness inflexibly to a relation between classes of objects and faculties. This effects two great changes in physics: 'the general is approached by the intelligence and the particular by the senses' (*Physics* 189a). Firstly therefore body and intellect are segregated, and likeness, instead of forming the identity of thought and nature, becomes attached to faculties: the general (the concept) to the intellect and the particular (the body) to the senses. There ensues therefore the domination of concepts and the conceivable by bodies and, at the same time, a segregation of thought and nature, taking the physics out of metaphysics. From now on, metaphysics is transformed into *meta ta phusika*, which is the play of intellect released from determination by sensibilia, so that it becomes possible to disparage metaphysics as an irresponsible distraction unnecessary to physics. 'It is whole entities that are more intelligible [*gnorimóteron*] to the senses' (*Physics* 184a). Of course, this does not go unchallenged; Plotinus will maintain a theory of incorporeal matter (*Enniads* III.6.viii–xix),[67] which follows from the problems Aristotle began to have with the substrate, 'the ultimate underlying subject common to *all the things of* nature' (*Physics* 192a). And the Stoics, trying to reassemble likeness, will develop a natural concept formation.[68] But the ground is laid for all the scientific revolutions, with their elements, earths, bodies, and 'first things': 'We may say that the science of nature is for the most part concerned with bodies and magnitudes and with their changing properties and motions' (*On the Heavens* 268a). Thus Denis Des Chenes, commenting on the *continuity* binding modern Cartesian physics to medieval, Scholastic physics, argues that 'Aristotelian philosophy of nature ... contains the principles common to *all* natural philosophy, and not just to the part that became our physics.'[69] All revolutions in physics have been governed by this single metaphysics, which we find in Kant: 'natural science ... in the strict sense belongs to the doctrine of body alone;'[70] and amongst particle physicists: 'science is the study of limited objects ... [the] investigat[ion of] an isolated part of the world by itself.'[71] Thus, as long as bodies dominate and thought is immaterial, there has never been a revolution in the natural sciences.

SPECULATIVE PHYSICS: THE MAGNETIC TRANSCENDENTAL AND THE DYNAMICS OF THE IDEA

A dynamical explanation in physics means exactly what a transcendental explanation means in philosophy. To explain a phenomenon dynamically means that it has been explained from the original conditions of the construction of matter in general ... All dynamic movements have their final ground in the subject of nature itself, namely in the forces of which the visible world is only the framework.

(Schelling: IV, 76)

What after all can work upon the mind other than itself, or that which is akin to its nature? It is therefore *necessary* to conceive of matter as a product of *forces* for *force* alone is the non-sensory in objects.

(Schelling: II, 222; *Ideas*, 175)

'The identity of the dynamic and the transcendental' (III, 452; STI, 91) is little developed in Schelling, but follows of necessity from the philosophy of forces we have been pursuing. If 'an original antithesis of forces in the ideal subject of nature appears necessary to every construction' (IV, 5), then anything constructed must evince that original antithesis, including thought. Before moving to naturephilosophy's conceptual core, therefore, the developments that Schelling drew from Plato (against Kant) need to be established.

One such development is the principle of likeness. To turn this principle or hypothesis into a component of speculative physics, Schelling will establish that it has its physical expression in the form of Identity. Identity is given physically in every organization on the Earth, and paradigmatically in the magnet's indifference point (1^0 or $\mathbf{A} = \mathbf{A}$). Identity can therefore be dynamically explained as the involute of a dynamic process (the production of individuality); it can also be explained transcendentally, from the concept itself, insofar as identity can never not be itself (IV, 120). But it is not a conjunctive predicate between two entities, nor will Schelling have anything to do with identity inhering in anything since neither matter nor *Ich* have any interiority (III, 368; *Ideas*, 26). Schelling goes on: 'everything that is, is (considered in itself) not the appearance of absolute identity, but rather *identity itself*' (IV, 120). Two questions arise: (1) what of infinite individuation; and (2), where does this leave the thesis of the identity of the transcendental and the dynamic? To answer them, we must ask: *why is a theory of identity necessary at all* – especially since the so-called Identity philosophy is held to supersede the *Naturphilosophie*, despite its major works devoting at least half their content to the topic. Moreover, we can see the germ of identity in Schelling's recapitulation of the neo-Platonic theory of reciprocal likeness in the passage from the *Ideas*, above. To follow this passage entails that mind knows mind only, or that what mind *is*, is in fact reciprocating forces or forces with which it is in affinity, such that 'knowing' arises from this reciprocity or affinity. Yet we have seen the trouble to which the abyss of forces leads, beginning with the *First Outline* (III, 23n.): the conflict of the forces cannot be assumed to be such as to maintain indefinitely the current relations amongst the series of organizations on the earth, and will give rise, come the *Philosophical Inquiries*, to world-disorder, such as occurs when the World Soul loses control in the *Statesman*. Moreover, Schelling requires this ungrounding of the ground in order to demonstrate nature's capacity for individuation through the 'will of the depths' (not so much a geology of morals as a geological ethology).

On the one hand, then, identity is necessary as a means to grasp individuation in natural production; on the other, it seems completely to undermine it, because if there is an identity of natural production, all natural production must be identical, and there is no question therefore but that the current series of organizations will continue to populate the Earth. But this is only so if the phenomena are mistaken for the forces. As Schelling notes, 'an original antithesis of forces in the ideal subject of nature appears necessary to every construction'.[72] Identity is therefore dynamic – polar, magnetic: at one pole, the infinite individuation from the *World Soul*; at the other, the absolute identity of the *Presentation of My System*; between the two, magnetic relation, but no absorption, duplication, or third-stage parthenogenesis, such as would give 'life' to the concept. This means that infinite individuation and absolute identity are not contraries, but antitheses, such as only arise from an indifference point that, as the *Inquiries* put it, 'precede all antithesis' (VII, 406; HF, 87).

What, then, can be said of the identity of dynamics and the transcendental? Retaining the principle of the reciprocity of likeness, Schelling writes: 'In transcendental philosophy ... we rely solely on this, that intuition, like everything else, can only become objective to the *Ich* through outer objects, which objects, now, can be nothing else but intelligences outside us ... ' (III, 556; STI, 174). Several things follow from this; firstly, intelligence is a phenomenon of force, just as quality is the object of sensation, 'but all quality is simply electricity' (III, 452; STI, 91), and since nothing guarantees the maintenance of these forces, nothing guarantees the recognition of any object whatever, as Ritter found in his self-experimentation programme: 'First case: Zinc in the eye. Chain closed ... diminution of external objects; blue color ... Second case: Silver in the eye. Chain closed ... red color, enlargement of external objects ... [and so on].'[73]

Sensation is altered by electrophysiological changes, like closing one's body into a galvanic chain. Although these are relatively minor changes, Ritter is beginning a programme of un-conditioning with regard to the conditions of his capacity for sensation. Similarly, Schelling's balance between intelligences is subject to disruption from, for example, electrical storms. This parallel seems suspiciously linear, like Oken's recapitulation. But there is a second consequence: having generalized the forces responsible for the production of quality in sensation beyond the particular organic platform in which they are contingently instantiated, Schelling, too, is beginning a process of un-conditioning. Just as, because 'all chemistry is sensory dynamics' (II, 224; *Ideas*, 257), then where there is chemistry, there is sense *in potentia*, so too for electricity and sensation. The unit of likeness is unpredictable in advance, so that all that is predictable is that every physical instantiation of a function of intelligence makes *actual* rather than *analogical* claim to 'intelligent objects' and the like. What recapitulates, the unit of selection for genetic philosophy, is always and only forces; forces react with forces, producing phenomena. Thus the phenomena are just as actual and physical as the forces that produce them, so that Schelling can conclude, with Kant, that 'matter is a species of representation',[74] but only insofar as representations are thereby treated as material things, on an ontological monofilament of a planomenon. It is between the physics of the planomena (geology) and the dynamics of the concept (noo-phoronomy), on the one hand, and the recapitulating, auto-potentiating forces that produce both, that speculative physics attains a physics capable of geology and noology, without sacrificing the physicality of either, or questioning their physical reducibility to the permanently raging yet identical 'abyss of forces'. This is how a physics of the World Soul is possible.

Notes

1   *Schellings Sämmtliche Werke*, ed. K. F. A. Schelling (Stuttgart and Augsburg: J.G. Cotta, 1856–61). References to Schelling will be to this edition, using roman numerals for volume and arabic for page numbers. *Philosophical Inquiries into the Nature of Human Freedom*, trans. James Gutmann (La Salle IL: Open

Court, 1986). The English translation of this text will be marked as 'HF' followed by the page number from this edition.

2   Omnès, R., *Quantum Philosophy*, trans. Arturo Sangalli (Princeton NJ: Princeton University Press, 1999).

3   Leibniz, G. W. *Philosophical Texts*, trans. and ed. R. S. Woolhouse and Richard Francks (Oxford: Oxford University Press, 1998), 210.

4   Foreword to Eric Alliez, *Capital Times*, trans. Georges Van Den Abbeele (Minnesota: University of Minnesota Press, 1991), xii.

5   A. Gode von Aesch, *Natural Science in German Romanticism* (New York: Columbia University Press, 1941, reprinted 1966), 255.

6   Joseph L. Esposito, *Schelling's Idealism and Philosophy of Nature* (Lewisburg: Bucknell University Press, 1977), 100–1.

7   Of the nature of the Absolute, Schelling writes in 1803: 'the absolute must be thought of purely as matter, as pure identity' (II, 60; *Ideas for a Philosophy of Nature*, trans. Errol E. Harris and Peter Heath (Cambridge: Cambridge University Press, 1988), 47; henceforth *Ideas*). Likewise, according to Moiso, Schelling's *Weltseele* 'cleared the way for a physics of realities, that is, the living totality of material events' (Francesco Moiso, 'The Hegelian theory of physics and chemistry in relation to Schelling's Naturphilosophie', in R. Horstmann and M. Petry (eds), *Hegels Philosophie der Natur* (Stuttgart: Klett-Cotta, 1986), 55).

8   'I suggest that the World-Soul operates in Platonic cosmology rather like the governor on a steam-engine' Richard D. Mohr, *The Platonic Cosmology* (Leiden: Brill, 1985), 171–9. The cybernetic account is interesting, both insofar as, unlike many contemporary commentators, it grounds itself in the physicalist account of the World Soul Plato offers, and as a physicalist counterpoint to the exclusively conceptual disjunction of regulative/determinant for understanding organism in Kant. And Mohr adds, crucially for what concerns us here, that 'like a machine governor, the World-Soul is capable of maintaining order only within a certain range of natural disruptions' (Mohr, *The Platonic Cosmology*, 172).

9   Proclus infers that the 'whole fabric' that Plato's demiurge divides into two in order to construct the cycles of the Same and the Different is metallic. He writes: 'Plato all but speaks of the divine Craftsman as using the tools of Hephaestus, forging the whole heaven, giving it a pattern of figures, turning the bodies on a lathe, and shaping each into its proper form', *The Commentaries of Proclus on the* Timaeus *of Plato*, trans. Thomas Taylor (New York: Kessinger, 1997), 281. Francis M. Cornford, *Plato's Cosmology* (London: Routledge & Kegan Paul, 1937), citing this passage on p. 74, adds to it the specific hypothesis that the 'whole fabric' is 'copper'.

10 Johann Wilhelm Ritter, *Fragmente aus dem Nachlasse eines jungen Physikers*, ed. Steffen and Birgit Dietzsch (Leipzig and Weimar: Müller & Kiepenheuer, 1984), 85.

11 Plotinus writes of the 'generative soul in matter' (*Enniads* II.iii.17 and V.i.5) of the soul as 'number ... but number as substance'. While the number Plotinus considers is the One, Lorenz Oken, in his 1802–10 *Lehrbuch der Naturphilosophie*, 3 vols (Jena: F. Frommann, 1809–11) makes the same case for the number zero, which generates entities in a material-formal set-theoretic manner. Oken defines *Naturphilosophie* as 'mathematics endowed with substance' (*Elements of Physiophilosophy*. Alfred Tulk (London: Ray Society, 1847), 4), from which it follows that 'the universe or world is the reality of mathematical ideas' (p. 1). See pp. 1–10.

12 Translation taken from: Schelling, F., *Bruno or On the Natural and the Divine Principle of Things*, trans. and ed. with an introduction by Michael G. Vater

(Albany: SUNY Press 1984), 176. The English translation of this text will be marked by 'Bruno' followed by the page number in this edition.

13 Ritter, J. W., *Beyträge zur nähern Kentniss der Galvanismus und die Resultate seiner Untersuchungen*, 2 vols (Jena: F. Frommann: 1800–5), 148. Ritter also writes (*Beyträge*, 252): 'All the inner, dynamic senses are constituted by one and the same natural force, electricity.' In the same year, Ritter published *Das elektrische System der Koerper* (Jena: F. Frommann), in which he argued that not only was electricity the principle of organic life, but also constituted an 'electrical system of the earth itself' (p. 148). Finally, in the 1810 *Fragmente*, the full extent of the electrical World Soul is realized: 'The universe is a voltaic body' (p. 245), crediting Schelling as the 'philosophical electrician and electrical philosopher' (p. 247). Novalis, in *Die Christenheit oder Europa und andere philosophische Schriften*, ed. Rolf Thomas (Köln: Könemann, 1996), confirms that 'Ritter is searching everywhere for the real World Soul' (p. 472).

14 Badiou, A. and Deleuze, G., 'The Fold, Leibniz and the Baroque', trans. Thelma Sowley in *Deleuze: A Critical Reader*, ed. Paul Patton (Oxford: Blackwell, 1997), 63.

15 Ibid., p. 55.

16 Schelling *Timaeus*, ed. Hartmut Buchner (Stuttgart-Bad Canstatt: Frommann-Holzboog, 1794). Schelling continues to reference the *Timaeus* throughout and beyond what are usually entitled his *Naturphilosophische* works (II, 181; *Ideas*, 144. See also II, 370; VII, 360, 374; *Human Freedom* 35, 50–1; X, 374). Given this recurrence, it is worth noting another: even in this latter work, the *Darstellung des Naturprozesses* (1844), Schelling remarks, 'what has occupied us until now is *Naturphilosophie*' and that even 'man [who] stands at the limits of nature', and with whom Schelling is going to occupy himself, is still cast as 'the ideal aspect *of the universe*' (X, 390, emphasis added). In other words, *nature and idea* form a continuity that extends throughout Schelling's work. There is an echo in this passage of a similar one in HF, where Schelling writes: 'The author has limited himself *entirely* to investigations in the Philosophy of Nature ... The present treatise is the first wherein the author offers ... his conception of philosophy which treats of the Ideal' (VII, 333–4; HF, 3–4, emphasis added). The echo makes it clear that in 1844 Schelling regarded the 'Freedom' essay as continuing *Naturphilosophie*.

17 Badiou, *Deleuze: The Fold*, 67.

18 While denying the existence of a World Soul, Leibniz maintains the existence of an 'active created force in things', which things are themselves 'made up of an infinite number of other organisms' (*Philosophical Texts*, 210–11). He thus refuses to have a continuum as something from which particular 'substantial forms' arise, and constructs it instead from the infinite number of little organisms that populate each natural machine. If the number is infinite, a continuum can be established mathematically by considering the distances between the infinite organisms in the multiplicity of natural machines to be *infinitely small*, as in the infinitesimal calculus. Badiou, by contrast, affirms the 'singularity', which 'demands that the separating distance be absolute and thus that the vacuum be a *point* of Being' (*Deleuze: The Fold*, 66)

19 Badiou, *Deleuze: The Fold*, 63.

20 Schelling knew of what is now known as the *Opus postumum* under the title *Transition from Metaphysics to Physics* (VI, 8). Badiou is also Kantian insofar as he remains attached to the *ethos* of critical philosophy, presenting 'truth' as 'a process of making holes in what constitutes knowledge' (*Deleuze: The Fold*, 67); the subordination of *phusis* to *ethos* is in itself a Kantian event, becoming all the more apparent in Fichte, for whom nature is merely a 'not-I'.

21 Leibniz, G. W., 'Critical Thoughts on the General Part of the *Principles* of

Descartes', trans. Leroy A. Loemker, in Loemker, ed., *Gottfried Wilhelm Leibniz: Philosophical Papers and Letters* (Dordrecht: Reidel, 1969), 409.

22 Leibniz, *Philosophical Texts*, 210. Woolhouse and Francks translate *organis* as 'organisms', unlike 'the other translations', which give 'organs'.

23 Johann Wilhelm Ritter, *Beweis, dass ein beständiger Galvanismus den Lebensprocess in dem Thierreich begleite* (Wiemar, 1798), 171. The quotation is cited by Walter D. Wetzels, 'Aspects of Natural Science in German Romanticism', *Studies in Romanticism* 10 (1971), 44–59.

24 Ritter, *Fragmente*, 184.

25 Thom, R., *Morphogenèse et imaginaire* (Paris: Lettres Modernes, 1978), 52ff.

26 Deleuze G. and Guattari, F., *A Thousand Plateaus*, trans. Brian Massumi (London: Athlone, 1988), 411, 286.

27 Langton C., 'Artificial life', in Margaret Boden, ed., *The Philosophy of Artificial Life* (Oxford: Oxford University Press, 1996), 39–94.

28 Leibniz, *Principles of Descartes*, 409.

29 Kielmeyer's *Rede* (Discourse on the Proportions of Organic Forces in the Different Series of Oganizations, 1793), echoing Plotinus (*Enniads* III.8.iv), begins with NATURE's discourse: 'If I could only lead you *out of space and time and follow the path with you where it departs from your system* ... I have already on occasion extinguished stars from above, and you only experience this after one or two hundred years; I have wiped animal species from the earth – but what happened: another species arose, and soon, I again led this *great machine of the organic kingdom* along a path of development, which you may present to yourselves as the developmental path of the universe, as perhaps that of the individual, in the image of a parabola that never closes on itself, since I never once clearly show you an element of this path', Carl Friedrich Kielmeyer, *Natur und Kraft. Carl Friedrich Kielmeyers gesammelte Schriften*, F. H. Holler, ed., (Berlin: Kieper, 1938), 63–5; anti-Kantian emphasis added.

30 Kielmeyer is often singled out as a Kantian natural scientist, rejecting the excesses of the *Naturphilosophen* with appropriate scorn, although here he manifestly rejects Kantianism, and the implications of his theory such as Schelling exploits to form the theoretical architecture of the World Soul, and to account for the 'fluctuating between inorganic and organic nature', are completely justified. Timothy Lenoir ('The Göttingen School and the development of transcendental *Naturphilosophie* in the Romantic era', *Studies in the History of Biology* 5 (1981), 111–205), for example, transforms Dietrich von Engelhardt's (*Hegel und die Chemie* (Wiessbaden: Guido Pressler, 1976), 5) 'tripartite schema' of *Naturphilosophie* into the 'transcendental, metaphysical and scientific', to present Kielmeyer as a transcendental natural scientist against Schelling, Steffens *et al.*, as representing 'speculative' *Naturphilosophie*. Lenoir writes:

> On closer inspection the view that German biology in the early C19th was shaped by *Naturphilosophie* turned out to be illusory ... One would expect that the works of Kielmeyer and Treviranus, e.g., would be a good place to begin to trace the role of *Naturphilosophie* in shaping biological thought in Germany ... Treviranus is cautiously critical [of it] while Kielmeyer is violently opposed to *romantische Naturphilosophie* ... I have discovered ... that a common core of natural philosophy does run throughout the works of these individuals; it is a philosophy of biology proposed by Immanuel Kant. *The Strategy of Life*. (Dordrecht: Kluwer, 1982), 5–6

Frederick Beiser (*German Idealism: the Struggle against Subjectivity 1781–1801* (Cambridge MA: Harvard University Press, 2002), 508) forcefully rejects this view:

[T]his distinction [between the natural scientists who observed Kant's regulative principles and the *Naturphilosophen* who ignored them] is more a positivistic construction than an historical reality ... First, Kant's regulative doctrine was *not* the foundation of empirical science in the late eighteenth century; rather it was completely at odds with it ... Second, the fundamental program of *Naturphilosophie* – to explain life and the mind on a naturalistic yet non-mechanistic foundation – was shared by all the physiologists and biologists ... The history of science needs to cast off the legacy of positivism – especially that lurking under Kantian guise – and to realize that *Naturphilosophie* was nothing less than the normal science of its day, not some freakish philosophical or metaphysical alternative to it.

The desire on the part of historians of science to 'save' the experimental scientists from the speculators is manifest in practically all works on the *Naturphilosophie*. The reason for this is partly methodological, as Beiser suggests, but also confirms Carus' assertion of the 'metaphysical aphasia' (Carus, C. G., *Organon der Erkenntniss der Natur und des Geistes* (Leipzig: Breitkopf und Härtel, 1856), 127) of the sciences of the mid-nineteenth century in the historians of science of the present.

31 Schelling, F., *System of Transcendental Idealism*, trans. Peter Heath (Charlottesville: University Press of Virginia, 1978). References to the English translation will be marked as 'STI' and give the page number of this edition.

32 Wallace, W., *Prolegomena to the Study of Hegel's Philosophy and Especially of his Logic* (Oxford: Oxford University Press, 2nd edn, 1894), 107.

33 It is therefore false to say of Schelling that his dynamics presuppose an equilibrium or symmetry between the attractive and repulsive forces, as Dale Snow does in her *Schelling and the End of Idealism* (Albany: SUNY Press, 1996), 90. It is true that the emergence of natural things presupposes a *relative* equilibrium of the forces, but nothing guarantees *a priori* that these forces (a) *will* reach equilibrium, or (b) reach *this* equilibrium. 'Dynamic and living' yes; but on condition that the 'and' is a tension.

34 Kielmeyer, *Natur und Kraft*, 56, 27.

35 Recapitulation, according to Kielmeyer, often credited with having offered the first scientific theory of recapitulation, gave it thus: 'Since the distribution of forces in the series of organizations follows the same order as their distribution in the developmental states of given individuals, it follows that the force by which the production of the latter comes about, namely the reproductive force, corresponds to the force by which the series of different organisms of the earth were called into existence' (*Natur und Kraft*, 93).

36 Ibid., p. 29.

37 Ibid., p. 98.

38 With Guattari, F., *What is Philosophy?*, trans. Graham Burchell and Hugh Tomlinson (London: Verso, 1994), 11.

39 See Alcinous, *The Handbook of Platonism*, trans. John Dillon (Oxford: Clarendon, 1995), 4.7–8, 5.7, and especially 4. 8: 'For it is by virtue of possessing a natural concept of the fine and the good, by using our reason, and by referring to natural concepts as definite units of measurement that we judge whether certain given actions are of one nature or another.' See also John Dillon's commentary (p. 67), where he advances the translation 'natural concept formation'. The same issue is more broadly dealt with by Plotinus' discussion of the 'materiality of the Forms in general' (*Enneads* VI.6.vi), and stems from Plato's 'unwritten doctrines' (Aristotle, *Physics* 209b15), from which Plotinus draws his theory of the *logoi* as powers rather than ideas: 'Nature is a *logos* which produces another *logos*' (*Enneads* II.3.xvii). For a concise commentary on the unwritten doctrines,

which centrally revolve around the materiality of the ideas, see Martin, *Études sur Le Timée de Platon*, 2 vols (Paris: Ladrange, 1841), vol. 1, 349–53.

40 Deleuze and Guattari, *What is Philosophy?*, 241.

41 Horst Fuhrmans, *F.W.J. Schelling. Briefe und Dokumente II: 1775–1803* (Bonn: Bouvier, 1973), 195.

42 Steffens, H., *Lebenserinnerungen aus dem Kreis der Romantik* (Jena: Eugen Diederichs, 1908), 176–7.

43 Ritter, *Fragmente*, 140.

44 The annotated line clearly replicates the title of Kielmeyer's *Rede* (1793).

45 'The will of the ground [*Grund*] excites the self-will of the creature from the first creation' (VII, 375; HF, 52). Schelling makes clear that this *Grund* is naturalistic: 'The empirical concept of the ground, too, which will assume an important role in all natural science, must, if scientifically thought out, also lead to a conception of selfhood and individuality' (VII, 376; HF, 53).

46 Schelling here calls this 'evil', after the Neoplatonist equation of the theory of Platonic matter and its errancy; cf. Plotinus, *Enniads* I.8.vii f.f.

47 Schelling, F., (ed.), *Zeitschrift für speculative Physik*, ed. Manfred Durner, 2 vols (Hamburg: Meiner, 1800–2, reprinted 2001), vol. 1, 192.

48 Henrik Steffens, *Beyträge zur innern Naturgeschichte der Erde* (Freyberg: Craz., 1801), cited in Snelders, H. A. M. 'Romanticism and Naturphilosopohie and the inorganic natural sciences 1797–1840', *Studies in Romanticism* (1970) vol. 9, 193–210.

49 This is evolution understood in a mathematical sense. As D'Arcy Wentworth Thomson points out in *On Growth and Form*, ed. and abridged by J. T. Bonner (Cambridge: Cambridge University Press, 1966), 198, 'The mathematician can trace one conic section into another, and "evolve" for example, through innumerable graded ellipses, the circle from the straight line: which tracing of continuous steps is a true "evolution", though time has no part therein. It was after this fashion that Hegel, and for that matter Aristotle himself, was an evolutionist – to whom evolution was a mental concept, involving order and continuity in thought but not an actual sequence of events in time. Such a conception of evolution is not easy for the modern biologist to grasp...'

50 Gilles Châtelet notes in his *Les enjeux du mobile: physique, philosophie, mathématique* (Paris: Seuil, 1993), 137, concerning his reproduction of J.-F. Marquet's reproduction of the diagram in his *Liberté et Existence* (Paris: Gallimard, 1974), 115, that it first appeared in K. A. Eschenmayer, *Versuch die Gesetze magnetischer Erscheinungen aus Sätzen der Naturmetaphysik mithin a priori zu entwickeln* (Tübingen, 1798; date and title corrected).

51 Châtelet, *Les enjeux*, 139.

52 Georges Louis de Buffon, *Histoire naturelle*, ed. Jean Varloot (Paris: Gallimard, 1984), 191.

53 Proclus, *The Commentaries of Proclus*, 1.

54 John Sallis, *Chorology: On Beginnings in Plato's Timaeus* (Bloomington: Indiana University Press, 1999), 56.

55 Cornford, *Plato's Cosmology*, 28ff.

56 J. G. Fichte, *Science of Knowledge*, trans. and ed. Peter Heath and John Lachs (Cambridge: Cambridge University Press, 1982), 17.

57 Appended to Schelling's *Timaeus* essay (1794) (1994), 121–2.

58 Immanual Kant *Critique of Judgment*, trans. Werner S. Pluhar (Indianapolis: Hackett, 1987), 182.

59 Immanual Kant, *Lectures on Metaphysics*, trans. Karl Ameriks and Steve Naragon (Cambridge: Cambridge University Press, 1997), 419.

60 See Plotinus *Enniads* I.8.ii, III.4.iii, V.1.ix, and, especially, II.4.iv: 'Further, if there is an intelligible universal order [*kosmos noetos*] There, and this universe

here is an imitation of it, and this is composite, and composed of matter, then there must be Matter There too. Or else how can you call it a universal order except with regard to its form?' and II.4.v: 'intelligible matter [*noetois hules*]'.

61 Proclus, *Commentaries on the Timaeus*, 1.

62 Heidegger gives the clearest example of what Proclus calls 'illiteracy' and Schelling calls 'the common deficiency of modern European philosophy', in *The Fundamental Concepts of Metaphysics*: 'The *phusiologoi* are neither "physiologists" in the contemporary sense of physiology as a special science of general biology ... nor are they philosophers of nature. The *phusiologoi* is rather the genuine primordial title for those who speak out about *phusis*' (*Fundamental Concepts of Metaphysics: World, Finitude, Solitude*, trans. William McNeill and Nicholas Walker (Bloomington and Indianapolis: Indiana University Press, 1995), 28).

63 See Schelling, F., *Ergänzungsband zu Werke Band 5 bis 9: Wissenschaftlicher Bericht zu Schellings Naturphilosophischen Schriften 1797–1800*, eds Manfred Durner, Francesco Moiso and Jörg Jantzen (Stuttgart-Bad Canstatt: Frommann-Holzboog, 1994), 60–5 and *passim*. See also *Philebus*, 24a–30a.

64 This occurs most overtly in Schelling's *Freedom* essay, VII, 360, 374; HF, 35, 50–1, but also at II, 20, 106; HF, 15, 144; II, 356.

65 Badiou, A., *Deleuze: the Clamor of Being*, trans. Louise Burchill (Minneapolis: University of Minnesota Press, 2000), 101.

66 For the indefinite dyad in Deleuze and Guattari, see their *What is Philosophy?* 38ff: 'The plane of immanence has two facets as Thought and Nature, as *Nous* and as *Phusis*', write Deleuze and Guattari (*What is Philosophy*, 38). The standard modern derivation of this diphasic single substance is Spinoza's *deus sive natura*; but its true root is the classical One-Many relation stemming from Plato – as it is for Schelling. The overlooking of this in both cases, although especially in the former, is due, as Badiou is correct to note, to our 'not having done with overturning Platonism' (*Clamor of Being*, 102).

67 Echoed by Schelling: 'matter is precisely just matter, that is, the basis of bodies, but immediately therefore, not corporeal' (X, 328).

68 Alcinous, *The Handbook of Platonism*, 67.

69 *Physiologia: Natural Philosophy in Late Aristotelian and Cartesian Thought* (Ithaca NY and London: Cornell University Press, 1996), 2.

70 Immanuel Kant *The Metaphysical Foundations of Natural Science*, trans. James Ellington (Indianapolis and New York: Bobbs-Merrill, 1970), 8–9.

71 Omnès, *Quantum Philosophy*, 229.

72 IV, 5; although at III, 324n., Schelling questions the grounds for this dynamic identity.

73 Ritter, J. W., *Entdeckungen zur Elektrochemie, Bioelektrochemie und Photochemie*, eds Hermann Berg and Klaus Richter (Leipzig: Akademische Verlagsgesellschaft/ Geest & Portig, 1986), 87.

74 Kant, I., *Critique of Pure Reason*, trans. Paul Guyer and Allen W. Wood (Cambridge: Cambridge University Press, 1998), A370.

7

SCHELLING AND SARTRE ON BEING AND NOTHINGNESS

Manfred Frank
Translated and edited by Judith Norman

At several critical junctures in my Schelling book,[1] I draw upon some revealing parallels with Jean-Paul Sartre's *Being and Nothingness: An Essay on Phenomenological Ontology*.[2] Schelling's theory of our understanding of the existence of other subjects is extraordinarily similar to Sartre's critique of Hegel's 'master and slave', and even more similar to what I, following Sartre, have called the 'ontological proof of reflection'. In addition, both Sartre and Schelling (in his later philosophy) make identical appeals to the two ways in which something can be considered a 'ground' (a ground of knowing and a ground of being). Schelling conceives of the transition from the 'noetic result' in consciousness to 'real time' in a manner very similar to Sartre. As several readers have noted that I borrow Sartre's 'operative concepts' to interpret Schelling's basic intellectual operations, it is only right that I make some of these loans explicit. So, in what follows, I will discuss the interaction between the two ways of being a ground, the theory of the pre-reflexive cogito, the ontological proof, and Sartre's distinction between two ways of non-being (*Nicht-Sein*). It will be easy to see why this comparison really clarifies our understanding of Schelling; but when it comes to a distinction between two ways of not being a being (*Nichtseiendem*) (*ouk on* and *me on*) it is, on the contrary, Schelling who can help Sartre make important distinctions.

[. . .]

Gerhard Seel, in what is currently the best German-language book on Sartre's philosophy,[3] suggested that Sartre's method be interpreted as dialectical. Here, this notoriously obscure term just means that there is a real interference between two realms of being; in the present case: between the *en-soi* (in-itself) and the *pour-soi* (for-itself). A movement in one leaves traces in the other. But also: what now looks like a movement in the *en-soi* (because our speculative gaze has been focused on it) proves equally to be a structural alteration in the *pour-soi*. And thus the dialectical ball keeps flying back and forth. (When it comes to the quick-witted Sartre, you have to be a deft and agile player in order to stay on the ball and keep up with his rapid dodges.)

To begin with, let me sketch a rough outline of the steps traced by the 'Introduction' to *Being and Nothingness*. They are called (with a nod to Proust) 'The Pursuit of Being' ('A la recherche de l'être') (BN 3). The discussion starts with the 'phenomenon' and how contemporary phenomenology has succeeded in getting past all possible dualisms, such as those of being and mere appearance, inner and outer, act and *potentia*, force and effect, and so forth. We are clear that 'being' has no meaning for us if there is nothing to appear. Of genius (as the *potentia* of a person) we only notice what presents itself, which is to say its deeds. We only know forces through their effects – so, for instance, we know the electrical current through something like electrolysis, or, even more simply, through the functioning of the refrigerator or the light bulb. We know the supposedly unfathomable interiority of the subject only from its style (the style of the subject's life, taste, speech, behaviour, and so forth). Accordingly, the theme of being – promised in the announcement of an ontology – seems to merge harmoniously into the project of a phenomenology. Sartre even talks about a new 'monism of the phenomenon' (BN 3).

But then a new dualism unexpectedly emerges: that of essence (as the synthesis of appearances into a conceptualized whole) and individual appearances. This is similar to the Kantian distinction between the manifold of individual appearances and the synthesis of these appearances once they have been unified and conceptualized in the object. The essence, as Sartre says, is 'the synthetic unity of the manifestations' of a thing; and the authority that this unity bestows and establishes is the concept. The appearance's manifold, gathered together into a unity under a concept, is called an object. But 'anyone saying object says probably'.[4] This is because I have never gathered *all* aspects (Husserl calls them profiles) together in my intellectual or sensible eye. An object is always richer than the totality of all the impressions that I can register of it in the course of a perception (or indeed in the course of a life). Sartre talks about a genuine 'inexhaustibility [*inépuisablilité*]' of the appearances of a thing (BN 6), about the genuine 'transcendence' of an object (BN 6). This transcendence moves the intended object outside the scope of the subject: it is something more than the subjective impression that empiricism, à la Berkeley and Hume, wants to reduce it to (BN 6). And thus a dualism of the infinite and finite arises. Certainly, when I have observed a multi-sided briefcase, I can express its 'essence' by means of a concept. But what I am doing is a *'passage à la limite'*, an anticipatory running ahead to the limit at which all information has been exhausted. Sartre called the synthesis of appearances 'the transcendent limit of the synthesis, the reason for it and its end' (BN 18). And it will never be given. So all concept formations are hypotheses: they use the mind's freedom to supplement what the experience of reality does not give them. In Husserl's language objects – unlike consciousness – are never 'adequately' given.

More: anyone saying 'appearance' (be it individual or synthetically united under a concept into a unified essence) is saying: appearance-for-a-*subject*. And with this, the supposed independence of the phenomenon switches in a sudden dialectic over to the subject on whose existence it depends. If there is no subject – if the subject does not have an independent *being* – then there is no phenomenon either.

But things grow worse: among all the phenomena (or appearances), one is special: the phenomenon of 'being'. It is the *esse apparens* (according to the scholastic usage) – being, to the extent that it itself appears. If it did not appear, how could we talk about it? So being's appearing has to correspond to a state of consciousness: while Heidegger would have being appear in the so-called *existentiale*, (which is, above all, understanding and care), Sartre has fun spoiling the appetite of the intellectual elite: being appears in the feelings – and feelings are modes of consciousness – of disgust and boredom. I will not discuss why Sartre picks precisely these feelings (we should bear in mind that, unlike Heidegger, he thinks of being as naked, senseless existence, as something that cannot be digested by the subject and therefore needs to be 'thrown up').[5] If we accept Sartre's claim that there is a consciousness in which being-itself manifests itself, then here we are only concerned about this claim (and not about whether someone might suggest another feeling as the manifestation of being). Now we have reached the point in Sartre's major work where the course is first set. Specifically, Sartre says that *the appearing of being presupposes the being of appearance.*

Not that this will be particularly surprising. In fact, we have already heard that being *qua* existence 'precedes' essence (as the synthesis of appearances). And this claim, which has not yet been demonstrated, must naturally also apply to the relation between the *phenomenon* of being and the *being* of the phenomenon, and, in fact, in such a way that the being of the phenomenon anticipates the phenomenon of being and first lays a foundation for the latter.

And so the dialectical ball returns from phenomenon (which we initially had to think of as independent) to being, which we now experience as providing a basis for essence. (Essence is certainly on the same level as the phenomenon; they are of the same type ('homogenous', Sartre says (BN 7)); the difference between them is only that the phenomenon is an individual appearance and essence is an (ideal) synthesis of all the appearances of an object. That is why the thesis of the ontic primacy of being over essence concerns appearance/phenomenon too, *ipso facto*.) But being-itself, being in-itself (*an-sich*) or rather within-itself (*in-sich*) *does not appear* on its own. It is in no way a quality (*quidditas*) of the object, but rather it is the non-apparent *real* ground of all appearing: 'condition of all development [:] It is being-for-revealing (*être-pour-dévoiler*) and not revealed being (*être dévoilé*)' (BN 8). I can, of course, change the qualities of a thing – for instance, by taking some paper with writing on it, crossing it out, writing on it again, erasing it, and cutting it into pieces or burning it. In doing these things, I am not cutting or burning its existence. Being is in no way something that I can get power over by laying hold of its qualities (its characteristics, the manners in which it appears). It is, in the words of Kant's famous insight, 'not a real predicate'. It does not belong among the qualities that I can articulate about an object. Because I can only say about something (*ti kata tinos*) *what* that something is: in other words, its essence (as – we already know – the synthetic unity of its appearances which belong to it as so many qualities).

[. . .]

So the difference between existence and essence is not like the difference between two concepts, but rather like the difference between actuality and concept: they have nothing in common although the latter refers to the former. I can change the outer shape of an object (like the piece of paper) as much as I want, but I will not disturb its being in the least. It will not dissolve into any of the parts or the appearances of the object – it remains whole and undivided down to the atom. Yet the paper (along with all its ways of appearing, down to the smallest atom) simply *would not be* if it lacked existence. So, being-as-appearance (*esse apparens*) seems to require something that does not appear, a subsistent being, as its ontic presupposition. Appearance (and with it, the appearing being, the *phenomenon* of being) 'needs in turn a being, on the basis of which (*sur le fondement duquel*) it can reveal itself [i.e. come to appear]' (BN 8). In an analogy with Anselm of Canterbury's ontological proof of the existence of God, Sartre calls this (ontic) dependence of the *phenomenon* of being on the *being* of the phenomenon, the 'ontological proof'. In it, appearances call for their *being*: 'it requires, as phenomenon, a foundation which is transphenomenal' (BN 9). Thus, the dialectical ball is suddenly thrown – it seems – from the subject back to being.

To recapitulate: the first step was to remove ontology through a monism of the phenomenon: being *is* only as appearing. This was the position of (Husserlian) phenomenology. Then it became evident that something can only be a phenomenon *for somebody*, which is to say for a subject. Now it seems (third) that the appearance would dissolve into nothingness if it were not ontically grounded in being. So now all eyes are fixed on the *subject*. Either it can give the phenomenon back the foundation in being that it lacks (in which case being would be located in the subject, and it would make sense for the subject to be considered a philosophical point of departure). Or – second possibility – it is evident that the subject (as an empty appearing-to-self which has to leave all content *outside* itself) is also ontically dependent on a being that it has to look for outside its own sphere. And then the effect of the 'ontological proof' on the subject would be ultimately to force it to hand over the baton of independence to subsistent being.

But for the time being it looks to the contrary as if there is no phenomenon (thus no appearing, and so no appearing of being) other than *for a subject*. And since the subject – as the place where all appearing becomes comprehensible – is the nerve-centre in which all questions of comprehensibility must be decided, we can also confidently delegate the question of being to the subject. Only here can the decision be made as to what should receive the honour of priority. The elegance of Sartre's 'ontological argument' consists in the fact that it allows *the proof of the ontic priority of being over appearing* (and, since all appearing is only for-a-consciousness, over self-consciousness as well) to be adduced from *the Cartesian evidence of self-consciousness itself*. Descartes' claim means not only 'cogito', but rather 'cogito, ergo *sum*': it implies a guarantee of being ... Now we should understand what Sartre makes of the existential implications of self-consciousness.

The idealistic position, into whose vortex we have been drawn, makes being dependent on being knowable. That is the position of the bishop Berkeley quoted by Sartre: *'esse est percipi'* (which means: to be is to be known).[6] Being can be accepted only relative to a consciousness that derives knowledge from it. But then the question suddenly arises about knowledge itself: *is* it (BN 10)? The answer to this question is clearly either 'yes' or 'no'. First possibility: no, knowledge itself *is not*; then being would be grounded in a nothingness (*Néant*), in a relative non-being: a *reductio ad absurdum*. Second possibility: yes, knowledge (on which we could ground the thought of being) *is*. Now for the sake of consistency we would once more have to employ the definition of being used above (that to be is to be known) and say: the being of knowledge also comes from being known. Again, we come to the same alternative: the knowing (the *perci*piens), in which the *being* of the previous knowing is founded, *is* it or is it *not*? And through a renewed application of Berkeley's formula *'esse est percipi'* we come to an infinite regress in which being is left incomplete, and with it also *that* being without which an idealistic position could never be consistently carried through: namely the being of the knowing subject.

Now if we accept Descartes' conclusion 'cogito sum' as certain (and that means as an unshakable truth), then the being of consciousness must be grounded in something other than another consciousness. To be more exact: there must be a consciousness whose *being* would resist being reflexively appropriated by another consciousness. In other words, there must be a consciousness whose awareness of itself does not rest on needing another (second) consciousness to reflexively thematize it in the first place. Now if we define 'knowledge [*connaissance*]' as the explicit reference of consciousness to something different from itself (including to another consciousness that is numerically distinct from itself), then we have to say: self-consciousness cannot be a type of self-knowledge. Because the *being* of consciousness could only be saved if the subject-pole of the consciousness could *not* be separated from the object-pole. In other words: in the case of a *being* of consciousness, the proposition *'esse est percipi'* must be suspended with respect to the awareness that consciousness has of itself. Consciousness must be certain of its being, without making itself into an object. *If* consciousness *is*, then this cannot be in such a manner that its being can be the *object* of an act of knowledge. So the self-knowledge (that most assuredly exists) must be grounded in an *im*mediate self-consciousness in which the subject and object of consciousness *are* one and the same, and know themselves *as such*. And this immediate consciousness (which is untouched by any mediation) is, according to Sartre, the very 'trans-phenomenal dimension of the being of the subject' that we are looking for.

Since we absolutely must accord to consciousness-of-self a mode of being that is not to be objectified, we are in a position to understand another theme: remember that we are alerted to the transcendence of the object by the fact that it is always more than the set of subjective appearances through which it makes itself known to us. That is why it is true that 'anyone saying object says merely what is probable' (*'celui qui dit "objet," dit probable'*: CC 51,6). The mere probability of object awareness is connected with the fact that something about the object is always lacking for me, something that I must ideally complete through a *passage à la limite*. That is why no perception of the object is adequate, let alone apodictic. But precisely these characteristics are true of subject- (or self-) consciousness: it is given as apodictic to itself and adequate, where 'adequate' means: immediately in all of its aspects. For this reason alone, self-consciousness could never be a consciousness of objects; and for this reason alone, the subject could never have any content (or rather: every content must be *external* to it: kept far away, on the side of the object). Sartre occasionally says: every object is 'a center of opacity for consciousness; it would require an infinite process to inventory the total contents of a thing' (BN 11). No, the subject is not characterized by opacity, but rather by transparency. It cannot 'ignore' any of its aspects. It is entirely apparent to itself. Where 'itself' means: not with its contents on the side of objects – which, according to Sartre, includes everything 'psychic' that 'psycho'-analysis investigates. Sartre calls this reference to something outside-yourself the transcendence of consciousness or – with Husserl – intentionality.[7]

[. . .]

[T]he self-transparency of self-consciousness is bought at the cost of the self-consciousness having no content in or through itself. It is totally insubstantial or empty (like the Kantian 'I think', in fact; it does not even have a Husserlian *hyle* (see BN 20)). All content must be given to it from outside.[8] This is true of its acquaintance with being too. If being were literally to enter consciousness, then, as Sartre says with a drastic metaphor,[9] it would spoil the transparency of consciousness, as if an opaque blade were slid into it and set up an inner contradiction in it. Apart from this, the presupposition still holds that being and essence are heterogeneous: they have absolutely nothing in common. But consciousness is pure appearing-to-itself, which is to say: a being-for-self. Descartes, Sartre says, did not deal carefully enough with the evidentiary experience of the cogito: he made it into a substance or thing ('*substantia*' or '*res cogitans*'): he reified it. But self-consciousness is an '*Absolutum*' in that it is not comprehensible in relation to anything (it is non-relative, which means: absolute). I quote Sartre:

> Likewise it is a non-substantial absolute. The ontological error of Cartesian rationalism is not to have seen that if the absolute is defined by the primacy of existence over essence, it can not be conceived as a substance. Consciousness has nothing substantial, it is pure 'appearance' in the sense that it exists only to the degree to which it appears. But it is precisely because consciousness is pure appearance, because it is total emptiness (since the entire world is outside it) – it is because of this identity of appearance and existence within it that it can be considered as the absolute. (BN 17)

So self-transparency belongs to self-consciousness along with certainty of being. It *too* makes self-consciousness conscious of the fact that it is empty, insubstantial, outwardly in reference to being, but itself not a being. It is – compared to a being in the emphatic sense – a non-being, the *néant*. Consciousness understands itself as relative nothingness, and it can precisely thereby hand over ontic primacy to being. Through this renunciation it can even make its epistemological structure intelligible: because something itself lacking content, something that has to draw its content from somewhere else, exists as intentionality. And now we can in conclusion explain how consciousness is ontically dependent while at the same time transcendentally independent of being: consciousness arises in an intentional relation to a being (and is carried by it: *portée sur*), that is not the same as itself (BN 22f.). To say that consciousness is ontically dependent on being is not to say that it is comprehensible through the thought of being: expressed transcendentally, 'nothing is the cause of consciousness'. And if we admit that it is not the cause of its being (but rather ontically dependent on it), then it is unproblematically 'cause of its own way of being' (BN 16n.). We can then provisionally determine it as a non-being (compared to the true being) that can do nothing to its being, but is accountable for everything *that* it lets happen to being (moreover, it is *what* interprets being: consciousness has a monopoly on hermeneutics).

The 'ontological proof' of consciousness would be more appropriately called the 'me-ontological proof'. It implies that consciousness is ontically dependent on being due to its 'absolute emptiness and insubstantiality'. If consciousness is insubstantial but in an intentional relation to subsistent being, then the latter's existential characteristics can be derived negatively (*per contrarium*). 1. 'Substantiality' or 'independence' (BN 27: 'it [*l'être-en-soi*] is its own support'). 2. Having the identity or simplicity of the *en-soi* ('the principle of identity ... is also a regional synthetical principle of being' (BN 28)): being is what it is, it is the same as itself, it is completely filled by itself, it has no emptiness or internal differentiation. Since all determination

is negation, then 3. being-in-itself is undetermined or indifferent to determinations: 'it is itself indefinitely and it exhausts itself in being' (BN 29). 4.
The en-soi is characterized by actuality: '[Being in-itself] can neither be
derived from the possible nor reduced to the necessary': it is actual ('*en acte*')
and contingent, where 'contingent' means: not ennobled by a potentiality or
any sort of 'necessary' ground. In short: all the characteristics of being-in-
itself are in contradiction to those of consciousness: it is filled with itself, it is
pure position and positivity, it is absolutely and unvaryingly together-with-
itself, it is wholly unconscious and independent of all determinations. It does
not need consciousness to subsist; in contrast, consciousness *would not be* (as
the 'ontological proof' holds) without the *en-soi*, 'on which it is directed and
by which it is carried'. But this does not mean that being-in-itself would
achieve the status of '*phenomenon* of being' without the help of consciousness,
that a (Heideggerian) disclosedness (*Erschlossenheit*) would come to it from
somewhere other than consciousness. But since consciousness – opposed to
being in every respect – is an empty void, we need a fuller determination of
its 'me-ontological' status (and here we can throw light on Sartre using a
central distinction from Schelling's late philosophy).

Sartre first distinguishes between two ways in which we can talk about
'nothing': between nothing as '*néant*' and as '*rien*' (BN 48). Each is (in
comparison with being en-soi) non *being*. 'It is striking in this connection',
Sartre writes 'that language furnishes us with a nothingness of *things* and
("*Rien*") a nothingness of human beings ("*Personne*")' (BN 48). However, the
non-being of things (their non-existence) and the negation of the presence of
people ('nobody') occur on the basis of a preceding being.

> This means that being is prior to nothingness and establishes the
> ground for it. By this we must understand not only that being has a
> logical precedence over nothingness but also that it is from being that
> nothingness derives concretely its efficacy. This is what we mean when
> we say that *nothingness haunts being*. That means that being has no need
> of nothingness in order to be conceived and that we can examine the
> idea of it exhaustively without finding there the least trace of noth-
> ingness. but on the other hand, nothingness, *which is not*, can have only
> a borrowed existence, and it gets its being from being. Its nothingness
> of being is encountered only within the limits of being, and the total
> disappearance of being would not be the advent of the reign of non-
> being, but on the contrary the concomitant disappearance of noth-
> ingness. *Non-being exists only on the surface of being.* (BN 49)

I think that Sartre's idea is understandable: the *néant* that we came to
know as consciousness (transparent to itself, empty, insubstantial) is the
ground of both negation and of what Sartre calls mundane, negative magnitudes (*négatités*) (BN 56)[10] such as uncertainty, resistance, prohibition,
denial, inconsistency, unfaithfulness, inaccessibility, fragility, and so forth –

entities that feign some negative in-itself by virtue of their quasi-objectivity. Still, we are well aware that such entities can come into the world only through a being whose existential characteristic is to be a *néant d'être*, which is to say a being that denies its *own en-soi* and, through negation, gives determination to *those* beings that it relates intentionally to (in accordance with Spinoza's famous phrase, '*omnis determinatio est negatio*' (BN 47)). But now the question arises of the sense in which this being *is*, if it is characterized by the fact that it refuses being. And at this point, the distinction between '*rien*' and '*néant*' can be referred to that between absolute and relative nothingness.

It clearly makes sense to say: 'there *is* consciousness'. But *how* is there consciousness when its ontological characteristic is 'to-be-nothing' (or more precisely, 'to-be-nothing-en-soi')? We have already gained some insight into this from the ontological (or better: me-ontological) proof. The nothing-in-being that we know as consciousness *exists* as supported by (and intentionally related to) a being that it itself is not. This is what Sartre means when he writes that the being of consciousness is a borrowed being. And this is what he means when he appeals to formulas that are not immediately intelligible, like '*être été*', consciousness being 'made-to-be':[11] 'Nothingness is not, Nothingness "is made-to-be", Nothingness does not nihilate itself; Nothingness "is nihilated" '(BN 58). In German [and English] there simply is no passive voice for the verb 'to be'. That is why Schelling had resuscitated the medieval '*wesen*'[12] when he wanted to say that consciousness being itself robbed of independent being, needs to be supported and carried by a being that is in-itself if it is not to dissolve into 'nothing at all' (*rien*). So consciousness is transitively 'made-to-be' by a being, and is thus maintained in its quasi-being.

In his *Aphorisms on the Philosophy of Nature* (of 1806) Schelling already had tried to describe the pantheistic idea that God's being is actively at work in all creation by using a bold, transitive formulation of 'to be', followed by an accusative. (Sartre will do the same when he says 'I do not *have* my body, I *am* my body.') Schelling writes:

> The sentence: A is B, in fact says nothing other than: A is the *esse* (the being [*Wesenheit*]) of B (which as would not *be* for itself as such; but *is* by virtue of the connection with A). This is the meaning of the sentence: *God is all things*, which in Latin is not expressed by *est res cunctae* as well as (*invita latinitate*) by *est res cunctas*. (SW I/7, 205, n. 1)[13]

More about this transitive meaning of being can be found in Schelling's later work, for instance in lectures 10 and 11 from his *Philosophy of Revelation* (SW II/3, 217ff. (on the meaning of identity as substantial) and particularly 227 ff.). There, Schelling compares being 'in a *transitive* sense' (227; see also II/1, 293) to the faculty or ability to do something. In Arabic, the copula 'is' is even constructed with the accusative as if it were the faculty, the potentiality of having been by it. So an Arab would not say '*homo est sapiens*', but something more like '*homo est sapientem*'. And this nuance implies that a human is not wise pure and simple, but rather only that he has the potential, the faculty, the possibility to be wise (while in reality he very rarely comes across that way). This is just what Sartre means: the *en-soi* works transitively in consciousness (which is lacking its own being) and in so doing lends it that little bit of being or quasi-being that it needs in order not to entirely lack all potential and be no being at all, which is to say *rien* or *ouk on*.

Unfortunately, the German language does not offer any distinction comparable to the Greek. Greeks distinguished between the *me on* and the *ouk on*. The former is non-being as compared to an emphatic being (comparative), such as when I respond to the question: 'so how was your exam?' with the answer: 'oh, it was nothing!' which does not mean that the exam did not exist at all (that is, did not take place) or that I failed to write a single line, but rather that in comparison to the standards that I set for myself, the outcome was trivial, not worth talking about. We can understand Gottfried Keller's famous verse in the same sense: 'a single day can be a pearl / and a century nothing', by which he does not mean that a hundred years fail to pass, but rather that they are not worth mentioning. *Ouk on*, not at all and being in no respect is, by contrast, the exclusive property of nothingness: things that I just hallucinate: a unicorn, the Matterhorn in the lecture hall, a square circle, and heaven on earth. In discussing creation out of nothing (although the context is not of interest here) Schelling makes the very useful distinction between non-being and something that just is not a *being*. Particularly in his *Presentation of Philosophical Empiricism* (in a Munich lecture from 1836) he does this in an entirely Sartrean sense, even defining terms in the same way. I will quote two lengthy passages that are enormously useful in understanding the Sartrean concept of Néant:

> To denote things that are not beings in the primary sense (that is, *conscious* of themselves), I could say that, in *contrast* or comparison to these primary beings, they are not *beings*, which only expresses a relative non-being and is certainly fine to say that they are, in themselves or when compared with themselves alone, not nothing, but by all means something – something that is. *In this sense*, Greek philosophers have discussed *me on* which has seemed contradictory to many since they are talking about non beings as if they somehow are. The explanation for this contraction can be found in Plutarch, who says at one point: you must distinguish between *me einai*, non-being, and *me on einai*, not being a being. For the Greeks, something that is not a being only means something that is not a being in a higher and pre-eminent sense; it does not mean something that is not a being at all. In this sense, the recognition that things that are not beings are beings too is one of the first steps to true knowledge (SW I/10, 235)[14]
> ... But the *ouk on* is entirely and in every sense a *noṇ* being – it is denied not only the *actuality* of being but also being overall, which is to

say possibility as well. What is denoted by the expression *me on* is denied only the *position*, the actual positing of being – but in order for this to be denied to it, it has to be in a certain manner. But in the expression *ouk on*, the negation of being is *affirmed* and even posited. I think I can prove that the distinction between the two negated particles refers to this, by the fact that the *me* is explicitly used in imperatives that mention something that is still to come and has not happened (and consequently has not been posited) but can happen. When I say: do not do that, this only means: do not let the action be posited; I thus deny in the soul of what is discussed only the position, the actuality of the action, and presuppose its possibility, because I would not otherwise forbid it. Another example! If someone has an intention to act, such as having decided to commit a crime but not having carried it out, I could easily say in Greek: *me epoiese*, because he only has not *done* it yet, only the execution, the actual occurrence, the position is denied; but when the crime has been committed and the perpetrator is in doubt, people will have to say about those who did not even formulate the intention, and who are therefore denied even the possibility of the crime: *ouk epoiese . . .*

One could cite the fact that in French, for instance, 'nothing' in the *genuine* sense, the *ouk on*, is expressed through a particular word (*rien*) and what simply does not have *being* is expressed through another (*le Néant*). Accordingly, if someone were to say that it is doubtful what sort of nothing is at issue in the idea of a creation out of nothing, I would answer that this is not doubtful, because it can be correct that God both created the world from nothing (*de rien*) and that he pulled it from something that did not have being (the *Néant*); in fact, according to the universally accepted conception, both *are* correct. (SW I/10, 283–5; see II/1, 288f. and 307[ff.])

I think that Schelling's explanation is really lucid and a great help in understanding Sartre's concept of the subject. Sartre's idea of the subject includes being (Schelling would say: being in the pre-eminent or emphatic sense). But this being is not the subject's own. The subject is an ontically dependent quality that helps being appear: that is – since appearances are 'ways of being' or quiddities – it allows it to have a What, an essence. But the subject *is* in some sense – it is not that it is nothing at all; it is just not a *being* itself, but rather exists as ek-static (intentional) reference to a being. The How of its being (in other words: its way of being) is being-made-to-be-by-the-*en-soi*. The subject is nothing compared with the en-soi; but it is not *so much* of a nothing that it *is* not in a particular sense. And this sense – once more – is that of *être été par l'En-soi*.

If you have any more patience (and it will be rewarded), I would like to give Schelling another word, since his late ontology has, of all that I know, the most stupendous similarities to that of the early Sartre. Like Sartre,

Schelling distinguished between 'different species of being' (SW II/1, 288).
He explains quite vividly:

> ...the inorganic has one way of being and the organic another, in
> whose cycle plants have yet another and animals another still. But who
> does not feel that these species of being could not possibly be original?
> We should rather assume that these species, which we learn about
> through experience, are ultimately derived from original, non-
> contingent differences that belong to the nature of being itself. This is
> because the differences are apparent to even basic observation. Who
> could say, for instance, that the pure *subject* of being is not itself a
> being, without admitting instead that precisely this is the first pos-
> sibility of being, namely to be a subject. Because whatever is an object
> presupposes what it is an object of. So a subject cannot at the same time
> *be* a being, and it is posited as having a deficiency, but it is deprived of
> only a particular *species* of being, not being overall, because how could
> something that is a complete non-being also be a subject? The subject
> has one type of being, the object another; if we do not mind using
> unfamiliar expressions, we could (with Novalis) call it pure *wesende*;[15] it
> will also seem unfamiliar to many if we call the one static [*gegen-
> ständliches*] and the other ex-static [*urständliches*] being; but it will be
> understood if we say that with the one species, being is just *itself* and
> with the other it is *outside* itself.
>   A deficiency is therefore posited with the pure subject: but defi-
> ciency is not an unconditional negation, but rather contains an affir-
> mation of another sort in itself, as we will show when the time comes
> ...not being (*me einai*) is not being nothing (*ouk einai*), since Greek has
> the advantage of being able to express the contradictory and merely
> contrary negation of each through its own particle. The mere deficiency
> of being does not exclude ability-to-be. Pure *ability* (and we can
> determine the pure subject as this) is non-being. (SW II/1, 288/9)

And Schelling quotes book IV of Aristotle's *Metaphysics* (IV, 4, 73, 1–3)
where the *dunamei on* is identified with the *me on*. Sartre's subject is just such
a being according to its ability. It is – in Schellingian vocabulary – indeed
deficient in being-*en-soi*, but is not for that matter *non*-existent, which is to
say: without any reference to existence. Itself evacuated of all *être en-soi*, it
refers itself to the thing that allows it – as potency (ideal ground) of being –
to 'be made to be [*wesen*]'. So being – *toto coelo* different in kind from
consciousness, with which it has nothing in common – is its ground of
being. And since consciousness *refers to being* (and thus guards itself against
descending into nothing), it makes being appear and thus be known. Thus it
is, although ontically dependent, nonetheless the ideal ground or epistemic
ground of the *en-soi*. Or: it is through consciousness that outward know-
ablility (Heidegger would say: disclosedness (*Erschlossenheit*), intelligibility

(*Verständlichkeit*)) occurs to being, which itself exists apart from consciousness. By the way, this entails that consciousness *as* subject of being is
independent with respect to being. The fact that it is empty or insubstantial
or *néant* does not accrue to it through being (how would that be possible,
since being is pure position, pure positivity and fullness?); rather it is its own
doing (and, as we will show later, the ground of its being *free*). This is what
Sartre says in the passage that I interrupted by the terminological excursus
into Schelling's late work:

> Nothingness is not, Nothingness 'is made-to-be,' Nothingness does
> not nihilate itself; Nothingness 'is nihilated.' It follows therefore that
> there must exist a Being (this can not be the In-itself) of which the
> property is to nihilate Nothingness, to support it in its being, to
> sustain it perpetually in its very existence, *a being by which nothingness
> comes to things*. But how can this Being be related to Nothingness so
> that through it Nothingness comes to things? We must observe first
> that the being postulated can not be passive in relation to Nothingness,
> it can not receive it; Nothingness could not *come* to this being except
> through another Being – which would be an infinite regress. But on
> the other hand, the Being by which Nothingness comes to the world
> can not *produce* Nothingness while remaining indifferent to that pro-
> duction – like the Stoic cause which produces its effect without being
> itself changed. It would be inconceivable that a Being which is full
> positivity should maintain and create outside itself a Nothingness or
> transcendent being, for there would be nothing in Being by which
> Being could surpass itself toward Non-Being. The Being by which
> Nothingness arrives in the world must nihilate Nothingness in its
> Being, and even so it still runs the risk of establishing Nothingness as a
> transcendent in the very heart of immanence unless it nihilates
> Nothingness in its being *in connection with its own being*. The Being by
> which Nothingness arrives in the world is a being such that in its
> Being, the Nothingness of its Being is in question. *The being by which
> Nothingness comes to the world must be its own Nothingness*. By this we must
> understand not a nihilating act, which would require in turn a foun-
> dation in Being, but an ontological characteristic of the Being
> required. It remains to learn in what delicate, exquisite region of
> Being we shall encounter that Being which is its own Nothingness.
> (BN 57–8)

Let us not get upset about Sartre's many equivocal uses of the expression
'to be' (which stands, alternatively, for a way of being, an essence, a being, for
reality altogether, or for the *en-soi*). The meaning of the passage is nonetheless clear. The *néant* naturally cannot be the doing of the *en-soi*. For one
thing, the *en-soi* is *toto coelo* different from the *néant* (they are as radically
distinct from each other as sensibility and understanding are for Kant). For

another, a pure fullness of being cannot create a lack of being. Nonetheless, Sartre talks about a 'being' that comes into the world through the nothing. And this being, which the concluding sentence makes us curious about, is naturally the subject (later called the *pour-soi*). It is the subject through which the nothing appears in the world. Consequently, the nothing is a structural element of self-consciousness and has no independent existence apart from it (as was the case with the *en-soi*). But we need to pay attention to something else as well: the being through which nothing comes into the world – that is, the subject – 'must [Sartre says] be its own nothing'. At first, this sounds incomprehensible. But it follows logically as a consequence of the insight that – if there are only two types of being, the *en-soi* and the *pour-soi*, and no third, and if the *en-soi cannot* be its ground – then nothing could only come into the world through the subject. And then the relative nothingness of the subject – Schelling would say: the fact that it is not *being itself* – must be its own doing. Put another way, the subject determines itself not to *be* (thus to be a *'néant de son propre être'*) or – as this is just saying the same thing in a different way – to exist as an intentional reference to the *en-soi* (and literally to ek-sist: that is, to stand outside of itself, to be ecstatically open to being). And this self-negation and self-imposed deprivation of being is the seed of the subject's *freedom*, for Sartre no less than for Schelling, the other great theorist of freedom in the tradition. (Remember the excellent, striking formulation, that the subject does not have its being in being *itself*, but rather in being *outside itself*. Schelling elsewhere says the same thing as Sartre, it is the essence of the ex-static, and thus non-hypostasized subject to be 'the nothing of itself' (Pos. Ph. 423).)

Earlier, in the chapter on the pre-reflexive cogito, Sartre emphasized this quality of self-determination (as ontological harbinger of the structure later to be revealed as freedom). This will be entirely comprehensible only to those familiar with Sartre's philosophy of self-consciousness as stated in the early works such as *Transcendence of the Ego* and especially in *Consciousness of Self and Knowledge of Self*. But *you* certainly remember this: in the dialectical struggle for (priority in) independence that went back and forth between the *en-soi* and the subject, the subject seemed at first to have won with the thesis that it alone has a being that is not mediated through an appearing-for-others. In the world, it might be true that 'being = being-known' (Berkeley's *'esse est percipi'*)[16] (since how would we encounter being if it were not a possible object of experience?). In the subject, being and being-disclosed are one and the same. And it is true of the subject – and *only* of the subject – that in it, *being* is measured in being *conscious*. This means, that it is enough to be conscious of your being in love in order to really be in love; and it is enough to feel conscious of a desire in order to really have that desire. Sartre writes in the chapter on 'the pre-reflexive cogito and the being of the *percipere*':

> There is no more first a consciousness which receives *subsequently* the affect 'pleasure' like water which one stains, than there is first a pleasure

(unconscious or psychological) which receives subsequently the quality of 'consciousness' like a pencil of light rays. There is an indivisible, indissoluble being – definitely not a substance supporting its qualities like particles of being, but a being which is existence through and through. Pleasure is the being of self-consciousness and this self-consciousness is the law of being of pleasure. This is what Heidegger expressed very well when he wrote (though speaking of *Dasein*, not of consciousness): 'The "how" (*essentia*) of this being, so far as it is possible to speak of it generally, must be conceived in terms of its existence (*existentia*).' This means that consciousness is not produced as a particular instance of an abstract possibility but that in rising to the center of being, it creates and supports its essence – that is, the synthetic order of its possibilities. (BN 15)

Naturally, Heidegger would never allow Sartre to confuse the notion of 'existence [*Existenz*]' with the scholastic '*existentia*' which means *quodditas* (that something is). And he would feel himself totally misrepresented (1) when Sartre places this quote in the context of self-consciousness (which is precisely what Heidegger wanted to get away from) and (2) when Sartre wants to use his thesis of the priority of existence (*that* something is) over essence (*what* it is) in order to explain the freedom of the subject. Sartre's real but unconscious model here as elsewhere is Schelling, who understood freedom as the independence of the essence from the That, and spoke of the subject's '*freedom from its own being*' (Pos. Ph. 443); he also said: '*Man must tear himself loose from his being in order to begin a free being ... To free yourself from yourself* is the task of all education.'[17]

[...]

Notes

1   [Translator: Frank is referring to *Der unendliche Mangel an Sein: Schellings Hegelkritik und die Anfänge der Marxschen Dialektik*, 2nd edn (extensively expanded and reworked), (Munich: Wilhelm Fink Verlag, 1992). The present essay is taken from part III of the introduction to that book (pp. 50–92). The parallels are drawn in Chapter 3 (Section 3), Chapter 4 (Section 2) and Chapter 8 (Section 1).]

2   [Translator: All references are to the English translation (BN) by Hazel E. Barnes (New York: Philosophical Library, 1966).]

3   *Sartre's Dialektik. Zur Methode und Begründung seiner Philosophie unter besonderer Berücksichtigung der Subjekts-, Zeit- und Vertherie* (Bonn: Bouvier, 1971).

4   'Conscience de soi et connaissance de soi' ['Self-consciousness and Self-knowledge'] in: *Bulletin de la Société Française de Philosophy*, vol. 42, 1948, 49–91 (quoted as CC), here pp. 51–3; compare 64. This important text was reprinted in a volume: *Selbstbewußtseins-Theorien von Fichte bis Sartre* (Frankfurt: Deutscher Klassiker, 1991) which I edited and provided commentary for.

5   This feeling is described in the famous scene of *Nausea*. Sartre's model is the phenomenological analysis of a Hungarian author in the *Jahrbuch für*

Phänomenologie und phänomenologische Forschung, in which vol. 1 of Husserl's *Ideas* and Heidegger's *Being and Time* also appeared: and thus in the journal of the phenomenological school.

6   [Translator: 'Sein ist erkannt werden.' Berkeley's famous comment is usually and better rendered into English as 'To be is to be perceived' but both Frank and Sartre rely on a distinction common to French and German – but missing in English – between objective knowledge (*Wissen* or *savoir*) and 'acquaint-anceship' (*Erkennen* or *conaissance*) using the latter terms to translate Berkeley's *percipi*.]

7   See Sartre's lively and intuitive short essay, 'A Fundamental Idea in Husserl's Phenomenology: Intentionality,' in: *Situations*, I (Paris: Gallimard, 1947), 29–32.

8   In *La Transcendence de l'Ego. Esquisse d'une description phénoménologique*, ed. Sylvie le Bon (Paris: Vrin, 1978) (the text itself is from 1936). (*The Transcendence of the Ego: An Existentialist Theory of Consciousness*, trans. Forrest Williams and Robert Kirkpatrick (New York: Farrar, Straus & Giroux, 1960).) Sartre had written 'In one sense, [the transcendental field] is a *void*, since all physical, psychophysical and psychic objects, all truths and all values are external to it.'

9   Ibid., p. 23 (English translation, p. 60).

10   'Nothingness must be given at the heart of Being, in order for us to be able to apprehend that particular type of realities which we have called *négatités*. But this intra-mundane Nothingness can not be produced by Being-in-itself; the notion of Being as full positivity does not contain Nothingness as one of its structures' (BN 56).

11   [Translator: a literal translation of '*être été*' would be something like: 'to be been'. In the standard English translation, Hazel E. Barnes renders the phrase as 'made-to-be' and explains that she is doing this 'because Sartre seems to be using *être* as a transitive verb … in the passive voice, thus suggesting that nothingness has been subjected to an act involving being' (BN 22, n. 14).]

12   [Translator: There is no modern English equivalent of 'wesen', which is most closely related to the term 'gewesen', the German perfect tense of 'to be'. Significantly, used as a noun, 'Wesen' means 'essence'.]

13   All references to Schelling are to *Friedrich Wilhelm Joseph von Schellings sämmtliche werke*, section I vol 1–10, section II vol 1–4, ed R. F. A. Schelling (Stuttgart: Cotta, 1856–61). The section number is given in roman numerals followed by the volume number in arabic numerals.

14   In the original, these lines precede the passage cited above:

> Grammaticians do not seem to have completely sorted out the difference between these two negative particles [*me on* and *ouk on*]; to be clear about this myself, I would ultimately have to resort to my philosophical concepts. Accordingly, I will explain myself as follows. The *me on* is that non-being, that merely does not have being, to which is only denied being that really *is*, but which has the possibility of being a being. So, since it has being as a possibility, the non-being indeed *is*, but it is still not the case that it could not be a being.

15   [Translator: see note 12 above.]

16   [Translator: see note 6 above.]

17   In *Philosophie der Offenbarung* (*Philosophy of Revelation*) (1841–2) (Paulus-Nachschrift), ed. Manfred Frank (Frankfurt: Suhrkamp, 1977); see the introduction for further quotations, p. 66f.

8

SCHELLING'S METAPHYSICS OF EVIL

Joseph P. Lawrence

Hell is ontologically prior to evil.

Unravelling this Schellingian insight assumes monumental importance in the light of the most glaring failure of contemporary thought, the failure to make sense of evil. Left numb by the Holocaust and its repetitions, by wars that have increasingly targeted civilian populations, and, most recently, by the renewal of international terrorism, thinking has by and large reneged upon what is surely its primary duty: to illuminate the frightening abyss of pain and death, so that the brute contingency of existence might be rendered into a clearing fit for living, if not into that which would answer our deepest yearning, the experience of life as something for which we could be genuinely thankful.

Evil is, of course, as old as man. And, one might well enough assume, its depth and scope have expanded as the instruments of power themselves have expanded.

More debatable, perhaps, is the old 'Ring of Gyges' claim from Plato's *Republic*, the claim that power not only extends the reach of evil, but itself has the tendency to corrupt and deform the soul, making it more evil than it already was. A frightening claim for a humanity bound to the principles of state, money, and technology. The goal of bringing everything under rational control has long been identified in our minds with the promise of abolishing evil altogether. Asserting that its pursuit may actually strengthen evil is rather like asserting that the God of our childhood was all along the devil in disguise. Such paradoxical reversals are not appreciated. When it comes to good and evil, we demand simplicity, even in the face of a continuous history of flawed judgments: saints are denigrated; tyrants are idolized. And with such flawed judgment, evil continues its exasperating ascent from the heart of the good.

Nor is the problem solved by following Nietzsche and declaring power itself our good. Even power can disappoint. Not only is it more vulnerable than it would like to admit to outbursts of irrational frenzy, but it seems actively to provoke them.[1] The conduits of universal will, from science to liberal democracy, from machine to money, are held in check by the unspeakable burden of pain that encircles the globe. The result is that vicious dialectic between the narcosis of a mechanized and endlessly self-duplicating form of reason and the irrationally frenzied grip on tradition that a recent commentator has designated the battle between Jihad and McWorld.[2] It is a battle that erupted in flame in the terrorist attacks on New York and Washington. During a few months of fear, Jihad seemed to have scored a victory. But with the scandalously quick return to the orgy of consumption, McWorld proved its resilience.[3]

Jihad and McWorld are possibilities that co-exist within reality itself. From a Schellingian point of view, they can be regarded as perverse distortions of the fundamental polarity that goes through all things. In the early philosophy of nature, Schelling depicted this polarity as the opposition between the forces of contraction and expansion that constitute the field of material reality. In the late philosophy, the polarity recurs in a historical version, as the opposition between the tribal (mythology) and the cosmopolitan (revelation). It is this formulation that comes closest to what is going on in the Jihad–McWorld relationship. To understand Schelling is above all to understand that he is not Hegel: ontological polarity can never be resolved in a developmental process. Mythology is neither subsumed nor obliterated in revelation.[4] Health and perversion reside as possibilities in both principles.

Their perverse manifestations are fully apparent in the contemporary context. While the spirit of Jihad, blinded by the fervour of its love for the particular, is the spirit of hatred and violence, the case of McWorld is harder to assess. Although its moving principle is clearly greed, its cosmopolitan emphasis on toleration and inclusiveness seems to give it a moral advantage – until one realizes that its goal is still domination. Its violence is not directed against any recognizable group, but only against those few and far between who refuse to embrace any group identity whatsoever. 'Be whatever or whoever you want to be, except this one thing: the person who, unique and alone, you yourself really are.' McWorld, together with its post-tribal ethic of endlessly diverse conformities, is what emerges when all limits are removed from capitalism. Within these conformities, the lie is disclosed that capitalism sanctifies the individual.[5] What it in fact sanctifies is the generic, the trademark. What it wants from the individual is only his greed – and not even that in its raw immediacy. When the advertising industry sets out to manufacture desire, its goal is to accommodate it to the range of available commodities. Its actual achievement, however, is something profounder and more dubious: desire is so thoroughly mediated that it becomes a social rather than individual phenomenon. The subject has acquiesced to its own destruction.

On the highest level, Jihad and McWorld reflect a rupture within the nature of God himself. Schelling asserts the assurance of the idealist: 'in the divine understanding there is a system'. Yet, he quickly qualifies it by adding: 'God himself is no system, but a life' (VII, 399). In the language of his metaphysics, there is a tension between the dark ground of reality and its actual (and thus rationally comprehensible) existence. Because reality is construed as becoming, as emergence into existence through the steady (but always incomplete) transformation of ground, this fundamental opposition can also be articulated as a relationship within the heart of temporality. Both Jihad clinging to the past and the McWorld attempt to manufacture the future on the pattern of the present are variations of the same error, the refusal to acknowledge that true origin is radically future. This refusal, and here lies Schelling's great insight, is not wilful and arbitrary obstinacy, but the necessary (and forgivable) consequence of something fear-evoking in the heart of being itself.

I

While other ages look outward, to God, for a guarantee of justice and stability, the modern age looks to humanity and places its faith in science, which seems to operate under the cheerful assumption that the principle of sufficient reason is the only guide we really need. It is this optimistic humanism that Schelling has in mind when he asserts that modernity 'pushes its philanthropism all the way to the denial of evil' (VII, 371). Instead of evil, we have problems. And for problems, explanations can be found, so that technological intervention will provide solutions.

Despite the fact that in peaceful times this is the view that forms the common sense of entire scholarly and scientific disciplines, it can be called naïve – and in a precise philosophical sense: it excludes the lesson of Kant's antinomies.[6] For it is based on the pre-critical belief that reality as a whole is an actually existing object held together by fully discernable causal relations: a given problem (for example melancholy) has a given solution (for instance, Prozac).

When violence rips through this assurance, modernity rediscovers the demonic. A deeper layer of its guiding ideology rises to the surface: order has been fashioned out of chaos. The reassuring idea that the world is rational yields to the desperate project of trying to make it so. Hobbes and Nietzsche are perhaps the two modern philosophers who best represent this view. It is tempting simply to assimilate Schelling to this tradition:

Everything is rule, order, and form in the world as we now see it. But the unruly still lies in the ground like something that could break through once more. Nowhere does it appear as though order and form were original, but rather as if something initially unruly had been brought to order. (VII, 359)

The neediness that elevates rationality to the status of a secular religion is intimately bound to the discomfiting intuition that reality itself is irrational. How else is the modern prohibition of metaphysics to be understood? If reality were recognized as truly rational, we would encourage the attempt to understand its inner meaning. Of course, if reality were deemed rational, we would also place our trust in it, instead of relying as heavily as we do on politics and technology to hold the world at bay. Metaphysical irrationalism is thus the deep premise of modern rationality. It alone provides the explanation for why practical and instrumental reason have achieved such dominance over theoretical reason. There is a certain kind of hope that is little more than the frenzied attempt to banish despair. Too many modern rationalists are rationalists by desperate conviction, compelled by the never articulated belief that reality itself is anything but rational. The rejection of metaphysics is thus based on a very specific, but unexamined, metaphysical assumption. The world threatens to fly apart: we *must* be rational.

The refusal to examine this root premise (to consider the possibility of a metaphysics of evil) is the fear that truth is too unbearable to be faced. Until harsh reality intervenes, lies always supplant truth. For normal liberal democracy, evil exists indeed: but only 'out there' somewhere, beyond the purview of healthy society. Somewhere in the dangerously other – in the underclass, in the impoverished worlds of Eastern Europe or of the great monstrous 'South' – evil lurks that is truly evil. When it remains hidden from view, it can be tolerated and forgotten. Suburban bliss has as its condition the terror that it shuts out. When that terror is asserted, bliss defiled knows no response but to search it out and exterminate it. If Jihad's ultimate act of evil was Auschwitz, hands-on extermination of the outsider within, McWorld's parallel act was Hiroshima: the sanitary and distanced extermination of the outsider without, collateral damage rendered acceptable by keeping the incinerated remains decently off camera.

The denial of evil assumes two forms. In times of peace, it is the optimistic assumption that evil is little more than an unfortunate residue of our animal heritage, the survival of aggressive instincts that can ultimately be overcome by reason. In times of crisis, it is taken more seriously as a demonic force, but in a way that still allows us to speak of denial: for the demonic is viewed as abiding only in the other. In fact, it is the very assumption that we ourselves are without evil that generates the conclusion that our enemies must be demonic: who else would oppose anyone as good as we are? In this supposition, the denial is apparent. The evil that we suffer is simply placed beyond the pale of what can be understood. Thus, in the study of the Holocaust, the focus is on purely empirical issues. The Nazis were evil; their deeds so diabolical that the only appropriate way to deal with them is by maintaining a posture of shocked silence. 'Don't try to understand this', we are effectively told. There are places where reason and understanding are not supposed to go. There are, however, just as assuredly moments in history when the game of denial can no longer be played. Evil has to be confronted. If this confrontation is to be carried out with any degree of real insight, we will have to discern the possibility of evil within nature – and within ourselves.

Within the Enlightenment framework, Kant's conception of radical evil is the most serious attempt to grasp the universality of evil. Instead of denying evil or projecting it into the hostile other (so that ultimately it cannot be thought at all), Kant maintains that it is something we can understand.[7] It is, indeed, nothing other than our own wilful, and universally human, subordination of moral to prudential reason. The assertion of the universality of evil, which evokes the traditional Christian conception of original sin, prepares the way for Schelling's more metaphysical conception. Even so, Kant's emphasis on wilfulness remains characteristically modern. According to Kant, evil is not the simple inheritance of a natural predisposition to self-interest. Instead, it is the transcendentally constituted decision to elevate that self-interest into life's guiding maxim. Yes, we will be moral, but only as long as morality does not interfere with our more fundamental pursuit of happiness.

Before articulating this conception of radical evil in his old age, Kant had identified freedom solely with the moral good, the autonomy that is achieved when the will casts off heteronomous impulses and conducts itself in accord to practical reason. In radical evil, however, impulsive desire is not construed as merely given, an animal condition from which we have to extract ourselves, but as something we have actively willed and bear responsibility for. Freedom is now the freedom to do good *or evil*.[8]

This remarkable extension of the idea of autonomy comes at a cost, rendering problematic the progressive view of history that celebrates practical reason's success in extricating itself from the contingency and heteronomy of nature. Such a view survives only as a regulative idea ('would that it so were'). On the field of actual history, the ongoing possibility of evil has to be taken more seriously. Instead of regarding it as a natural condition that we escape when we become autonomous, Kant assimilates evil to the autonomous will itself, identifying it with the universal maxim of self-interest (not the natural propensity to self-interest, but the wilful decision to elevate that propensity to the status of a maxim). Yet because this act lies so close to the heart of the self, Kant is forced to the conclusion that it is *'inextirpable* by human powers'.[9] This is where he makes a remarkable concession to traditional religion, agreeing that salvation is possible only through a divine gift of grace.[10] This is not so different from Heidegger's verdict, delivered in defiance of the very project of autonomy, that 'only a god can save us'.

Even so, Kant himself stopped short of ontologizing evil. While he did construe evil as universally human, he did not entertain the thought that it somehow contaminates the ontological ground of reality. Quite the contrary, his attempt to bind evil into the structure of autonomy can be read as a way of completing Enlightenment's unstated goal: the completion of the old project of philosophical theodicy.[11] Faith in reason: if man is to assume the task of restructuring nature to suit his own ends, he has to operate under the assurance that the ground of nature is benevolent. Humanism requires the notion of a God that is, at worst, metaphysically neutral. From this perspective, atheism itself is a form of theodicy: if there is no God, he can hardly be blamed for evil. Rousseau's story of a bungling series of utterly contingent (and thus reversible) mistakes replaces any notion of a metaphysics of evil.

Much of this is foreshadowed in the classical form of theodicy found in the *Genesis* story of Adam's Fall.[12] The narrative is familiar: God was good; His creation was good; then man chose evil. Evil is solely the fault of man. While a serpent made the story in *Genesis* a little more complex (and Kant himself accommodates that serpent in the form of desires that do in fact well up from animal nature), the gist is the same: evil is ours. The justification of God lies in the affirmation of our own guilt.

This concept of radical evil (where Kant meets St Augustine) is a necessary correction to the tendency to cast evil into the demonic other. But the very definition of evil as an unconditioned insurrection of the subject legitimates society's system of domination. If evil is radical in the Kantian sense, that is, formed from a root that precedes all heteronomous influences or impulses, then it is in principle unforgivable. This has serious consequences. If what the victim has suffered is decisively *someone's fault*, then he (or his friends) can be excused for lashing out at the perpetrator of such unforgivable wrong. This is of course the origin of the dialectic of revenge, cause of so much evil in the world. Violence begets violence. By feeding into the operative mechanism of evil, the radically moral conception has undermined itself (insofar as morality assumes freedom from mechanism).

Against this danger, Kant knows only the traditional strategy: substitution of the measured response of punishment for the immeasurable fury of revenge. But punishment (the hell that follows evil instead of preceding it) requires first of all a guilty party. Assuming that radical evil is at bottom the wilful assertion of prudential reason, guilty ones should always be lurking in the shadows. But the suicide bomber is nowhere to be found. He has sacrificed his very life in a way that Kant has denied is even possible.[13] By refusing to acknowledge that radical evil can intensify into what he calls diabolic evil, the psychotic distortion that allows one to will evil as one's good, Kant preserves the imperative of philosophical rationality, whereby reality itself is construed as rational and hence good. But by doing so, he eliminates the possibility of comprehending what stands outside of the *Gestalt* of such rationality. The concentrated fury of Jihad has no place in his scheme. Evil has been pushed back into the incomprehensible other.

Punishment cannot be successfully allocated to a purely rational framework. Kant tries to do precisely that when he situates punishment within the impersonal apparatus of the state: reason that, by virtue of institutionalization, has become alienated from the purview of the thinking self. To function justly, law must function mechanically. Its agent must not be allowed to think for himself. The autonomy of moral reason falls outside of the rational structures that are required to enforce it. To illustrate the full catastrophe of this thought, I need allude only to one agent in particular:

Adolph Eichmann. On the face of it, Eichmann's self-defence ('I was only doing my Kantian duty') rings false: one's duty derives solely from the moral law, not from the command of the *Führer*. On the other hand, the need for punishment (and for Kant this includes the need for capital punishment) cannot be delivered over to the purely formal ideal: its kingdom of ends withholds itself in an ever-receding future. It requires its concrete embodiment in the state. But Eichmann was simply the state's representative. Who was he to decide that the Jews were not to be punished? *Not deciding*, suspending moral judgment, is in fact the proper Kantian stance for an agent of the impersonal apparatus of the state.[14]

Schelling's own answer to these strange constrictions of reason cannot be understood apart from his more general philosophical answer to Kant's (and Fichte's) notion of the self-constitution of the self. Self-consciousness, he asserts, is ultimately derivative: it is grounded in an identity that precedes all reflection and consciousness.[15] Radical evil must likewise be derivative. The evil self was not evil before it made itself so. For that very reason its 'making itself so' cannot be thought of as a simple act of self-constitution. If it is derivative, however, it is not derivative of anything in the field of experience, for then it would not in any obvious sense be *radical*. Its originative condition must therefore lie both beyond the field of experience and beyond the horizon within which the self constitutes itself as itself. Its ground is rooted in nature, creeping up on us from behind, as it were, just as the state itself is not an autonomously posited construction of practical reason, but a burden placed on us by nature, pre-conscious punishment for pre-conscious sin (XI, 547).

In other words, radical evil has to be metaphysically understood. Heidegger is the one who most fully argued this thesis.[16] What distinguishes my own interpretation from his is that I retain Schelling's sense that, although evil does in fact have to be understood out of its ontological ground, that ground itself, because it is pre-moral, is not evil. In other words, Heidegger goes too far in the direction of ontologizing evil. The result is that we are left with no way out, fully at the whim of the gods. Between Heidegger and Kant, I settle for a middle option, which I take to be Schelling's own. It retains the moral conception of evil but modifies it by situating it within its ontological ground. This is different from Heidegger's strategy of reading evil itself back into the ground, with the result that its violence ends up determining the nature of good itself. This entanglement of violence in the good is in fact a problem that infects both Heidegger's ontological amorality (evil as birth contraction of the good) and Kant's exaggerated moralism (evil as the overture to punishment).

The move I propose takes the problem beyond the order of guilt and punishment. To uncover the condition of evil is to uncover at least the possibility of forgiveness. This has, however, nothing to do with the reduction of evil into the natural order. Construing the condition of evil metaphysically situates it beyond the field of causality, enabling us better to understand the *diabolical* evil that the history of fanaticism pushes upon us. But, because the diabolical is not to be construed as a separate being that exerts causality upon the self, it does not imply anything as fixed as a *diabolis*. As real as the ground itself may be, the demons that inhabit it can still be understood as projections of human fear.[17] Schelling thus enables us to think the diabolical without falling into a Manichean form of dualism. His primary commitment is still a commitment to reason.

But what is important for him is not so much theodicy as *theogony*.[18] The undetermined condition of freedom is a metaphysical condition. In other words, the ground of reality must contain the possibility of both good and evil. If that ground is taken to be God, then God must be thought of as having a history (possibilities distinct from his goodness). The unforgivable scourge of self-constituted evil is lifted once we understand something of freedom's condition: it is the tail of the snake that extends beyond the phenomenal into the forgotten 'before' of creation. Kronos and his cohorts rear their ugly heads and shatter the delusions of theodicy. That Schelling strives to resurrect the forgotten gods (forgotten in philosophy, if not in poetry) without positing actual evil in the divine should not be dismissed as an unfortunate recurrence of the metaphysics of presence (as if the Manichean alternative would somehow be more liberating!). By providing a theoretical alternative to the hell of hatred, his move affords us a glimmer of hope. But it offers nothing like a guarantee that we can be released from that hell. From beginning to end, Schelling's one thought remains that of *freedom*. In that regard, he is thoroughly (and reassuringly) modern. That he is able to combine the thought of freedom with a restoration of the tragic sense (the most important consequence of theogony) is what makes him directly relevant to a modernity that has suddenly discovered the illusory nature of its pretence to invulnerability. Looking beyond the pain of this discovery, we might take solace in one thought. Living with vulnerability offers a distinct advantage: it restores to the human the full energy and vitality of the ground.

II

Schelling's thought will emerge more clearly if we continue to develop the contrast with Kant's concept of radical evil. It is a concept that, first of all, seems too narrowly focused on the individual. Cruelty can, of course, manifest itself as the psychotic rage of the solitary individual against the sheer facticity of existence. Even so, as Kant himself emphasizes, the instinct of the individual, bound as it is to awareness, still remains at its healthiest before it is exposed to society's mordant offer to exchange the comfort of solidarity for the discomfort of thought.[19] Even within the rage of the solitary individual, there is a clearly discernible social moment: for solitude is the result of social exclusion. Solidarity comes at an awful price.

My primary point, though, is not that evil is a social phenomenon, but that it is an imbedded phenomenon. If it emerges out of an unconditional act of freedom, that freedom cannot be envisioned as an act of detached subjectivity. Instead, it operates through and upon a ground (which it carries within itself). The primary ground is nature, not that nature 'outside' of us, but that nature, which we *are*. Evil does not arise *ex nihilo*. It is not the simple play of selfishness, but the self-deception and cruelty that surface when we blame suffering, originally a function of the limits imposed on us by nature, on something that we are able to *control*. To attain my selfish desire, I work to frustrate the desire of the other. It is a conception that clearly leaves rooms for different modalities of evil. From Schelling's point of view, evil already exists in the epistemological act whereby the knowing subject casts all nature outside of itself, transforming it into an *object* of scientific understanding and technological manipulation. This is the tacit and seemingly innocuous evil of McWorld. It is carried to a higher power when it involves the objectification and manipulation of other human beings. Jihad's emotionally charged loathing, 'the other tribe is filth', is the local and (once televised) highly conspicuous version of what unfolds silently and universally in McWorld's dispassionate reduction of humanity to 'resource' and 'consumer'. The irony is that the former serves as the ground and justification of the latter: fear of Jihad is the origin of McWorld.

Our resolve to remain 'in control' leads us to substitute what we can manipulate and eliminate for what irremediably presses itself upon us. To sever evil from its ground in suffering, as Kant does, radicalizes it by enhancing its blameworthiness. The dilemma this causes is that the very attempt to analyse evil, to take it seriously, becomes implicated in the fundamental mechanism that gave rise to it in the first place. By illuminating the guilt of the individual, Kant comes perilously close to inviting a response that is itself evil: the guilty individual can be exterminated; suffering cannot. Modernity's crusade against suffering leads to genocide on an unprecedented scale.

The contrast I want to develop shows itself in the different ways in which Kant and Schelling read the Book of Job, traditionally construed as the Bible's great contribution to the study of evil. Schelling sets himself solidly in this tradition, by focusing his primary attention on the prologue and the question it raises: why does God allow Satan to inflict so much torment on Job? (XIV, 247–51). Kant, on the other hand, leaves aside the prologue and the metaphysical issues it raises and concentrates his attention instead on the dialogue between Job and his friends.[20]

Prologue left aside (with its fearfully pious Job), the dialogue reveals a man of remarkable courage. Against the instinct of the herd, its tendency to cave in to the charge of arrogance as if deviation from the group were the greatest of all possible sins, Job withstands the relentless accusations of his 'friends' and maintains his innocence to the end. Hell may simply be hell. It is not necessarily a punishment for wrong committed. In this case, the darkness is in God.

Kant seems to accept this. Although he does not directly assert darkness in divinity, he does emphatically affirm the viewpoint that Job (who accuses God of permitting injustice) speaks the truth. The metaphysical issue is not, however, what interests him, but rather the fact that Job's sincerity serves as a foil for the hypocrisy of his friends, who, according to Kant, sense the pain of existence but choose to live in denial, hoping to save themselves by flattering God.

Except for the hypocrisy of Job's friends, the Book of Job would not, on Kant's reading, be about evil at all, but only about suffering. His understanding of radical evil, as a flaw within the specifically human self, makes him uninterested in any explicit indictment of God. In the same way, Job's sufferings are also uninteresting, precisely because they are the sufferings of an innocent. By discarding the notions of natural and metaphysical evils, Kant is able to maintain his focus on what he regards as the only real evil, which is moral. Earthquakes and plagues (and loathsome sores) are simply to be endured, until science gains the knowledge that will enable us to fix them.[21] It is not pain that is evil, but only the person who wilfully inflicts it.

I have already hinted at one problem with this interpretation. While it is certainly possible that Job's friends do not truly think God always acts justly, it is clear that they have a good enough reason for not saying so: their fear that what God has let happen to Job, he could just as well let happen to them. If God himself is not trustworthy then the moral imperative loses its bite. The insistence that the world is founded upon justice is not simply the wishful thinking of Job's friends, for Kant himself is caught up in the same pious wish. It is, moreover, so utterly understandable in human terms that it can be regarded as the foundational act of all human societies. Job's friends have something to fear: if they flatter God, it is because they recognize the horror of what he has permitted. What else can they do but flee into the fantasy that he might have his reasons? Their denial of truth seems to be a reflexive and thus easily forgivable denial.

On the other hand, one wonders how Kant could have come to Job's defence. If radical evil is universal (which is Kant's way of agreeing that we have all sinned in Adam), then Job's friends are telling the truth: Job is guilty. The curse delivered to Adam was a curse delivered to all humanity. Divine justice is a heavy burden to bear.

But is it justice?

The God who closes the dialogue by speaking out of the whirlwind certainly suggests that it is not. Suffering is not a punishment imposed upon sinful humanity, but instead, it is the collateral damage of creation itself. 'What does it matter that you suffer?' God effectively tells Job. 'The spectacle of nature is so gloriously beautiful.'

Because Schelling anticipates Nietzsche in providing an aesthetic rather than a moral justification of existence, this point is worth unfolding more fully.[22] But to really make it deliver, I need to reiterate the strange claim I made above that viewing the shadow side of God simultaneously makes evil both more forgivable and more diabolical.

In order to clarify the diabolical side of the issue, I will start with an observation that René Girard makes absolutely convincing.[23] The sin of Job's friends is far more serious than the rather innocent lie that Kant is able to see. For they are not only the witnesses of Job's suffering, but also the *causes* of it. This is a point that really should be obvious to anyone, who (like Kant) sets the prologue aside. Girard begins his counter-interpretation by taking seriously Job's statement (which, once discovered, can be multiplied *ad nauseum*): 'All my dearest friends recoil from me in horror: those I love best have turned against me.'[24] The pain of solitude is a social imposition. Like Oedipus, Job has been made into the scapegoat of a suffering community. His friends are not simply speculatively inferring plausible reasons for divine disfavour. They know those reasons with the full certainty granted by social unanimity, which is why they utter their accusations (that Job is the cause of everything wrong in their world) with the acid venom of the righteous. His friends know the mind of God, for their God is nothing other than the will of society.

The reduction of God to the social order is older than the Enlightenment, although the Enlightenment (McWorldian theology) is what makes it appear irreversible. Despite his emphatic view that the only evil in the Book of Job is the evil in Job's friends, Kant remains blind to the diabolical extent of that evil. The source of his blindness is his own implicit identification of God with humanity. If this seems to reconcile poorly with his Rousseauian conviction that society is responsible for the corruption of the individual, it is apparent in his assurance that for that very reason society alone can be the vehicle of his redemption. The vehicle is the ethical commonwealth (the philosophically comprehended Church).[25] Its goal is the kingdom of ends, the completed community of mankind, in which alone God becomes fully real.

Schelling's deviation from that fundamental dogma of modernity[26] enables him, in his own interpretation of the Book of Job, to restore to its place of honour the prologue in heaven, the opening dialogue between God and Satan, who is strangely glorified by being called one of God's sons.[27] A quick sketch of the broad outline of Schelling's interpretation reveals the following.

For Schelling, Satan, like Christ, was 'begotten, not made' (XIV, 256). If Christ ultimately preceded the creation as the eternal Word through which it was spoken into being, Satan preceded it as the original chaos out of which it emerged. Himself torn forth from that chaotic ground by the act of creation, Satan assumes the entire series of personalities depicted in pagan theogony, but first and foremost the personality of the accuser.[28] What God stabilized into being with the pronouncement of its essential goodness, Satan destabilized with the insistence that true goodness requires the full repetition of all that God himself endured in the initial act of creation. Satan is thus Nemesis, unable to tolerate any creature's enjoyment of undeserved happiness (XIV, 260). To deserve happiness, the creature must find its own way to divinity, just as God himself had to find that way by traversing the hell of his own incomprehensible facticity, the Father born as Father only in the Word that he himself uttered into being. Job suffers the horror of exclusion from the community for a reason. Only in the deepest solitude of being does the original freedom, fulcrum of the unspeakable plenitude of creation, begin to show itself. Job hears the divine voice only when his suffering leaves him with nothing more to hold onto. It is the role of Satan to destroy Job's God (the honour that had been conferred upon him by human society) so that he can enter into the purifying fire. The most important moment in the Book of Job is given when Job realizes that the god he has always feared, the violent god of justice (who, like the god of modernity, is identical with society as a whole) is evil and thus no God whatsoever. He is a phantom god, with no being apart from the all-too-human fear of social oppression and exclusion. The terrifying features of the world we live in, the twin facts that the innocent suffer and the guilty go free, must be encountered before the laughing God of creation can be disclosed. Unable and unwilling to extinguish the flames of the hell that is the condition of free creation, he points instead to Behemoth and Leviathan (hippopotamus and crocodile) as proofs that chaos can be subdued, if not entirely and completely tamed.

These images are of course too 'thick' for the modern taste, too dangerously near Jihad madness. If they are not simply to be thrown aside in anger, they have to be rendered understandable.

I will try to do this in two steps. The first involves a short reflection on Schelling's *Ages of the World*. The second will unfold out of a direct encounter with the metaphysics of evil, the heart of the 1809 *Philosophical Investigations into Human Freedom*.

III

What I will present here is restricted to the element of image and vision. It ignores the fact that Schelling's primary effort was to elevate such intuitions into the language of rational dialectic. For those who want the 'concept', the work of Wolfram Hogrebe is indispensable.[29] Manfred Frank is another author who has successfully taken the concern for argumentation into the profound obscurities of Schellingian metaphysics.[30] But one condition for his being able to do this is the detour he has always taken around the one work in which Schelling directly poses the question of evil: the 1809 treatise on human freedom. What Hogrebe and Frank have correctly understood is that it is possible to express the poetic project of the *Ages of the World*, the attempt to lay out the path through which divinity extricates itself from hell, in the more neutral language of philosophy. The path then can be conceived as the process through which a rationally understandable world emerges from the ungroundable contingency and facticity of being. But it is too Hegelian a move to conclude that, because the dialectic can be achieved in thought, it has been achieved in reality. If divinity is thinkable, it does have to be comprehended as the result of a process of becoming. The problem, however, is that the only evidence we have that such a result has been attained is the relative order and stability of the world as we perceive it. But the absolute is not the relative. The only possibility of actually *knowing* divinity is the completion of the process *within us*. Precisely this is what we are missing.

What we are left with is really no more than what Kant called a 'regulative idea' of reason. While it is reasonable to speculate that reality might ultimately be elevated into the full luminosity of reason, there is no guarantee that this is the case. Doubly so, because more is at stake than the inertia of matter that clings to the infinite past of an irretrievable origin.[31] Evil represents a force far greater than inertia, a force capable of actively opposing the glorious march to divinity. The dramatic failure of the *Ages of the World*, the fact that Schelling became caught in a series of rewritings that were never able to advance beyond the dark abyss of the past ('*O Vergangenheit, du Abgrund der Gedanken!*'), indicates that something more than the power of dialectic is required to facilitate the birth of the new man out of the old.[32]

Let me concretize this, by citing a beautiful passage from the first version of the *Ages of the World* (which has yet to be translated into English), a passage that is part of a much longer section missing from the two later versions. It represents, quite possibly, Schelling's moment of highest inspiration and has appropriately been likened to the completion of Dante's *Divine Comedy*: the delivery, through divine love, of the beatific vision. Strangely enough, this is where I want to locate the real problem of evil.

> Thus after objective being is most completely unfolded and articulated through time, the force of contraction, in its guise as world-sustaining past, steps fully into its own and delivers its final accomplishment, through which the entire process comes to a close: the drawing together of all that has been unfolded, none of which can again fall into the past, so that it is posited as one whole, effecting a simultaneity between everything that has emerged in the process of becoming, with the result that the fruits of different times live together and share a common center, like leaves and organs of one and the same blossom, turning slowly about its middle.[33]

In the case of Dante, this final falling away of the past occurs where we no longer try to force the vision, so that 'desire and will were moved already – like a wheel revolving uniformly – by the Love that moves the sun and the other stars.'[34] It is essentially the same in Schelling. The will to achieve, regardless of the nobility of its goal, is exasperated by the force of its own endeavour. Only divine love can ripen the fruit of time.

Where I discern the shadow of evil in this beautiful vision is in the intractable nature of force. It shows up in Schelling's text in the notion of a divine *contraction*. From the standpoint of the blossoms and the fruits of time, the past may simply fall away. From the standpoint of that past, however (and Jihad's entanglement in it), the violent movement of assertion and mutual destruction sustains itself by the indomitable will to be. Were we to get over to God's side, such a will would be unnecessary. But this is still hypothetical, for *our present is that past*. We are where God always already *was*, with no guarantee whatsoever that we will 'blossom' into the fullness of presence rather than catapult ourselves into the awful abyss. If we fail to engage the past, to actively overcome it in heart and mind, choosing instead to allow it slowly to grow longer and longer behind us, then we are its prisoners.[35] Instead of leaping into the abyss, we get dragged into it.

In this regard, it is important to focus on what Schelling's metaphor leaves out. Blossoms and fruit require supporting branches and stems, which in turn require roots and dirt and water. Light and air on one side, to be sure, but rotting compost on the other. (Martin Luther is said to have had his religious awakening while sitting at the privy.) The mind may indeed have the potential to awaken to a luminosity that transcends the ravages of time. Even so, it remains an embodied mind, precariously poised over the possibility of destruction. Its epiphanies are unthinkable apart not only from the force of contraction, but also from what contraction expels: more rot for the compost. Nothing takes flight without the struggle against gravity's pull into darkness.

I will tie these observations to another passage from the first version of the *Ages of the World*, a passage that once again did not make it into the two versions that have been translated into English. Too long to quote, I will indicate its import by locating it within the more general development Schelling sets forth. The entire project is the narrative of God's becoming, beginning with the emptiness and purity that would have prevailed, even if the birth into being had never occurred. In the *Ages of the World*, this principle is referred to as primal *Lauterkeit*; in the treatise on human freedom, it is the *Ungrund* (it is tempting to put them together: 'the purity of the unground'). Within the primal essence of this 'unborn God', the heart of pure freedom, Schelling divines just enough of a quiet joy (freedom from the burden of existence!) to permit him the suggestion that it awakens the craving to be from the abyss of what absolutely is not. Instead of presenting here the details of the dialectic that ensues, let me comment on its literary features. The life of the primordial will as it awakens to consciousness is portrayed with the imagery of complete innocence, a simple play of forces that generate the bliss of the primordial child god. This state of innocence is disrupted, however, as the opposing forces become heightened in their intensity, until the meek inner will experiences the desperate severity of its counterpart, the will to be something. Fear ensues; chaos erupts, and the rotary wheel of forces that anticipates the revolving heavens begins to turn.[36] Schelling's description of these movements is a truly powerful mixture of dialectical precision and poetic licence. The attentive reader gains a sense of privileged access to the first miraculous phase of God's inner becoming.

Completely absent in the final two versions, which proceed to a dialectical description of how God might have extricated himself from the deep necessity of eternal recurrence, is a curious *repetition* of the darkest moment, the cataclysmic fall into chaos. Schelling introduces the repetition by saying that it is time to 'go back into the *inner life* of the being that exists within this conflict' (WA, 39). The words that follow soon thereafter set the tone of the next few pages: 'Pain is something necessary and universal, the un-avoidable passageway to freedom' (WA, 40). The creator has no alternative but to lead his creatures through the nightmarish path that he himself had to traverse. The previous movement from the idle play to the violent clash of forces is now repeated from the perspective of the suffering subject. Con-forming to the stage of innocent play are the idyllic visions through which the forms of the creatures first surfaced in the divine imagination. The force of contraction gives them progressively more colour and intensity until fear transforms them into nightmarish apparitions. There follow paragraphs that have few equals outside of Dante's *Inferno* and the *Tibetan Book of the Dead*. As fear gives way to panicked anxiety, the nightmare visions erupt into the flaming fires of hell. There is no dialectical path that assures extrication from eternal recurrence, for the very need to escape is what gives fuel to the flames. The demonic will to eradicate the ground of existence is the very device through which that ground gains the impenetrable depth of infinity. Even the purity of the primordial essence, which still underlies this horrific eruption, offers no solace, because its freedom and emptiness of form threatens to strip from the will the faint residue of familiarity that it strives to hold onto. All of this is prelude to a final great collapse into what Schelling calls divine madness (WA, 42).

At this juncture, two vivid images are juxtaposed. The first is the wagon of Dionysus, accompanied by music that is 'now stupefying, now lacerating'. It is pulled by lions, panthers, and tigers, and followed by swirling masses of whatever has been infected with the horror of Dionysian insanity. The second image is even more disturbing. Against this chaotic flood, Schelling evokes the horror of divine solipsism: 'For human beings are helped by other human beings, helped even by God; however, there is nothing whatsoever that can come to the aid of the primal being in its stultifying solitude; it must fight its way through chaos for itself, utterly alone' (WA, 43).

This hell is real enough, the very ground of all being. In God, though, there is no evil. Job finally has his real answer. It is God himself who is the prototype of all suffering innocents.

IV

We now have before us the vision of a hell that is ontologically prior to evil. Because hell is first and foremost a state of spirit and mind, we can also see clearly how Schelling's understanding of original chaos differs from that of Hobbes and of materialist metaphysics in general. From the perspective of the latter, chaos is a consequence of the principle of entropy. It belongs to matter itself and awakens the need for rational control. On this view, spirit stands in opposition to nature, much as in the older Neoplatonic and Christian traditions, which viewed evil as sensuality and good as the power of the spirit to bridle and tame the unruly forces of nature. Schelling's image of divine madness suggests the need for an entirely different scheme. The possibility of evil is rooted in a deformation of reason and spirit, a deformation that penetrates into the ground and condition of creation itself.

Once again, a comparison to Kant might prove helpful. The strength of the idea of radical evil is that by focusing on the intellectual act of constituting maxims, it correctly situates evil in the rational sphere. The weakness, however, is that by framing the maxim as an elevation of self-interest over the interest of the whole, Kant lets the actual content of evil collapse once again into the sphere of animal desire. But, as noted above, the suicide bomber clearly breaks with the principle of self-interest, in a way that allows evil to exhibit an uncanny proximity to good. The pain and horror of being pushes spirit, already on its deepest and still unconscious levels, beyond the animal quest for feeding appetites. For Schelling, man's problem is not that he tends to be an animal when he should be more than that. No animal can be called evil precisely because animals are securely guided by an instinct for survival. 'Animals can never step out of unity', as Schelling puts it, 'whereas man can voluntarily rip apart the eternal bond of forces. For this reason Franz Baader is right when he says that it would be something worth wishing for, if man's depravity went only as far as becoming a beast; but unfortunately man can only stand above or beneath animals' (VII, 373). The division of forces that gives order to the primordial chaos through the slow evolution of living beings does not simply place man above the entire sequence, for the entire process constitutes a progressive intensification of the forces and tensions that lie latent in the ground. Man comes up from the deepest and ugliest part of the ground. As such he contains within himself something that is more crocodile than any crocodile could ever be.

All things, for Schelling, are instantiations of will, having stepped into being by progressively overcoming the darkness of desire, the unfocused craving for being. Evil erupts from a will that is more primordial than my own will, for my will is constituted out of the conflict of that will with its opposite. It is the will not only to self-destruction but to the destruction of all that exists: 'Evil is the most purely spiritual of principles, for it carries out a vehement war against all objective being, intending finally the obliteration of the very ground of creation' (VII, 468). The existence of the world gives evidence that God himself withstood this temptation. For him, evil was no more than a possibility. But for God to become manifest and real, man, as the latent god, must be placed before the very same temptation and possibility. The nuclear arsenals of the present age have a metaphysical grounding that reaches into the inner being of God himself. The goodness of God, who preserves the world, receives its measure against the destructiveness of mankind. That goodness is a morally significant goodness, however, only to the degree that God stands in the same temptation as man.

This, then, is the first chapter of theogony. In Schelling's treatise on human freedom, a prolonged discussion of the metaphysical possibility of evil, that is, an exploration of the temptations that stood before God himself, precedes any discussion of radical evil (VII, 357–73). The self-constitution of evil is a mediated one. Eternity itself presupposes the abyss of an eternal past. What surfaces in man, and constitutes the real possibility of evil, is the oldest and most hidden part of the ground, that principle of radical freedom which, preceding all causality, is capable of fully lacerating the order of the world.

It is this principle from the deepest past which erupts in nature and creates the gulf between animal and human, opening thereby a space for all culture and, indeed, morality itself. The first *human* acts had to be evil acts.[37] This is so much the case that even the most sublimely good actions bear within them the appearance of evil. It is not an accident that saints get burned as heretics. Only separation in time allows us to comprehend as the sign of divine humility the words of Christ, 'it is not I who speaks but the Father in me.'[38] Were one of our contemporaries to use such words, he would be declared an arrogant lunatic. Were he to prevail in such statements, he would be crucified for his evil. Communities are bound together by the collective pursuit of need and desire, which is why good appears as evil to the collective imagination. This in turn is why the banal forms of evil (which mask their destructiveness by hiding behind self-interest) ultimately outweigh the demonic. McWorld (the attempt to secure the world by eradicating the ground) is more of a threat than Jihad (the retreat into ground that wants to eradicate the world). The enforcers of everyday political correctness can be as violent and vicious in their exclusions as the tyrants they hold out against. Their danger lies less in their power and fury than in their numbers (particularly after one considers how many ideological permutations of the politically correct there are). Trivial evil multiplied by the cowardice that keeps the common person from being either good or evil exceeds in magnitude the diabolical evil of the aloof and aberrant: global warming may provide the ultimate proof of this. It is thus within the state, according to Schelling (and he is thinking here not of tyrannical regimes but of the just and rational state of bourgeois hope), that we find 'evil in large measure', which serves finally to reduce humanity to the 'struggle for existence' (VII, 462). It is the dubious contribution of our own age to have shown that this reduction is possible even in the midst of unfathomed wealth. Real poverty and spiritual poverty have this in common: the flattening of concern and interest to a purely material plane. This occurs as a consequence of the most vulgar and widely distributed form of evil, whereby the animal instinct for survival, a mere means and condition for life, detaches itself from the rest of nature and makes itself into an end.

This utterly banal form of evil is the principle of capitalism, with its explosive power to rip apart cultural identities and constitute the counterfeit culture of McWorld. Schelling situates this principle within the more general history of imperialism and completes thereby a second chapter of theogony (VII, 373–82). The actuality of evil in the world at large thus precedes (and conditions) the emergence of radical evil in the individual. Its presuppositions are a selfishness that human beings share with animals in conjunction with a tendency to flee the natural order, so that the principle of selfishness, instead of sustaining nature as its ground and condition, can be set against it in radical opposition. If greed is the face of such evil, the death wish is still its hidden premise: the culmination of McWorld is Disney, reality not so much denied as eradicated. As for why human beings take flight from reality, Schelling's answer is clear: 'The fear of life itself drives man out of the center in which he was created' (VII, 381). It is a fear to which, as we have already seen, God himself was not impervious. Its trigger is the sheer contingency of existence (what is this strange world in which I find myself encased?). Its feedback mechanism, which can make it accelerate into full-blown anxiety and panic, is the frightening discovery that running away is not really an option. The world of fantasy beckons. But what has no ground in reality is vulnerable to destruction (which feeds fear even more). 'Evil in large measure' is the ever-growing desert that captured the attention of Nietzsche and Heidegger.

Schelling does pose the question that Kant had placed in the centre of his own investigation: how does an individual actually *choose* evil? He does so, however, only after first establishing that the possibility of evil lurks in reality itself (so much so that it has to be taken seriously as a possibility for God himself) and then revealing that the actuality of evil is the great engulfing premise of history. In response to the question of how the individual then chooses evil for himself, he emphasizes his agreement with Kant and Fichte that this has to be conceived as a free and therefore eternal act. He complicates the intuition, however, by adding the emphatic assertion that self-positing 'presupposes true being' so that it is *real* or unconscious self-positing (VII, 385). The free act by virtue of which a human being has established his nature is a fully unconscious act that is rooted in the abyss of being itself. It is an unconscious act that, as eternal, accompanies the self into this world and into this very present. While it itself cannot be recollected, it bequeaths a moment that certainly can: the conscious awareness that the act (itself unconscious) was in fact my own act (VII, 386). In other words, although we do not recollect how we made ourselves so, we do recollect, through our sense of guilt, *that* we made ourselves. At the same time, the intensity of this guilt is obviated by the fact that this self-constitution was a mediated one. Before radical evil arises, there is an inclination to evil, which itself is grounded in the metaphysical insurrection of the ground against the power and luminosity of the world-creating Word (VII, 388).

A good example of the seductive force of that insurrection can be found in the writings of Slavoj Žižek who, from the thoroughly correct observation that our symbolic constructions are fantasies, infers that the word itself is inherently a lie. He likens, for instance, Schelling's sublime vision of the completed blossom of eternity (a version of which I quoted from the *Ages of the World*) to:

> The already-mentioned 'posthumanist' utopia of a new 'bionic angel,' of a wired subject who, by means of 'downloading' consciousness into the machine, cuts the links that attach the subject to the material body and turns into a spirit freely floating in the ethereal materiality of cyberspace.[39]

This is, of course, an accurate description of the fantasy world we live in, but an inaccurate portrayal of the 'word' Schelling endeavours to express, which is always emphatically the word of the ground itself.[40]

The 'virtual-world' reflex is rooted in fear and confirms our notion that evil perpetuates itself by the will to escape. The past cannot be escaped, eradicated, or left behind. It can only be transformed in the moment of insight and creation. The Disney fantasy of a 'world without evil' deserves the scorn that Žižek levels at it, for it is a world without life. But to unmask that lie is not to shatter the word itself, which is always the word of the ground.[41] '*Wirkenlassen des Grundes*' – allowing the ground to operate – is the way love stepped forward to create a world (VII, 375). Had God refrained from creating a world, out of fear of that evil which is its condition, then, as Schelling clearly states: 'evil would have triumphed over the good and love' (VII, 402). 'Resist not evil' is, of course, the most emphatically Christian and the hardest of all commands.[42] It is opposed absolutely to the fantasy worlds of both Disney and the Pentagon. It dissolves both Jihad and McWorld, leaving in their place the world *just as it is*. The rotating vortex of desires and drives is not itself reality; it is the hell that is reality's ground and condition. At some point the 'fear of life' has to be overcome, so that one can enter into that hell and be cleansed by its flames. 'Hence the general necessity of sin and death as the actual dying away of selfhood, through which all human will must make its way as through a fire in order to be purified' (VII, 381). The goal of this purification is that radical openness that allows future, the temporal correlate of the formless *Ungrund*, to win back its position as origin.[43]

Merely human words are of course lies enough – and they stand opposed to the ground. There are, however, other words that carry within themselves a mysterious power and authority and go beyond the human. 'It is not I who speaks', proclaims the Son, 'but the Father who speaks in me.' It is a proclamation that Schelling renews and makes plausible for our own age. As the descent into the abyss becomes more evident and urgent, the capacity to listen to such speech will grow.

Notes

1   This relationship stands at the centre of the highly controversial essay that Baudrillard wrote in response to the terrorist attacks of September 11, *L'Ésprit du Terrorisme*. It originally appeared in *Le Monde*. A German translation quickly followed in *Der Spiegel* and an English translation in *Harper's Magazine* (February 2002, 13–18). Because the idea that suicide bombers are somehow a necessary manifestation of an irrational system ('as if every means of domination secreted its own antidote') appears to be cynical, Baudrillard's remarks were initially dismissed as being both insensitive and so fatalistic that they obliterate the possibility of moral comprehension. When one remembers, however, that morality is more fundamentally about action than judgment, everything changes. For what action requires above all is *space*. The disclosure that what postures as absolute power is not absolute is the necessary premise to any moral action whatsoever. If suicide bombing is a response blinded by hatred, other responses can be imagined, which retain the clarity of actual understanding.

2   Barber, B. R., *Jihad Vs. McWorld: How Globalism and Tribalism Are Reshaping the World* (New York: Times Books, 1995).

3   Zengotita, T. de, 'The Numbing of the American Mind', *Harper's Magazine*, April 2002, 33–40.

4   This emerges with fullest clarity when Schelling discusses philosophy's relationship with both mythology and revelation. Its goal is to understand both, not within their conceptual consequence, but within their historical truth. See XI, 250. The references are to Friedrich Wilhelm Joseph Schelling, *Sämtliche Werke*, ed. K. F. A. Schelling, volumes I–XIV (Stuttgart and Augsburg: Cotta, 1856–61). References to the *Ages of the World* are cited as WA and come from *Die Weltalter*, ed. Manfred Schröter (Munich: Biederstein, 1946). All translations are my own.

5   Barber's notion of McWorld is a popularized and updated form of the kind of social and cultural critique found in Horkheimer, M. and Adorno, T. W., *Dialectic of Enlightenment*, trans. John Cumming (New York: Seabury Press, 1972). While the call to authenticity is evocative of Nietzsche and Heidegger, it retains a more pronounced *social* horizon: how should society be structured, if the individual is to be set free? This concern with the social and historical dimension of the project of authenticity is what links critical theory back to Schelling, who occupies an interesting kind of middle position: with Heidegger, he views the social as essentially religious and cultural rather than political; with Horkheimer and Adorno, on the other hand, he is still intent to rescue an understanding of *reason* that, while always irremediably an individual accomplishment, nonetheless suffices to reconcile the individual with the social ideal. An interesting case for Schelling's compatibility with critical theory can be found in Dieter Jähnig, 'Philosophie und Weltgeschichte bei Schelling', in Jähnig, *Welt-Geschichte: Kunst-Geschichte: Zum Verhältnis von Vergangenheitserkenntnis und Veränderung* (Köln: Verlag Dumont Schauberg, 1975), 38–67.

6   This point is well made in Slavoj Žižek, *Tarrying With the Negative: Kant, Hegel, and the Critique of Ideology* (Durham: Duke University Press, 1993), 83–8.

7   Kant's theory of evil makes up the first book of *Religion Within the Limits of Reason Alone* (New York: Harper & Row, 1960), 15–39.

8   For a full discussion of this shift, see Gerold Prauss, *Kant über Freiheit als Autonomie* (Frankfurt: Klosterman, 1983).

9   Kant, *Religion*, 32.

10   Ibid., p. 70.

11   Odo Marquard, *In Defense of the Accidental* (New York: Oxford University Press, 1991), 8–28. An interesting response to Marquard's reading of theodicy (first put forth in 1965) can be found in an article by Cavallar, G. 'Kants Weg von der Theodicee zur Anthropodizee und retour', *Kant-Studien*, 1993, 90–102.

12   See Paul Ricoeur, *The Symbolism of Evil* (Boston: Beacon Press, 1969), 235–43.

13   Kant, *Religion*, 30–2. See also: Žižek, *Tarrying With the Negative*, 95–101.

14   The issue is discussed in Hannah Arendt, *Eichmann in Jerusalem* (New York: Viking Press, 1964). For a discussion of the specific relationship to Kant see Ranasinghe, N., 'Ethics for the Little Man: Kant, Eichmann and the Banality of Evil', *The Journal of Value Inquiry*, vol. 36, 2002, 299–317.

15   An extraordinarily clear discussion of Schelling's argument can be found in Manfred Frank, *Eine Einführung in Schellings Philosophie* (Frankfurt: Suhrkamp, 1985), 23–70.

16   Martin Heidegger, *Schellings Abhandlung Über das Wesen der menschlichen Freiheit* (1809) (Tübingen: Niemeyer, 1971), 125–98.

17   'This fear, this outrage in the face of the loss of the unity of consciousness ... is what drove them to project at least a partial unity [the pagan god], in the hope of surviving, if not as humanity, at least as a tribe' (XI, 115).

18   Hesiod, *Theogony* (Indianapolis: Bobbs-Merrill, 1953). See also Dodds, E. R., *The Greeks and the Irrational* (Berkeley: University of California Press, 1951). For a thorough presentation of what is at issue in the contrast between theodicy and theogony, see Ricoeur, P., *The Symbolism of Evil*, 211–78.

19   Kant, *Religion*, 85ff.

20   Kant, *On the Failure of All Attempted Philosophical Theodicies*, published as a supplement to Despland, M., *Kant on History and Religion* (Montreal: McGill-Queen's University Press, 1973), 283–97. See also Kant's letter to J. C. Lavater from 28 April, 1775 (10: 176–9), that can be found in A. Zweig's translation of Kant's *Philosophical Correspondence, 1759–99* (Chicago: University of Chicago Press, 1967).

21   This is made clear in Kant's response to the Lisbon earthquake of 1755. See I. Kant, 'Geschichte und Naturbeschreibung des merkwürdigen Vorfälle des Erdbebens', in Kant's *Werke*, Academy edition, vol. 1: *Vorkritische Schriften I 1747–1756*, Berlin 1910, 460.

22   It is easiest to provide the Nietzsche reference because he is the one who explicitly states the idea, for example, in section #5 of *The Birth of Tragedy* (London: Penguin, 1993), 32. Dieter Jähnig demonstrates convincingly that the same thought stood at the very centre of Schelling's philosophy. See D. Jähnig, *Schelling: Die Kunst in der Philosophie*, two volumes (Pfullingen: Neske, 1966 and 1969).

23   René Girard, *Job: The Victim of His People* (Stanford: Stanford University Press, 1987).

24   Job 19:19.

25   Kant, *Religion*, 88 ff.

26   This is most clearly discussed in lectures 23 and 24 of Schelling's *Philosophy of Mythology* (XI, 534–72).

27   One result of this restoration of the prologue is that Schelling's interpretation

falls in line with the general project of Goethe's *Faust*. While Goethe had no patience for Kant's moral conception of evil, he was generally enthusiastic about Schelling's notion of ground, particularly as it was expressed in the early work on the philosophy of nature.

28   It should be pointed out that what is true of Satan, that in his pre-Christian manifestation he was identical with all of the gods of theogony, *is also true of Christ*. The difference between Satan and Christ emerged only when Christ renounced the temptation to become prince of this world. Evil and good are identical in the ground, which itself is therefore neither evil nor good. For a wonderful overview of these relationships, see Benz, E., 'Theogony and the Transformation of Man in Friedrich Wilhelm Joseph Schelling', in *Man and Transformation: Papers from the Eranos Yearbooks* (Princeton: Princeton University Press, 1980), 203–47.

29   Hogrebe, W., *Prädikation und Genesis: Metaphysik als Fundamentalheuristik im Ausgang von Schellings 'Die Weltalter'* (Frankfurt: Suhrkamp, 1989).

30   Frank, M., *Eine Einführung in Schellings Philosophie*.

31   Frank, M. *Der unendliche Mangel an Sein: Schellings Hegelkritik und die Anfänge der Marxschen Dialektik* (Frankfurt: Suhrkamp, 1975).

32   The quotation ('Oh, past, thou abyss of thought!') is from WA, 218.

33   WA, 87.

34   *The Divine Comedy of Dante Alighieri: Paradiso* (Canto xxxiii, 143–5), trans. Allen Mandelbaum (New York: Bantam, 1982).

35   The necessity of this positive engagement in the past is what leads Horkheimer and Adorno to the recognition that the political revolutionary has to be a cultural conservative of a very specific sort: 'The task to be accomplished is not the conservation of the past, but the redemption of the hopes of the past' (*Dialectic of Enlightenment*, xv). This statement is completely in the spirit of Schelling's *Ages of the World*.

36   Within the rotary movement (Nietzsche's eternal recurrence) we find the primal need for what can variously be called redemption, salvation, creation, resurrection, and emancipation. It is mistaken to try to historicize the relationship as Žižek does when he asserts that Schelling has projected onto the Absolute the breakdown of the traditional, pre-modern community in the emergence of capitalism. See Žižek, 'Selfhood as Such is Spirit: Schelling on the Origins of Evil', in Copjec, J. (ed), *Radical Evil* (London: Verso, 1996), 2–3. Such a transition is emancipation from rotation only in its initial unfolding. Precisely because the relationship is metaphysical before it is historical, the rotation makes its way with necessity back into the new age (eternal recurrence is *eternal*): thus the image of Charlie Chaplin in the wheel of the machine – or of the disappearance of time in the age of the time-saving machine. There is no possibility of institutionalizing emancipation in such a way that the project of emancipation will be thereby rendered superfluous. Rotation is the cycle of nature that comes before the eruption of human history; it is pagan fatalism that precedes Christian hope; it is traditional community that yields to modern society; it is global capitalism – with no liberation of Prometheus anywhere in sight. Perhaps the best gloss on Schelling's intuition in the *Ages of the World* is Mahler's Symphony No. 2: *Resurrection*. These are matters I have discussed elsewhere, particularly in the conclusion of Lawrence, J., *Schellings Philosophie des ewigen Anfangs* (Würzburg: Königshausen & Neumann, 1989), 203–6.

37   Žižek, *Tarrying With the Negative*, 96f.

38   John 14: 7.

39   Žižek, S., in Schelling, *The Abyss of Freedom/Ages of the World* (Ann Arbor: University of Michigan Press, 1997), 77.

40   To render such a word plausible, I refer the reader to the second volume of

Dieter Jähnig, *Die Kunst in der Philosophie*. An even bolder attempt creatively to rethink the possibility of a 'word of the ground' can be found in Martin Heidegger, *Der Ursprung des Kunstwerkes*, a translation of which appears in Heidegger, M., *Basic Writings* (New York: Harper & Row, 1977), 143–88.

41 Žižek would certainly acknowledge that the creative word derives from the ground, but he would deny that it embodies anything more than a flight into fantasy. The result is that while he quite correctly emphasizes Schelling's anarchism (which can easily enough be inferred from my own contrast of Schelling with Kant), he seems to think that what holds for the state must hold for religion and culture as well. The artificiality of the state (and thus its inherent evil) I see myself. But I believe that, if one derives one's understanding of culture from something deeper and more lasting than Hollywood, one will see how a cultural form might be understood as not only having roots in the ground, but as taking the ground into itself and preserving it in the beauty and openness of the word. For his complete Schelling interpretation see Žižek, *The Invisible Remainder: An Essay on Schelling and Related Matters* (London: Verso, 1996). What I set in opposition to it is not only the Jähnig volumes I have already mentioned, but also Schulz, W., *Die Vollendung des deutschen Idealismus in der Spätphilosophie Schellings* (Pfullingen: Neske, 1975), especially pp. 259–70. If I had space fully to develop my critique of Žižek, I believe I could show how Schelling makes it possible to be simultaneously politically radical and culturally conservative, whereby by 'conservative' I do not mean Matthew Arnoldesque fixation on the past, but something else entirely: the realization that the deepest moments of culture can only be comprehended in a response that is so thoroughly creative that it opens up access to the future. To understand that relationship is to understand 'ground' by Schelling.

42 Matthew 5: 39.

43 I discuss Schelling's conception of such a future in 'Philosophical Religion and the Quest for Authenticity', which is forthcoming in Wirth, J. (ed.), *Why Schelling Now?* (Bloomington: Indiana University Press). The guiding intuition is that, just as philosophy completes itself by restoring openness to the fundamental questions out of which it initially arose (questions that have rightly been called not only 'unanswerable' but 'religious'), religion completes itself by achieving the openness of philosophy. This is not accomplished in New Age eclecticism or eradication of sectarianism (this is the religion of McWorld), but in the philosophical understanding of the entire history of religion. Trying to eradicate Jihad only makes it stronger. The act of understanding alone has the power to make friends of enemies.

9

SCHELLING AND NĀGĀRJUNA: THE 'NIGHT ABSOLUTE', OPENNESS, AND *UNGRUND*

Michael Vater

A key feature of Schelling's Philosophy of Identity, modelled on Spinoza's metaphysics, is its assertion that there is a doublefold of being that can be expressed, but never simplified or explained away: identity *and* difference, absoluteness *and* relativity – infinitude *and* finitude in Spinoza's parlance, or noumenon *and* phenomenon in Kant's. A scant seven years after Fichte declared Kant's thing-in-itself the chief obstacle to adopting his transcendental idealism as the gold standard of philosophical explanation and led German philosophy into a position we might call 'systematic phenomenalism', Schelling apparently reverted to the practice of pre-critical metaphysics, postulating a unified ground of being that, if not directly experienceable, serves at least as a reflexive unification of more prosaic cognitive modes. This paper explores the similarities between Schelling's moves made between 1801 and 1815 and the tradition of Mahayana Buddhist anti-metaphysical argumentation called 'Madhyamika', initiated by the second-century Indian thinker Nāgārjuna and elaborated by the seventh-century thinker Chandrakirti and subsequent commentators in India and Tibet.[1] I argue that the radical simplicity of Madhyamika theory of knowledge and reality, which – in its insistence that, if we distinguish 'absolute' and 'relative' truths or ways of speaking, we are factually acquainted with only one set of conditioned entities to which these labels apply in different ways – provides a benchmark of conceptual clarity by which we can assess Schelling. Still freighted by the West's concept of substance, modelled on the identity and permanence of the 'thing', Schelling continually finds himself forced to reify and then dissolve his Absolute, to both posit and deconstruct substance within it, in order to discover spontaneity or 'will'. Nāgārjuna's contribution to his tradition was, by contrast, the simplifying and consolidating move of identifying what previous thinkers had distinguished, phenomenal being (*saṃsāra*) and its extinction (*nirvāna*), or conditioned arising (*pratītya-samutpāda*) and openness (*śūnyatā*).[2]

The upshot of Madhyamika thinking is to expunge all ideas of the doubleness of absolute and relative truth: openness, the anti-metaphysical character of being, *is* the thoroughly conditioned nature of appearances, no more. Judged by this standard – which long centuries of Buddhist thinking found difficult to achieve and maintain in its purity – Schelling seems constantly to slide into a problematic reification of his 'Absolute' and thus leave himself open to Aristotle's classic objection to the Platonic theory of forms: such discourse reduplicates entities, but fails to explain them.[3] Only if the absolute *is* the relative, is talk of an 'absolute' level of knowing and reality not redundant.

THE ABSOLUTE AND THE RELATIVE

Before we can explore the details of Schelling's and Nāgārjuna's two-layered theories of knowledge and reality, we must see what motivates a thinker to adopt such a double-aspect theory. As far back as Parmenides in the West and Shakyamuni Buddha in early India, thinkers have acknowledged a difference between the sharp-edged particularity that characterizes the items of common experience taken one by one – even if (as in early Buddhist traditions) the 'individual' of ordinary discourse and perception is dissolved by analysis to nothing more than a 'flow' or confluence of atomic sensory moments – and such general features as reflective philosophical thought can assign to the whole order of being. It is interesting that while Parmenides finds the 'Way of Truth' to point away from the multiplicity and variation of appearances to a monolithic 'being' that does not appear, but that must be thought if there is to be *any* thinking or assertion at all, the Buddha, on the basis of the direct experience of his 'wake-up' visions – the seeing-through of his own karmic journeys, those of all suffering migrators, and the interdependent nature of all phenomena – comes to reflectively stamp the endless cycle of worldly being with the 'three characters' (impermanence, suffering or 'dis-ease', and lack of self) that the Mahayana sages will later render by the term *sūnyatā*, emptiness or openness.[4] Things, apprehended in their appearing, one by one, are deceptive – cognitively untrue and affectively unsatisfying. Both thought and desire demand, as Spinoza saw, that finitude must be 'thought away', that philosophy must establish, both by intuition and by argument, a domain where reality is one, undivided, and the object of pure or non-reactive willing. Of course, finitude, particularity and the flow of discrete appearances will not just go away once they are denounced as partial and unsatisfying. If both logic and heart conspire to demand that reality be one, undivided and uncoloured by affect (whether positive or negative), the ordinary materials for cognition – sensation, feeling and the perceptual habits for constructing everyday objects – do not simply evaporate. One is left with a double account of knowing and reality: *being* as I think it ought to be when prompted by the demands of logic and desire and being as it continues to happen under feral conditions. Obviously, this 'double'-thinking is not finally satisfying, any more than double vision would be useful for guiding the motions of one's body. Spinoza swiftly draws the conclusion: *there is no explaining finitude* or its connection to unitary non-finite substance; the finite is its own point of view, and a thoroughly idiosyncratic one in logical terms, even if its fragmentary point of view is our usual *modus operandi*.[5] From the Buddhist side too, the same conclusion is reached: samsaric being, the objects of our perceptions and the items of our grasping, is illusory – it is both *there*, and deceptive and disappointing, in the way a mirage, a dream or a hallucination is.[6]

Schelling is not an idealist in this practical, Buddhistic or Spinozistic sense; he is not impelled by suffering or buffeted by the power-fluctuations (affects) entailed by perceiving and reacting to finite things. He is a theoretical or structural idealist, nurtured by reading Plato's *Timaeus* alongside Kant's *Critiques*, whose chief intellectual motivation is to see the order and organization of nature welling up from the self-constituted spontaneity of the transcendental I.[7] As he approached the break with Fichte and the launching of his Identity Philosophy, Schelling conflated the literal idealism of Platonic natural science with the structural view of nature he learned from Spinoza, wherein being was articulated into discrete orders of attributes or qualitative phenomenal orders, not sundered into individual entities contingently ordered and only randomly associated – by external motion, for instance. It is this structural vision of nature – reality expressed in media both real and ideal, giving rise to phenomena that express nuanced forms of ideality and reality (as gravity and light do, respectively), and ordered by the repeated expression of similar structures – that Schelling is unable to reconcile with the dead objectivity of the Fichtean check or limit and that drives him to reconfigure the whole of his philosophy – to expunge the dynamism and agility of Fichte's introspective 'intellectual intuition' from the naturalized idealism of Identity Philosophy as 'subjectivism' or anthropomorphism.

The 1801 'Presentation of My System' begins with a claim to a self-constituting and self-authorizing 'reason' that is fundamentally different from ordinary finite cognition, whether object-directed or reflective. Schelling argues that reason constructs itself 'between' the subjective and objective, in their 'indifference-point'. It simultaneously abstracts from object-oriented thinking and from its subjective counterpart too. 'Reason's thought is foreign to everyone; to conceive it as absolute, thus to come to the standpoint I require, one must abstract from what does the thinking.'[8] In this disembodied and transfinite knowing, philosophy constructs an absolute stance, and therefore posits an Absolute beyond phenomena whose medium is 'reason' and whose life is 'Philosophy', in the definitive or archetypal version which is the object of all systems and the effort of all philosophizing. Having thus talked or, more grandly, 'posited' his way into this self-inflating transfinite stance, Schelling's only problem is to return to earth now and then, or at least to survey the domains of finite being so that they can be noetically mapped onto the Absolute. The qualitative features of relative being offer no problem; a simple quantitative line ordered by three points – the subjective, the objective, and, in between them, the point of balance or indifference – serves handily enough to translate all phenomena into relatively 'subjective' or 'objective' amalgams of the basic real-ideal concrete being.[9] What the line cannot do, and no amount of fiddling with its formula or with Platonic-sounding incantations can do, is to derive the relative from the Absolute. The problem of individuation becomes the knot or tension point of Schelling's systems, and in succeeding decades Schelling often seems to drift into the hopeless task of 'deriving' the underivable finite, or explaining the inexplicable finite. The 'thing' of common experience becomes, in his philosophy, the ultimate surd: the theoretical counterpart of Nāgārjuna's tantalizing 'city of Gandharvas'.

Does Nāgārjuna encounter a similar problem, or does the fourfold logic of classical Buddhist thinking prevent the question of the ontological status of the individual from ever arising? If, in the West, the dubious being of particulars on the level of relativity forces thought to another level where being, value, and beauty are conceived in such purity that a subsequent reconnection of the absolute to the relative becomes problematic, in Buddhist thinking one moves from the problematic character of things – whether 'self' or 'object,' or indeed 'belief' or 'view' – to the level of *sūnyatā*, where one isolates that very character: openness (emptiness) or lack of any conceivable fixed character. The problem is not, as in the West, that one cannot reconceive relative being in relation to absolute being once that level has been achieved, but that one will repeat at the level of absolute analysis the fundamental mistake made at the relative: reifying or solidifying the flowing, evanescent, spontaneous and 'appearing' nature of reality, fixing it as *svabhāba* or 'self-nature'. The mistake lies in *grasping*: the 'taking-as-real' endemic to all dualistic perception, willing, and thinking that makes distinct entities of *what appears*, of its *appearing for* ... and of *that to which the appearing is*, viz., 'object', 'relation between' and 'subject'. The mistake of grasping is primarily cognitive: a 'mis-take' or misinterpretation, and not primarily an overreach of will or desire. The dissolution of grasping in perceiving, willing, thinking that Buddhism recommends as liberating therapy is the dissolution of the chief cognitive mis-take, the solidification of the various sensory, affective, hedonic, and dispositional streams of experience in a 'self'. This dissolution of the I's mistaken self-absolutization is the intent of first-order Buddhist teaching, which is soteriological, not philosophical, and which, once accomplished, indeed shows the fly the way out of proverbial fly-bottle.[10] Nāgārjuna compactly expresses this first-order teaching near the beginning of his chapter on the self:

> One who does not grasp onto 'I' and 'mine',
> That one does not exist.
> One who does not grasp onto 'I' and 'mine',
> He does not perceive.

When views of 'I' and 'mine' are extinguished,
Whether with respect to the internal or external,
The appropriator ceases.
This having ceased, [re-] birth ceases.

Action [karma] and misery having ceased, there is
liberation [mokṣa]
Action and misery come from conceptual thought.
This comes from mental fabrication [prapañca]
Fabrication ceases through emptiness.[11]

This whole passage, up to the last line, speaks of the 'realities' of conventional discourse, whose standing in appearance Buddhist teaching does not dispute (nor the usefulness of discourse about them, in everyday contexts). Perceivers, graspers, Is, appropriators, sufferers and migrators all pertain to the level of appearances and to the consequences of taking such appearances to be solid beings having permanent reality (or self-nature: svabhāva). The last line mentions the sole item of second-order teaching ('absolute truth'): sūnyatā – emptiness, openness, indeterminacy, flexibility or lack of fixity. The problem for Buddhist thinking, which starts out to be resolutely non-metaphysical, is to refrain from repeating the original mistake – grasping, solidification or 'reification' of first-order items (appearances) – on the second-order level, that is, to point to it without naming, conceptualizing, or substantializing it. To be true to its soteriological intent, Buddhist thought must be non-theoretical; it must *not* produce philosophy.

Nāgārjuna's next lines, which reproduce the *tetralemma* of early Buddhist texts depicting Shakyamuni's refusal to answer unanswerable questions by systematically denying *all* logical possibilities of formulating an answer, illustrate this 'path of non-thinking':

That there is a self [ātman] has been taught,
And the doctrine of no-self [anātman],
By the buddhas, as well as
The doctrine of neither self nor nonself.

What language expresses is nonexistent.
The sphere of thought is nonexistent.
Unarisen and unceased, like nirvāṇa
Is the nature of things [dharmatā].

Everything is real [tathyam: factual] and is not real,
Both real and not real,
Neither real nor not real.
This is Lord Buddha's teaching.

Unconditioned by another, peaceful and
Not fabricated by mental fabrication,
Not thought, without distinctions,
That is the character of real*ity* (that-ness) [*tattvasya*].[12]

The four possibilities of the tetralemma are that something exists, does
not exist, both exists and does not exist, and has no ontological status
(neither exists nor does not exist). When this is asserted of conventional
entities like the 'I' of ordinary discourse, as in the passage's third stanza, the
way is blocked to any *theory* of 'the self', for example, the Vedic and Upa-
niṣadic teachings about the abiding *ātman* or any competing materialistic
theory about the ultimate nonexistence of a subject that perceives, thinks,
talks, and so forth. This by no means undermines ordinary language, however, for – as the first stanza reminds us – the buddhas speak, for life
guidance, about the conventional self of everyday life and discourse in any
and all ways that are useful. A confession of absent-mindedness in most
contexts is not nihilistic, nor is answering 'present' to a roll-call
metaphysical substantialism.

If there is, in ordinary contexts, no *problem* with the items of ordinary
discourse, and in exact discourse, no formulating any *theory* of them – our
first and third stanzas define the territory of 'relative truth' – then any
putative 'nature of things' is wholly beyond any precise saying or thinking.
The unconditional or 'absolute' sense of things, indicated in Nāgārjuna's
second and fourth stanzas, is a matter of seeing (*if*, indeed, one sees it), and
not of saying – either on the conventional or technical level. The terms
dharmatā ('thing-ness'), 'suchness' and the like, though used in Buddhist
thinking as technical terms, have a 'loosey-goosey', non-referring function:
they indicate not being able to indicate anything. The Madhyamika
('Middle-Way') philosophy that Nāgārjuna elaborates holds that:

(1) The objects of ordinary discourse and practice – persons and objects –
appear as they appear and function as they function in ordinary life contexts.
If the 'I' did not grasp itself as entity rather than *perform* as a cognitive and
volitional *function*, no ontological problems would arise.

(2) If one asks about ontological commitment to these things, neither
assertions of existence or reality (*eternalism*) are appropriate, nor corresponding denials (*nihilism*), much less any logically exotic other possibilities.

(3) The 'Middle Way' between the rejected options of (2) can be expressed
only in *negative* terms – in one word, 'emptiness', or in many, 'unoriginated,
undestroyed' and so forth.[13] The negative ontology of the middle way
simultaneously affirms the phenomenal status of the items in (1) – along
with their non-problematic, non-theoretical character – and the impossibility of either formulating or denying their 'reality', as expressed in (2).

The whole weight of Nāgārjuna's thinking, then, is to deny that appearances have any reality, or to say the same thing, that they are *sūnya:* empty, open, flexible, spontaneously appearing and workable – susceptible to many, perhaps divergent interpretations and uses.[14] In a subsequent section we will work on the more difficult idea that the interdependent or infinitely conditioned character of phenomena in their appearing is the whole meaning of this lack of solid being or emptiness-openness. Nāgārjuna's distinctive contribution to Madhyamika thought is that emptiness is nothing other than this dense interconditioning of phenomena; it too is empty, even of emptiness. *Pratītya-samutpāda* (the webs of phenomenal conditioning that bring appearances to appearance) and *sūnyatā* refer exactly and only to each other.

The clarity of Nāgārjuna's view – one sole domain of appearances, described in two ways, once in terms of the conditioned laws of appearances and again in terms of their lack of substance – will serve as a standard by means of which to assess Schelling's thinking on the relative and the Absolute, as it evolved from 1801 through 1815.

THE 'NIGHT ABSOLUTE'

The canonical text of the System of Identity is the 1801 'Presentation of My System of Philosophy'. Patterned on Spinoza's *Ethics*, it preserves in broad outline Spinoza's distinctions among substance, attributes, and modes, and even more importantly, the dichotomy between infinite existence and finitude.[15] At its beginning, Schelling adumbrates the 'essence'–'form' distinction, on which so much of his philosophy turns, in terms of the 'identity of reason', meaning substantial or qualitative identity, and its conceptual or propositional expression in terms of the 'law of identity', A = A. This law is also said to be an 'unconditional *cognition* of identity'.[16] The Absolute is identity, therefore, but identity doubled in the lenses of essence and form or an 'identity of identity' – essential identity mirrored in an infinite cognition of identity.[17] Infinite cognition, however, is abstract or categorical, and so not *for a subject* nor *of an object*. Evidently – and here Schelling's text plainly leaps a gap rather than providing a transition – such cognition cannot be fully *realized* without being fragmented into myriads of finite cognizers or subject-objects, each with a correspondingly fragmented version of original identity: '*Absolute identity cannot posit itself infinitely without infinitely positing itself as subject and object.*' Schelling's proof is laconic (at best): 'This proposition is self-evident.'[18] Having established the fracture of the Absolute in its realization – though never offering any *a priori* explanation why there should be a divergence between essence and expression or 'reason' and 'reflection' – Schelling proceeds in the remaining general discussions of the 'Presentation' to unfold a double description of the realized or finitized cosmos – one description in which every individual is said to be itself a totality, or real, only insofar as it is embedded in the totality of a 'power' or order of being, and another description in which the individual as individual is unreal, illusory, and lacking any ground of being.[19]

Schelling deferred comments on the methodology of the System of Identity in the 'Presentation', but in a series of essays penned in the months following its publication, he finally confronted the unresolved issues of that first attempt: the need to demonstrate that an absolute stance is possible alongside the relative (or that philosophy rises to reason from reflection); and to address the question whether the individual can enter absolute philosophy as an individual or only as a variable in an abstract algorithm. In a passage that prefigures Hegel's infamous comments in the preface to the *Phenomenology*, Schelling laments that 'most people see in the essence of the Absolute nothing but empty night, and can discern nothing in it. It disappears for them into mere negation of difference, and is for itself entirely a privative entity. Therefore, they prudently make it the end of their philosophy.'[20] He later continues: 'The essence of the Absolute in and for itself says nothing to us; it fills us with images of an infinite enclosure, of an impenetrable enclosure and concealment, the way the oldest forms of philosophy pictured the state of the universe before He who is life stepped forth *in his own shape* in the act of his self-intuitive cognition.' This is the eternal form, the day that comprehends and illuminates the riches of the night Absolute. This cognition, otherwise called 'intellectual intuition', is 'the light in which we clearly discern the light of the Absolute, the eternal mediator, the all-seeing and all-disclosing eye of the world.'[21] What Schelling struggles to articulate with this notion of the Absolute's form is a cognition at once self-constituting and self-knowing, an archetypal mind or luminosity which is universal, not individual, and which constitutes the 'space' of articulation and knowing. It is evidently both the ground of our sort of knowledge, finite cognition or reflection, and of its connection to the self-constituting reality of the Absolute. 'Only in the form of all forms is the positive essence of [the Absolute's] unity cognized. But in us this is embodied as the living idea of the Absolute, so that our cognition has its being in it and it subsists in us.'[22] These are difficult ideas that Schelling lays out in language more prophetical than argumentative. The problems of the relation of the Absolute to the dual orders of phenomena, of the connection of the 'night Absolute' to the day of cognition – or of the way the Absolute's form or 'idea' is mirrored in reflective or discursive human knowing – are the central metaphysical and epistemic problems of Identity Philosophy. Schelling never managed to solve them in a straightforward and coherent way, although he continued to write as if they were soluble, if not solved.

OPENNESS

Nāgārjuna's teaching on emptiness or openness was not an isolated achievement; a moment of conceptual clarity and rigour, that once achieved, stayed fixed and ever accessible. His cryptic argument – culminating in the claim that the Buddha never offered any 'teaching' – spawned generations of commentators, and, once entered into the historical stream of Buddhist thought, evoked the paradoxical response of multiplying philosophies and metaphysical attempts to define what emptiness is or is not.[23] The crystallization of philosophical interpretations around the core idea that *there is no precise saying of what is the case* illustrates, at least, the plausibility of Buddhism's non-theoretical or soteriological thrust; one's grasping onto and defence of a conceptual scheme is every bit as much a grasping as is sensual desire or anger toward a perceived enemy – both in the solidification of the knowing situation, and in the attachment to one's view and one's arguments that arises along with 'intellectual certainty'. Almost despite itself, therefore, late Indian Buddhism elaborates subtly differentiated positions about the 'being' and 'non-being' of the self and its objects. The generation and exhaustive testing of argument for all plausible positions has traditionally been used as a training technique – not to arrive at any ultimate propositional truth or any theoretical resting place, but merely to exercise one's mind in the 'land of untruth' by refuting untruths until the process shuts down the mind and 'seeing' can occur.[24] In this context, of course, what is 'seen' is what is *not* there. This scepticism about whether the human mind is capable of simultaneously seeing and saying the true marks the unique approach and self-limitation of Buddhist thinking. The ultimate use of philosophy is to stop thinking!

That is easily enough said, but the only fruitful way to pursue the negative ontology of Madhyamika speculation is to speculate actively and then analyse self-critically and refute the positions spun out. That is roughly the process that Buddhist thinking followed in late India and Tibet, where a line of thought that goes from Nāgārjuna (second century) to Chandrakirti (seventh century) was continued by Tibetan scholars of various monastic allegiances, notably Tsongkhapa (1357–1419, founder of the Geluk order) and Jamgön Mipham (1846–1912, of the Nyingma order and the Rimé movement).[25] Though I cannot summarize the whole history of Madhyamika here, we can safely follow established designations and call Nāgārjuna's original position the 'Middle Way' or *prasangika.*[26] A *prasanga* is a 'consequential' argument (*reductio ad absurdum*): it invalidates an assumption by deriving a contradiction, but it does no more than make a negative statement. From Nāgārjuna's plain statement that in teaching emptiness (openness) the Buddha taught nothing, we can see why the tradition that follows him calls itself Prasangika (or Consequence School) and claims that it produces no theory, no philosophy, that in advancing the *non-affirming negations* that it generates, it aims merely to clear the ground of conceptuality or precisely stated untruth.[27]

A second position in the Madhyamika, opposed to the simple Prasangika line and refuted by Chandrakirti as too epistemically and metaphysically robust to be the 'middle-way' is *svatantrika*, the Independence School – so-called because it advanced independent inferences, or 'affirming negations', about relative being, viewed in the light of emptiness or absolute being. It is also rightly called the 'Independence' school because it argues that phenomena, though empty of reality on the level of ultimate truth, retain their relative qualities and functions on the level of relative truth or conventional discourse. Thus, we distinguish in appearances between our perceptions of a 'real' city and those perceptions which are eventually dismissed as mistakes and arising from a mirage. The effect of Svatantrika reasoning, as Chandrakirti and Tsongkhapa both argue, is to validate a common-sense realism on the level of appearances, but to claim on the unrelated level of 'ultimate truth' that appearances are nonetheless 'empty'.[28] They commit a triple fault: duplicating levels of reality, solidifying or objectifying ordinary appearances, and emptying the teaching on emptiness of any meaning or function. The Svatantrika view, it is argued, has no liberating function; it subtly encourages one to cling to everyday 'realities' and to adopt extravagant beliefs about domains of reality that one has not experienced.[29]

A third position we can identify is that advanced by Tsongkhapa and the Geluks, and refuted by Mipham in his commentary on Chandrakirti. This position is unnamed, but we could perhaps label it neo-svatantrika in that it sneaks around to a reification of the two levels of truth and to a subtle, 'functional' reification of phenomena on the relative level. The Geluks argue, for example, that if this stream of perceptions I am having is a 'pot', then the teaching on emptiness means *not* that the pot is empty of pot, but that it is empty of *true existence*. Emptiness, replies Mipham, does not mean that the phenomenal pot works so well on the level of appearances that we can have a theory of appearances and understand the reality of apparent objects, but that philosophical analysis cannot even find the 'pot' in the pot, much less anything as exotic as 'true existence'. Emptiness or openness, as the ultimate but wholly negative character of appearances or conventional things, means the whole conceptual apparatus used to talk about and manipulate them falls apart — that we cannot find entity, cause, effect, agent, process, arising, dwelling, disappearing — in appearances. Like Froggie's car, appearances go without saying, but when we try to say why they go, they stop going, as does our saying. Mipham puts it this way — and in my estimation recaptures the simple core of Nāgārjuna's teaching about the identity of emptiness and interdependent arising:

> If the eye is not empty according to its nature, it cannot be empty of true existence. For in that case, the nature of the eye is not emptiness. Indeed, since an other-emptiness is not a self-emptiness, such an (extraneous) emptiness cannot be the nature of the thing itself. It is instead something wholly alien to it, in the same way as a nonexistent sky-lotus cannot exemplify the nature of a lotus grown in water ... One must therefore affirm that the nature of all phenomena is emptiness: phenomena are empty of themselves.[30]

There is no character attributed to phenomena that they *have*; everything attributed to them is imputed, nothing more. There is nothing to be said about the character they have other than that they appear; if there appears even to be an 'arising', a 'dwelling', or an 'extinction' of their appearance, it cannot be found if you look for it, and, if you think you see it, you cannot express it. There is no theory of appearances; their whole function is their appearing. Anything more one wants to say about them must be phrased negatively: they are empty, open, indeterminate, and when they arise, they arise relatively, in reference to one another, conditioning one another. *Nothing* in any way exemplifies what Spinoza correctly said must be thought and said about substance (if there is any) – it *is* and is *conceived* through itself. Phenomenalism is negative ontology – nothing is and is conceived through itself – or, said in a less nihilistic manner, everything is let free to happen, though none of it can be referred to itself, or be isolated, single, detached in its appearances. 'Appearance' refers to context, the background of cognition; there is no end to context, just as there is no end to space – though at a certain point of course, we lose the will to continue on and on to verify this view.

Do we now have the correct reading of Nāgārjuna's openness? Of course it will not stay still for thinking, because thinking wants to pin it down and fix it, make it an essence. Have we missed it? Probably not; it is likely we have had a glimpse or two beneath the garments of language and thought as we reviewed the merry dance of Madhyamika positions and switched from essence of existence, absolute to relative, and pot to no pot. Would we get it if we did it again tomorrow? Probably yes, a bit, and no. Would we ever really *get* it? No, says Nāgārjuna; at least not *as philosophy:*

> The Conquer taught openness as the refutation of all views.
> But those who hold openness as a view are beyond remedy.[31]

UNGRUND

To this point we have explored the origin of the problem of the absolute and the relative in Schelling and Nāgārjuna, and we have found that in the first thinker there tends to be a reduplication of entity in thought and discourse when one posits the Absolute alongside finite being, whereas in the second the two levels, once posited, tend to disappear into less than one under the pressure of philosophical analysis. In general we can dimly see that all problems disappear if there is a sheer symmetry of reference between the absolute and the relative, so that they are differentiated but interdefined aspects, but both ultimately referred to appearances, and our recent Madhyamika voyages have taught us that one needs to keep one's thinking moving in order to keep this paradoxical view in view.

We turn now to a later phase of Schelling's thinking, to his 1809 essay on human freedom and his attempt there to refound his system on a new basis, that of 'will' or 'freedom' rather than being.[32] I wish to carry into this investigation two lessons from Nāgārjuna – on the positive side, that we must keep moving in order to see, in some sense, items that do not appear as a steady presence for a seeing that is itself not a steady presence, and on the negative or cautionary side, the warning that one errs the most when one tries to make a 'philosophy' of openness, or a 'philosophy of freedom'.

The Philosophy of Identity was a monstrously boring construction, an imposition of the same on the different by the manipulation of a sterile formula: *the quantitative difference* (or in the highest case, the indifference) *of the subjective and the objective*, or the *identity of identity and opposition*.[33] It was encyclopaedic without being really systematic; one could not see the articulation of the principle of system, one could only read about it after the fact. The bellows of the hurdy-gurdy were well creased and tightly folded, but who or what pulled and pushed the folds and what reed provided the voice remained hidden from view.

Schelling now realizes that what he had discussed in earlier versions of 'the system' as the mechanism of counter-systematic aberration – the individual's self-positing as finite, self-temporalization, or 'the fall of ideas from the Absolute' – can provide the clue if he can but separate the idea of action from action in time. Being is now grasped as *will*, a term that imports into the basis of all explanation both a subjective and objective aspect – on the one side, something like a psychological process and, on the other, factual limitation or determining placement in situation. By virtue of the first, reality is invested with yearning, drive, resistance, and desire – a process that finally culminates in decisive choice and which makes space in it for unforeseen event – sheer happening or spontaneous action. By virtue of the second, unforeseen consequences arise in the fluid situation – quite outside the territory of desire, intention, foresight, or planning – but they impart to it an *after the fact* intelligibility, such as the feeling of 'chosen fate' or 'destiny embraced'. The mechanisms of human motivation – action, dispositional formation, and the grey determination of repetition and habit *as well as* the opposite movements of prescient choice, foresight, intention, and self-transforming desire – are built into the nature of things when freedom or will is made the system basis. But if nature is psychologized in this new version of system, human choice is naturalized, removed from the censoring discourse of at least Kantian morality and religion. Instead of the abstract logical formulae of formal, negative freedom, Schelling demands that the system principle incorporate a real, naturalized and positive idea of freedom – freedom for good or evil.[34] The joint of system folds not only the lateral dimensions of nature and consciousness and maps their structures upon one another; their midpoint or centre of indifference is articulated along the vertical axis, and the natural-and-conscious regions of divine love (ideality, the *telos* of union) and history (reality, the divided and divisive material backdrop of human actions, good and evil) emerge as mirror and counterpoint. If Schelling were visually to represent the situation of categorial willing in the freedom essay, it would look something like this:[35]

God

Nature   Consciousness

Historical Existence

Space does not allow us to trace out all these complicated relationships in detail, nor to pose basic methodological questions about the philosopher's access to knowledge of such things. Our interest is in the more logical features of Schelling's metaphysics of freedom – the double emergence of being or appearances (nature and consciousness) from the indifferent primal state he calls *Ungrund* and the articulation of structures of intelligibility and production (ground and existence) within appearances. Schelling's key idea is that freedom and necessitation coexist in the highest case, God or the Absolute, and within that categorial overlap, produced or derivative absoluteness can occur; this is the situation of humankind's standing *vis-à-vis* the divine, a freedom that is thrown or necessitated.[36] Humankind is created or derivative, argues Schelling, 'but dependence does not exclude autonomy or even freedom. Dependence does not determine the nature of the dependent, and merely declares that the dependent entity, whatever else it may be, can only be as a consequence of that upon which it depends; it does not declare what this dependent entity is or is not.'[37] The model for this dependent independence or derived freedom is to be sought in language and logic. The *statement*, in making an assertion or expressing a content, does not (except in the case of tautology) express a bald identity; if there is content expressed, the identity of the copula signifies not sheer identity but the relation of grounding as well: ground and consequence, antecedent conditions and emergent results.[38] Schelling claims that this understanding of identity as grounding was advanced as early as the 1801 'Presentation of My System'. What he cites in his earlier discussions of gravity, forces, and light, is the intriguing reciprocal relationship between an essential identity of opposite powers in the 'ground' – gravity, to this day an idea that must be thought as one of the bases for the action of matter, but whose actual or existent force or particle cannot be empirically located – and its manifestation in phenomena as the existing co-presence of opposed repulsive and attractive forces.[39] On this understanding of the ground-existent relationship, Schelling can posit a latent but necessary connection of necessity and freedom (or even of good and evil) as essence or possibility in the primal ground, and can at the same time think of their expressed distinction as realized inside the 'created absoluteness' of humankind, whose historical existence is given over to realizing these opposites in all their contrariety.

In the early stages of the freedom essay, therefore, Schelling employs his new understanding of identity as grounding (or sufficient reason) to explain how the identity of nature and spirit in the Absolute can be the basis for the emergence of conscious and social being from natural conditions, how the essential identity of freedom and necessitation in primal willing can ground the emergence of human conduct, free in some respects, necessitated in others, and leading to historical situations, some marked by good, others by evil. We have a fairly satisfactory explanation of the fourfold of being in appearances, but Schelling's whole description there seems to move on the level of the ontic, rather than the ontological. The initial description has the further defect of asserting, without explaining, the counterpart 'existential' movements of the personalization of God and the actualization of evil in humans. If the existential 'histories' of the deity – in the process of becoming person or love at the price of having stepped out of absoluteness – and of humankind's adventures in good and evil – in order to effect an eventual separation of them and a purifying transmogrification of the latter – are to have any explanatory power, they too must be seen as produced or consequent moments in a grounding relationship as proceeding out of a prior undifferentiated state. When Schelling turns to this task, late in his argument, the ontological dimension of sheer Indifference or Absoluteness is introduced again, now with the dramatically negative-sounding name of *Ungrund* (the groundless).[40]

The contrast between the (logically, not temporally) original *Ungrund* or Indifference and the God and humankind that emerge from it is the contrast between the abstract pantheistic conception of deity and the conception of a living personal God. In the prior state, opposites lie together as disjuncts inclusively disjoined; when opposition is actualized in transition to existence, disjunction is exclusive, active, and, in time, 'critical' or divisive. Actualization effects judgment, cosmic division and differentiation. Schelling says:

> Reality and ideality, darkness and light ... can never be predicated of the groundless *as antitheses*. But nothing prevents their being predicated as non-antitheses, that is, in disjunction and each *for itself*; wherein, however, this duality (the real twofoldness of principles) is established. There is in the groundless itself nothing to prevent this. For just because its relation toward both is a relation of total indifference, it is neutral (*gleichgültig*) toward both. If it were the absolute identity of both, it could only be both *at the same time* ... Thus out of this neither-nor, or out of indifference, duality immediately breaks forth (which is something quite different than opposition ...) – and *without* indifference, that is, *without* the groundless, there would be no twofoldness of the principles. Instead of undoing the distinction, as was expected, the groundless rather posits and confirms it.[41]

This passage represents Schelling's most careful thinking about the so-called identity of the Absolute: it is an essential distinction without active opposition (*Gegensetzung*). It accounts for the duality of coordinated real principles, once the opposites are posited as nature and consciousness, for example, as the mutually mirroring evolving principles of divine personality and humankind in history.

Note that Schelling argues that actualized duality 'directly breaks forth' out of the neither-nor of indifference. The 'will' in this 'philosophy of freedom' is unmotivated, or spontaneous. A psychology of desire in the divine imagination could be added to the story, but as it is in *Ages of the World*, the most that systematic philosophy can do to *explain* willing is to explain the conditions of willing and the antecedent-consequent logic of grounding. Activity or volition cannot be deduced. Schelling achieves the simple inter-referentiality of Nāgārjuna's Madhyamika account of the absolute and the relative: one set of items, two descriptions, reduplication of content as *explanans* and *explanadum*. If, pictured at this level of abstraction, the reduplication seems a bit obvious and the explanation a bit tautological, we can ask whether any explanation achieves anything more. It is simply 'logic in, logic out' − and other than that there is just the sensory manifold, raw sensory *qualia*. As Nāgārjuna and his Madhyamika brethren can teach us, logic and language work at a coarse, conventional level, but beyond moving us through the texture of inter-coordinated appearances, they do not function, and when pressed, they show only that there is nothing to see. The bright day of appearances fades into the 'night Absolute'.

What about the comparative success of the two philosophies, Buddhist Madhyamika speculation and Schelling's Philosophy of Freedom? Schelling certainly seems to have more positive content in his philosophy, but much of it is smuggled in from the existing discourses of morals and religious doctrine. Platonist that he is, with a positive sense to be imparted to being or actuality, he first has to argue from the relative to the Absolute, then somehow argue for the descent or derivation of the relative. Nāgārjuna has the cleaner, more phenomenological task of noticing the lack of being on the level of relative being, of formulating the absolute as a generalization of this lack of characteristics, no more, and of pointing out the identity of reference between the two levels of discourse. The Buddhist thinker, however, faces the additional and daunting task of learning to see as she thinks, not as she wishes.

Notes

1   For a brief history of Madhyamika thought in India from Nāgārjuna to Chandrakirti, see 'Translators' Introduction', *Introduction to the Middle Way: Chandrakirti's* Madhyamakavatara *with Commentary by Jamgön Mipham*, trans. Padmakara Translation Group (Boston: Shambhala, 2002), 5–32. Cited hereafter as Chandrakirti.

2   McCagney, N., *Nāgārjuna and the Philosophy of Openness* (Lanham MD and Oxford: Rowman & Littlefield, 1997), 51, 59.

3   See Aristotle, *Metaphysics* i.9, 991a2–10 and 991b1–5.

4   For an account of Gautama's enlightenment experience and its significance,

with a brief investigation of the twelve links of interdependent arising (*pratītya-samutpāda*) which *Aśvagosha* claims was its chief cognitive content, see Robinson, R. H., Johnson W. H. *The Buddhist Religion: A Historical Introduction*, 4th edition (Belmont CA: Wadsworth, 1997), 15–20, 23–9. Cited hereafter as Robinson and Johnson. For the 'three characters' of saṃsaric being, see *Dhammapada*, trans. and notes by John Ross Carter and Mahinda Palihawadana (New York and Oxford: Oxford University Press, 2000), XX, 277–9, 49.

For an introduction to 'emptiness,' including an accessible paraphrase of Nāgārjuna's chief line of argument in the *Mūlamadhyamakārikā*, see Sue Hamilton, *Indian Philosophy: A Very Short Introduction* (New York and Oxford: Oxford University Press, 2001), 94–100.

5   For Spinoza, a finite thing is finite if and only if it is limited by another finite being of its own kind or within its own qualitative order. It cannot be conceived as a non-finite limitation of the one God/Nature, but only as following within one of the infinite modes that is already cut up into chains of finite causal determination. Though we can understand how one finite being causes, limits and determines another, we cannot conceive how being itself undergoes fundamental limitation. See Baruch Spinoza, *Ethics*, Book I, Def. 21, Prop. 28 and Proof, trans. Samuel Shirley (Indianapolis: Hackett, 1982), 31, 50–1.

6   Nāgārjuna ends his investigation of conditioned being (finite things) this way:

> Like a dream, like an illusion,
> Like a city of Gandharvas [fairies],
> So have arising, abiding
> And ceasing been explained.

The Fundamental Wisdom of the Middle Way: Nāgārjuna's Mūlamadhyamakārikā, trans. and commentary by Jay Garfield (New York and Oxford: Oxford University Press, 1995), VII, verse 34, p. 22. See also pp. 159–77. Hereafter cited as MMK-G.

7   Schelling's notes on the *Timaeus* show how struck he was by Plato's assumption that 'a single Idea in the divine understanding' underlies the genera that nature exhibits, that a 'noetic cosmos' makes possible the order of empirical nature. The syntax of nature is *ideal* – not factual, existent, or physical – and it is *prior* to everything empirical, not abstracted from it. Schelling breathlessly draws the conclusion: nature's *idea* can be nothing originated nor destroyed, so it is simply *not subject to the form of time*. Schelling, F., *Timaeus* 1794, ed. Hartmut Buchner (Stuttgart-Bad Cannstatt: Frommann-Holzboog, 1994), 30, 37.

8   Schelling, F., 'Darstellung meines Systems der Philosophie', §1, Def., in *Sämtliche Werke*, ed. K. F. A. Schelling (Stuttgart and Augsburg, 1856f.), vol. IV, 114–15. Hereafter cited as 'Darstellung', SW IV. See also Schelling, F., 'Presentation of My System of Philosophy', trans. Michael Vater, in *The Philosophical Forum*, XXXII, No. 4 (Winter 2001), 349. Hereafter cited as 'Presentation'.

9   SW IV, pp. 137–9. 'Presentation', 365–7.

10   Heidegger punningly suggests that the totality of the Absolute (if there is such an entity or order) lies its being ab-solved from extrinsic relation, in the intensification of its self-relation and self-reference. In contrast, the Buddhist dissolution of the false absolutization of the 'self' is the relocation of consciousness in centreless space, or the de-centring of the illusory (and pre-Copernican) cosmology which is the 'self'. See Heidegger, M., *Schelling's Treatise on the Essence of Human Freedom*, trans. Joan Stambaugh (Athens OH: Ohio University Press, 1985), 43. Henceforth cited as *Schelling's Treatise*.

11   MMK-G, XVIII, 3–5; translation altered. For the Sanskrit, see Nancy

McCagney, *Nāgārjuna and the Philosophy of Openness* (Lanham MD and Oxford: Rowman & Littlefield, 1997), 181. Cited hereafter as MMK-M.

12 MMK-G, XVIII, 6–9, 49; translation altered. Compare MMK-M, 182.

13 Nāgārjuna furnishes the complete formula in his famous dedicatory verses:

> Whatever is dependently arisen is
> Unceasing, unborn,
> Unannihilated, not permanent,
> Not coming, not going,
> Without distinction, without identity,
> And free from conceptual construction.

> (MMK-G, 2: see MMK-M, 137)

14 Nāgārjuna transformed earlier philosophical analyses of the interdependent nature of appearances – the Abhidharma of the Sarvastivadin – by denying any element of substance to the apparent succession of momentary events that make up the texture of appearance or any sense of linear time in consciousness's progression through the twelve nodes of *pratūya-samutpāda*. Appearances are densely interconditioned and coproduced; the appearing 'entity' or *dharma* floats on a sea of *tendrel*: interconnection, interinfluence, interaction. See Reginald Ray, *Indestructible Truth: the Living Spirituality of Tibet* (Boston and London: Shambhala, 2000), 369–72, 394–8. Cited hereafter as *Indestructible Truth*. See also Robinson and Johnson, 86–9.

15 Spinoza's conviction that the one substance is expressed in at least two irreducible orders (extension and thought) and that finite modes follow identically but separately in the two orders is captured by Schelling in the object-and-image world picture that articulates physical nature and consciousness along similar lines through the repeated instantiation of the subject-object relation – conceived geometrically as an extended line, whose extremes are 'subjectivity' and 'objectivity', and whose midpoint is the identity or indifference of these qualities. See Baruch Spinoza, *Ethics*, I Def. 2–6, II, Prop. 7, Cor. and Schol.; Schelling, 'Darstellung meines Systems', §§ 41–47. including corollaries and remarks, SW IV, pp. 134–9; 'Presentation', 362–6.

16 Schelling's 'Presentation' depends from the start on an unspecified difference between *reason* and *reflection*, the mode of cognition that gets expressed in propositions and which carries with it externality, succession, duration, and analysis in terms of mechanical causality. Their *convergence* in the single case of reason and the law of identity defines the standpoint of the Absolute; see 'Darstellung', §§ 1–7, SW IV, 114–18; 'Presentation', 349–51.

17 'Darstellung', § 16, Cor. 2–§ 20, SW IV, pp. 121–3; 'Presentation', 354–5.

18 'Darstellung' §21, SW IV, 123; 'Presentation', 355.

19 Compare §§ 35–8 (including corollaries, explanations and remarks) with §§ 39–43. §37 explains that quantitative difference of the subjective and the objective is the ground of finitude, while quantitative indifference is infinitude (SW IV, pp. 130–5; 'Presentation', 360–3.) Only for reflection, of course, and not for reason, is the *qualitative identity* of absolute Identity refracted into the *quantitative indifference* of subjectivity and objectivity. It is worth noting that this pseudo-mathematical approach to the problem of the Absolute and the relative is what forever after draws Hegel's scorn for his erstwhile colleague.

20 'Fernere Darstellungen aus dem System der Philosophie' (1802), SW IV, 403; hereafter cited as 'Fernere Darstellungen', SW IV. See also 'Further Presentations from the System of Philosophy', trans. Michael Vater, *The Philosophical*

Forum, XXXII, No. 4 (Winter 2001), 391; hereafter cited as 'Further Presentations'.

21 'Fernere Darstellungen', SW IV, 404–5; 'Further Presentations', 392.
22 'Fernere Darstellungen', SW IV, 404; 'Further Presentations', 391.
23 Nāgārjuna ends his analysis of *nirvāṇa* with these verses:

> Since all events are open, what is infinite, what is finite?
> What is infinite and finite and what is neither infinite nor finite?
>
> What has gone away? What identity? What difference?
> What is permanent and impermanent or neither, and so forth?
>
> Liberation is cessation of all thought, the quieting of phenomena.
> No doctrine was taught by the Buddha at any time, at any place, to any person.

MMK-M, XXV, 22–4; 210 (translation altered); see MMK-G, 76.

24 On monastic training in philosophy and debate, see *Indestructible Truth*, 200–4.
25 For a concise account of these orders in ancient and recent Tibetan Buddhism, see *Indestructible Truth*, 103–29, 189–225.
26 For the closest thing in English to a complete history of Buddhist philosophy and dialects see John Petit's extensive introduction to *Mipham's Beacon of Certainty: Illuminating the view of Dzogchen, the Great Perfection* (Boston: Wisdom Publications, 1991), 51–61, 101–24.
27 Chandrakirti, 'Translators' Introduction', 20–4.
28 Says Tsongkhapa, 'Even though the Savatantrikas do not actually say that things exist truly, nevertheless, because they do not refute them with a reasoning directed at the ultimate [level], and because they assert that phenomena have an existence according to their characteristics, they succeed, in effect, in proving the true existence of things, though this is not what they intend.' Cited by Jamgön Mipham, 'The Word of Chandra: The Spotless Crystal Necklace: A Commentary on the Madhyamakavatara' in Chandrakirti, 175. Mipham refutes the Svatantrika view in his own voice thus: 'When it is said that the eye is empty of eye, the thing that is empty is *the eye itself*. But what is it empty of? Again, it is the *eye* of which it is empty. The eye is empty of itself. If it is said that the eye is not empty of eye but is empty of an extraneous attribute such as a true appearance of the eye, this is not at all the meaning of emptiness. As Chandrakirti says … "The eye is empty of eye" (and so on for all other phenomena) expresses the nature of emptiness. Emptiness does not mean the absence of something from something else, as when one says that the eye is devoid of an inner agent or of the subject-object duality of perceptions.' 'The Word of Chandra', Chandrakirti, 314.
29 If Svatantrikas, thinking they are Madhyamikans, nonetheless abandon phenomenalism on the relative level and behave like realists, Mipham's refutation of their position is not to say that phenomena are unreal or nonexistent, but to say there is no coherent ontology (or even phenomenology) of phenomena themselves. On the level of their bare appearance, they are beyond existence or nonexistence, and so beyond saying or nay-saying. See Chandrakirti, 'Translators' Introduction', 34–7.
30 'The Word of Chandra', in Chandrakirti, 177.
31 MMK-M, XIII, 8, 169: translation altered.
32 The title of Schelling's essay, 'Philosophical Inquiry into the Nature of Human Freedom and of Objects Connected To It', indicates that Schelling has not changed his goal of forging a complete system – a total account of nature and human reality. He has, if anything, enlarged it, injecting an explicitly theological tone into the metaphysical basis of system, and ranging under the

208

account of consciousness or spirit (for the first time) considerations of morality, historical existence, and even the nature of evil.

Heidegger's discussion of Schelling's essay is illuminating, especially his initial discussions of the idea of system and of the attraction and repulsion the idea evokes in us. 'To be sure, the false form of system and the business of constructing systems must be rejected again and again, only because system in the true sense is one, indeed, *the* task of philosophy' (*Schelling's Treatise*, 27). As Heidegger reads Schelling, the true 'jointure' of being brought to light in this work – the fold or seam that simultaneously joins and divides – transmutes his earlier system-*formula*, the identity of nature and freedom, into the fundamental onto-theological *question* of the identity of *necessity and freedom* (*Schelling's Treatise*, 59–61).

33 'Darstellung', §§ 31 and 32, proofs and remarks, SW IV, pp. 128–29; 'Presentation', 359–60. Compare *Bruno*, SW IV, pp. 235–6; *Bruno, or the Divine and Natural Principle of Things* trans. Michael Vater (Albany: State University of New York Press, 1984), 136.

34 *Philosophische Untersuchungen über das Wesen der menschlichen Freiheit und die damit zusammenhängende Gegenstände*, SW VII, 350–4; hereafter cited as *Philosophische Untersuchungen*, SW VII. A curious feature of his recasting of ontology in volitional terms is Schelling's insistence that all the predicates of being – groundlessness, eternity, self-affirmation and *independence from time* – be transferred to the primal Will. As in Kant's problematic staging of the moral act of the will, volition decides outside of and beyond time, so without reference to any process of motivation or any physiology of action.

35 Heidegger says that Schelling reveals the territory of the fundamental question by bringing together the question of being (grounding) and that of the divine (truth, value, meaning). Heidegger's version of this fourfold is the 'onto-theological question'. Schelling sees in humankind a contingent separation and reconciliation of natural and conscious principles which are indissolubly (but only ideally) united in God; Heidegger can only advance problematically toward onto-theology, while Schelling thinks he can respond to the doubled questions of meaning and being in an assertoric or theoretical manner. See *Schelling's Treatise*, 64–6.

36 *Philosophische Untersuchungen*, SW VII, 347.

37 Ibid., 346; F. W. J. Schelling, *Of Human Freedom*, trans. James Gutmann (Chicago: Open Court, 1936), 18.

38 *Philosophische Untersuchungen*, SW VII, 341–2, 345–6.

39 *Philosophische Untersuchungen*, SW VII, 357. See 'Darstellung', §54, Anm., SW IV, 146–7, and § 93, n.1, SW IV, 163.

40 *Philosophische Untersuchungen*, SW VII, 404f.

41 Ibid., SW VII, 407; *Of Human Freedom*, 88.

SELECTED BIBLIOGRAPHY

GERMAN EDITIONS OF SCHELLING

(Listed chronologically in order of publication.)

Schelling, F. W. J., *Friedrich Wilhelm Joseph von Schellings sämmtliche Werke*, 14 vols, ed. K. F. A. Schelling (Stuttgart: Cotta, 1856–61).

—— *Schellings Werke. Nach der Original Ausgabe in neuer Anordnung*, 12 vols, ed. M. Schröter (Munich: Beck, 1927–59).

——*Die Weltalter. Fragmente in den Urauffassungen von 1811 und 1813*, ed. M. Schröter (Munich: Biederstein and Leibniz, 1946).

—— *Friedrich Wilhelm Joseph von Schelling. Ausgewählte Schriften*, 6 vols, ed. M. Frank (Frankfurt: Suhrkamp, 1985).

—— *Historisch-kritische Ausgabe, im Auftrag der Schelling-Kommission der Bayerischen Akademie der Wissenschaften*, 80 vols (projected), ed. H. M. Baumgartner, W. G. Jacobs, H. Krings (Stuttgart: Frommann-Holzboog, 1976–).

ENGLISH TRANSLATIONS OF SCHELLING

(Listed chronologically in order of original composition)

Schelling, F. W. J., *The Unconditional in Human Knowledge: Four Early Essays 1794–96*, trans. F. Marti (Lewisburg: Bucknell University Press, 1980).

—— *Idealism and the Endgame of Theory: Three Essays by F. W. J. Schelling*, trans. Thomas Pfau (Albany NY: SUNY Press, 1994) (Includes: 'Treatise Explicatory of the Idealism in the Science of Knowledge' (1797); 'System of Philosophy in General and of the Philosophy of Nature in Particular' (1804); and 'Stuttgart Seminars' (1810).)

—— *Ideas for a Philosophy of Nature: as Introduction to the Study of this Science* (1797), trans. E. E. Harris and P. Heath (Cambridge: Cambridge University Press, 1988).

—— *System of Transcendental Idealism* (1800), trans. P. Heath (Charlottesville: University Press of Virginia, 1978).

—— 'Presentation of My System of Philosophy' (1801) and 'Further Presentations from the System of Philosophy' (1802), trans. M. Vater, in *The Philosophical Forum*, XXXII, No. 4 (Winter 2001), 339–97.

—— *Bruno, or On the Natural and the Divine Principle of Things* (1802), trans. M. Vater (Albany: SUNY Press, 1984).

—— *On University Studies* (1802), trans. E. S. Morgan, ed. N. Guterman (Athens, OH: Ohio University Press, 1966).

—— *The Philosophy of Art* (1803), trans. D. W. Stott (Minnesota: Minnesota University Press, 1989).

—— 'Schelling's Aphorisms of 1805' (1805), trans. F. Marti, in *Idealistic Studies* 14 (1984), 23–56.

—— *Philosophical Inquiries into the Nature of Human Freedom* (1809), trans. J. Gutmann (Chicago: Open Court, 1936).

—— *The Abyss of Freedom/Ages of the World* (1813), trans. J. Norman with an essay by Slavoj Žižek (Ann Arbor: The University of Michigan Press, 1997).

—— *The Ages of the World* (1815), trans. F. de W. Bolman (New York: Columbia University Press, 1967).

—— *The Ages of the World* (1815), trans. Jason Wirth (Albany: SUNY Press, 2000).

—— *Schelling's Treatise on 'The Deities of Samothrace'* (1815), trans. R. F. Brown (Missoula, MT: Scholars Press, 1977).

—— On the History of Modern Philosophy (1827), trans. A. Bowie (Cambridge: Cambridge University Press, 1994).
—— On the Source of the Eternal Truths (1850), trans. E. A. Beach, in Owl of Minerva 19 (1990), 55–67.

ADDITIONAL SOURCES

(Listed alphabetically by author.)

Asmuth, C., Denker, A. and Vater, M. (eds), Schelling: Between Fichte and Hegel (Amsterdam: Grüner, 2001).
Baumgartner, H. M., Schelling: Einführung in seine Philosophie (Freiburg: Alber, 1975).
Beach, E. A., The Potencies of God(s): Schelling's Philosophy of Mythology (Albany: SUNY Press, 1994).
Bowie, A., Schelling and Modern European Philosophy: An Introduction (London: Routledge, 1993).
Breidebach, O., 'Zum Verhältnis von Spekulativer Philosophie und Biologie im 19. Jahrhundert', Philosophia Naturalis 22 (1985), 385–99.
—— 'Die Naturkonzeption Schellings in seiner frühen Naturphilosophie', Philosophia Naturalis 23 (1986), 82–95.
Brown, R., The Later Philosophy of Schelling: The Influence of Böhme on the Works of 1809–15 (Lewisburg: University of Pennsylvania Press, 1977).
Clark, D. L., 'Heidegger's Craving: Being-on-Schelling', Diacritics vol. 27(3) (Fall 1997), 8–33.
—— 'The Necessary Heritage of Darkness: Tropics of Negativity in Schelling, Derrida, and de Man', in Intersections: Nineteenth-Century Philosophy and Contemporary Theory, ed. T. Rajan and D. L. Clark (Albany: SUNY Press, 1995), 79–146.
—— 'Otherwise than God: Marion, Schelling', in Trajectories of Mysticism in Theory and Literature, ed. Phillip Leonard (London: Macmillan, 2000), 33–176.
Dews, P., 'Nietzsche and the Critique of Ursprungsphilosophie', in Exceedingly Nietzsche: Aspects of Contemporary Nietzsche Interpretation, ed. David F. Krell and David Wood (London: Routledge & Kegan Paul, 1988), 164–76.
—— 'The Eclipse of Coincidence: Lacan, Merleau-Ponty and Schelling', Angelaki vol. 4(3) (2000), 15–23.
Düsing, K., 'Spekulation und Reflexion: Zur Zusammenarbeit Schellings und Hegels in Jena', Hegel-Studien 5 (1969), 95–128.
Esposito, J., Schelling's Idealism and Philosophy of Nature (Lewisburg: Bucknell University Press, 1977).
Fackenheim, E., 'Schelling's Conception of Positive Philosophy', Review of Metaphysics 7 (1953/54), 563–82.
Fischer, K., F. W. J. Schelling (Heidelberg: Winter, 1895).
Frank, M., Eine Einführung in Schellings Philosophie (Frankfurt: Suhrkamp, 1985).
—— Der unendliche Mangel an Sein: Schellings Hegelkritik und die Anfänge der Marxschen Dialektik, 2nd edn., extensively expanded and reworked (Munich: W. Fink, 1992).
—— and Kurz, G. (eds), Materialien zu Schelling philosophischen Anfängen (Frankfurt: Suhrkamp, 1975).
Fuhrmans H., Schellings letzte Philosophie. Die negative und positive Philosophie im Einsatz des Spätidealismus (Berlin: Junker-Dünnhaupt, 1940).
—— Schellings Philosophie der Weltalter. Schellings Philosophie in den Jahren 1806–1825. Zum Problem des Schellingschen Theismus (Düsseldorf: Schwann, 1954).
Görland, I., Die Entwicklung der Frühphilosophie Schellings in der Auseinandersetzung mit Fichte (Frankfurt: Klostermann, 1973).
Habermas, J., Das Absolute und die Geschichte (Bonn: Bouvier, 1954).
—— 'Dialektischer Idealismus im Übergang zum Materialismus – Geschichtsphilosophische

Folgerungen aus Schellings Idee einer Contraction Gottes', in *Theorie und Praxis* (Berlin: Luchterhand, 1969), 108–61.

Hartkopf, W., *Studien zu Schellings Dialektik* (Frankfurt: Anton Hain, 1986).

—— 'Die Anfänge der Dialektik bei Schelling und Hegel', *Zeitscrift für Philosophische Forschung* 30 (1976), 545–66.

Hartmann, E. von, *Schellings philosophisches System* (Leipzig: Haacke, 1897).

Hasler, L. (ed.), *Schelling: Seine Bedeutung für die Philosophie der Natur und der Geschichte*, papers from the International Schelling Conference in Zurich, 1979 (Stuttgart: Frommann/ Holzboog, 1981).

Hayes, V., 'Schelling: Persistent Legends, Improving Image', *Southwestern Journal of Philosophy* 3 (1972), 63–73.

Heidegger, M., *Schelling's Treatise on the Essence of Human Freedom* (1809), trans. Joan Stambaugh (Athens OH: Ohio University Press, 1985).

Hogrebe, W., *Prädikation und Genesis* (Frankfurt: Suhrkamp, 1989).

Holz, H., *Speculation und Faktizität* (Bonn: Bouvier, 1970).

—— *Die Idee der Philosophie bei Schelling* (Freiburg, Munich: Alber, 1977).

Horstmann, R.-P., ' "Kant hat die Resultate gegeben": Zur Aneignung der *Kritik der Urteilskraft* durch Fichte und Schelling', in *Hegel und die 'Kritik der Urteilskraft'*, ed. Hans-Friedrich Fulda and Rolf-Peter Horstmann (Stuttgart: Klett-Cotta, 1990), 45–65.

Jähnig, D., *Schelling: Die Kunst in die Philosophie*, 2 vols, (Pfüllingen: Neske, 1969).

—— 'Philosophie und Weltgeschichte bei Schelling', *Studia Philosophica* 30 (1970–1), 126– 66.

Jaspers, K., *Schelling: Grösse und Verhängnis* (Munich: Piper, 1955).

Kasper, W., *Das Absolute in der Geschichte* (Munich: Matthias-Grünewald, 1965).

Krell, D. F., 'The Crisis of Reason in the Nineteenth Century: Schelling's Treatise on Human Freedom (1809)', in *The Collegium Phaenomenologicum*, ed. J. Sallis, G. Moneta and J. Taminiaux (Dordrecht: Kluwer, 1988), 13–32.

—— *Contagion: Sexuality, Disease, and Death in German Idealism and Romanticism* (Bloomington: Indiana University Press, 1998).

—— ' "Das Vergangene wird gewußt, das Gewußte [aber] wird erzählt": Trauma, Forgetting, and Narrative in F. W. J. Schelling's Die Weltalter', *Postmodern Culture* 11 (2001), http:// muse.jhu.edu/journals/pmc/v011/11.2krell.htm.

Lanfranconi, A., *Crisis: Eine Lektüre der 'Weltalter'-Texte F. W. J. Schellings*. (Stuttgart: Frommann-Holzboog, 1992).

Lawrence, J., 'Schelling as Post-Hegelian and as Aristotelian', *International Philosophical Quarterly* 26 (1986), 315–30.

—— 'Art and Philosophy in Schelling', *Owl of Minerva* 20 (1988), 5–19.

—— 'Schelling: A New Beginning', *Idealistic Studies* 19 (1989), 189–201.

—— *Schellings Philosophie des ewigen Anfangs* (Würzburg: Königshausen & Neumann, 1989).

Lukács, G., *Die Zerstörung der Vernunft* (Berlin: Aufbau-Verlag, 1954).

Marcel, G., 'Schelling fut-il un précurseur de la philosophie de l'existence?' *Revue de métaphysique et de moral* 72 (1957), 72–87.

Marquard, O., *Schwierigkeiten mit der Geschichtsphilosophie* (Frankfurt: Suhrkamp, 1973).

—— *Transzendentaler Idealismus. Romantische Naturphilosophie. Psycholanalyse* (Cologne: Dinter, 1987).

Marti, F., 'Young Schelling and Kant', *The Southern Journal of Philosophy* 13 (1975), 471–84.

Marx, W., 'Grundbegriffe der Geschichtsauffassung bei Schelling und Habermas', *Philosophisches Jahrbuch* 81 (1974), 50–76.

—— *The Philosophy of F. W. J. Schelling: History, System and Freedom*, trans. T. Nenon (Bloomington, Indiana University Press, 1984).

Norman, J., '*Ages of the World*. Metaphysics as Epic', in *Schelling: Between Fichte and Hegel*, ed. C. Asmuth, A. Denker and M. Vater (Amsterdam: Grüner, 2001), 169–83.

—— 'The Logic of Longing: Schelling's Philosophy of Will', *British Journal for the History of Philosophy* 10 (2002), 89–107.

O'Meara, T. F., 'F. W. J. Schelling: Bibliographical Essay', *Review of Metaphysics* 31 (1977), 283–309.

Oesterreich, P., 'Schellings Weltalter und die ausstehende Vollendung des deutschen Idealismus', *Zeitschrift für philosophische Forschung* 39 (1985), 70–85.

Sandkühler, H. J. (ed.), *Natur und geschichtlicher Prozess: Studien zur Naturphilosophie F. W. J. Schellings* (Frankfurt: Suhrkamp, 1984).

—— *Friedrich Wilhelm Joseph Schelling* (Stuttgart: Metzler, 1970).

Schulz, W., 'Das Verhältnis des späten Schelling zu Hegel: Schellings Spekulation über den Satz', *Zeitschrift für Philosophische Forschung* 8 (1954), 336–52.

—— *Die Vollendung des deutschen Idealismus in der Spätphilosophie Schellings* (Stuttgart: Kohlhammer, 1955).

—— 'Anmerkungen zu Schelling', *Zeitschrift für philosophische Forschung* 29 (1975), 321–36.

Seidel, G. F., 'Creativity in the Aesthetics of Schelling', *Idealistic Studies* 4 (1974), 170–80.

—— *Activity and Ground: Fichte, Schelling and Hegel* (Hildesheim and New York: Georg Olms, 1976).

Snow, D., *Schelling and the End of Idealism* (Albany: SUNY Press, 1996).

Steinkamp, F., 'Schelling's Account of Primal Nature in *The Ages of the World*', *Idealistic Studies* 24 (1993), 173–90.

Theunissen, M. 'Schellings Anthropologischer Ansatz', *Archiv für Geschichte der Philosophie* 47 (1965), 174–89.

—— 'Die Aufhebung des Idealismus in der Spätphilosophie Schellings', *Philosophisches Jahrbuch* 83 (1976), 1–29.

Tillich, P., 'Schelling und die Anfänge des existentialen Protestes', *Zeitschrift für philosophische Forschung* 9 (1955), 197–208.

—— *Mysticism and Guilt-Consciousness in Schelling's Philosophical Development*, trans. Victor Nuovo (Lewisburg: Bucknell University Press, 1974).

Tilliette, X., *Schelling. Une philosophie en devenir*, 2 vols (Paris: Vrin, 1970).

Vater, M., 'Heidegger and Schelling: The Finitude of Being', *Idealistic Studies* 5 (1975), 20–58.

—— 'Intellectual Intuition in Schelling's Philosophy of Identity 1801–1804', in *Schelling: Between Fichte and Hegel*, ed. C. Asmuth, A. Denker and M. Vater (Amsterdam: Grüner, 2001), 213–34.

White, A., *Schelling: An Introduction to the System of Freedom* (New Haven: Yale University Press, 1983).

Wirth, J., 'Schelling and the Force of Nature', in *Interrogating the Tradition*, ed. John Sallis and Charles Scott (Albany: SUNY Press, 2000).

Zeltner, H., *Schelling* (Stuttgart: Frommann, 1954).

Zimmerli, W., 'Die intellektuelle Anschauung beim frühen Schelling', *Proceedings of the XVth World Congress of Philosophy* 5 (1975), 839–43.

Žižek, S., *The Indivisible Remainder: An Essay on Schelling and Related Matters* (London: Verso, 1996).

INDEX